"I am offering my humble obeisances and prayers just to please You." *(p. 96)*

Kṛṣṇa brought forward the cows and played on His flute through the forest of Vṛndāvana.
*(p. 113)*

“Do not be afraid of the hill and think that it will fall from My hand.” *(p. 175)*

It appeared that Kṛṣṇa was a greenish sapphire locket in the midst of a golden necklace. *(p. 214)*

Kṛṣṇa appeared on the scene and touched the serpent with His lotus feet. *(p. 226)*

All day they simply make arrangements to steal our butter and yogurt. *(p. 61)*

The great sage Nārada Muni. *(p. 67)*

We think that this apparent punishment to Kāliya is actually some benediction. *(p. 123)*

Kṛṣṇa would praise them, "My dear friends, you are dancing and singing very nicely."
*(p. 132)*

Pralambāsura looked just like a cloud and lightning carrying the moon. *(p. 133)*

Due to remaining in the water for a long time, the *gopīs* felt cold and were shivering. *(p. 154)*

The god of the waters was holding Nanda captive underneath the sea. *(p. 184)*

Out of many thousands of *gopīs,* Rādhārāṇī is the most prominent. *(p. 211)*

# KṚṢṆA

## *The Supreme Personality of Godhead*

### *Volume 1*

## BOOKS by
## His Divine Grace A. C. Bhaktivedanta Swami Prabhupāda

Bhagavad-gītā As It Is
Śrīmad-Bhāgavatam, Cantos 1–9 (27 Vols.)
Śrī Caitanya-caritāmṛta (17 Vols.)
Teachings of Lord Caitanya
The Nectar of Devotion
The Nectar of Instruction
Śrī Īśopaniṣad
Easy Journey to Other Planets
Kṛṣṇa Consciousness: The Topmost Yoga System
Kṛṣṇa, the Supreme Personality of Godhead (3 Vols.)
Perfect Questions, Perfect Answers
Transcendental Teachings of Prahlād Mahārāja
Kṛṣṇa, the Reservoir of Pleasure
Life Comes from Life
The Perfection of Yoga
Beyond Birth and Death
On the Way to Kṛṣṇa
Geetār-gan (Bengali)
Rāja-vidyā: The King of Knowledge
Elevation to Kṛṣṇa Consciousness
Kṛṣṇa Consciousness: The Matchless Gift
Back to Godhead Magazine (Founder)

*A complete catalog is available upon request*

Bhaktivedanta Book Trust
3764 Watseka Avenue
Los Angeles, California 90034

# KṚṢṆA

## The Supreme Personality of Godhead

A Summary Study of Śrīla Vyāsadeva's *Śrīmad-Bhāgavatam*, Tenth Canto

*Volume 1*

*His Divine Grace*
**A.C. BHAKTIVEDANTA SWAMI PRABHUPĀDA**
*Founder-Ācārya of the International Society for Krishna Consciousness*

THE BHAKTIVEDANTA BOOK TRUST
New York · Los Angeles · London · Bombay

Readers interested in the subject matter of this book
are invited by the International Society for Krishna Consciousness
to correspond with its Secretary

**International Society for Krishna Consciousness**
**3764 Watseka Avenue**
**Los Angeles, California 90034**



Library of Congress Catalog Card Number: 74-118081
International Standard Book Number for Trilogy: 0-912776-60-9
International Standard Book Number for Volume One: 0-912776-57-9
International Standard Book Number for Volume Two: 0-912776-58-7
International Standard Book Number for Volume Three: 0-912776-59-5

First Printing, 1970: 30,000 copies (2 volumes, hardbound)
Second Printing, 1971: 10,000 copies (2 volumes, hardbound)
Third Printing, 1972: 20,000 copies (2 volumes, hardbound)
Fourth Printing, 1972: 150,000 copies (3 volumes, softbound)
Fifth Printing, 1972: 150,000 copies (3 volumes, softbound)
Sixth Printing, 1972: 300,000 copies (3 volumes, softbound)
Seventh Printing, 1973: 100,000 copies (2 volumes, hardbound)
Eighth Printing, 1973: 900,000 copies (3 volumes, softbound)
Ninth Printing, 1974: 300,000 copies (3 volumes, hardbound)
Tenth Printing, 1976: 300,000 copies (3 volumes, softbound)

Printed in the United States of America

*To My Father, Gour Mohon De (1849-1930)*

a pure devotee of Kṛṣṇa, who raised me as a Kṛṣṇa conscious child from the beginning of my life. In my boyhood ages he instructed me how to play the *mṛdaṅga.* He gave me Rādhā-Kṛṣṇa Vigraha to worship, and he gave me Jagannātha-Ratha to duly observe the festival as my childhood play. He was kind to me, and I imbibed from him the ideas later on solidified by my spiritual master, the eternal father.

# Contents

# Words from George Harrison

Everybody is looking for KṚṢṆA.

Some don't realize that they are, but they are.

KṚṢṆA is GOD, the Source of all that exists, the Cause of all that is, was, or ever will be.

As GOD is unlimited, HE has many Names.

Allah-Buddha-Jehova-Rama: All are KṚṢṆA, all are ONE.

God is not abstract; He has both the impersonal and the personal aspects to His personality which is SUPREME, ETERNAL, BLISSFUL, and full of KNOWLEDGE. As a single drop of water has the same qualities as an ocean of water, so has our consciousness the qualities of GOD'S consciousness . . . but through our identification and attachment with material energy (physical body, sense pleasures, material possessions, ego, etc.) our true TRANSCENDENTAL CONSCIOUSNESS has been polluted, and like a dirty mirror it is unable to reflect a pure image.

With many lives our association with the TEMPORARY has grown. This impermanent body, a bag of bones and flesh, is mistaken for our true self, and we have accepted this temporary condition to be final.

Through all ages, great SAINTS have remained as living proof that this non-temporary, permanent state of GOD CONSCIOUSNESS can be revived in all living Souls. Each soul is potentially divine.

Kṛṣṇa says in *Bhagavad Gita:* "Steady in the Self, being freed from all material contamination, the yogi achieves the highest perfectional stage of happiness in touch with the Supreme Consciousness." (VI, 28)

YOGA (a scientific method for GOD (SELF) realization) is the process by which we purify our consciousness, stop further pollution, and arrive at the state of Perfection, full KNOWLEDGE, full BLISS.

If there's a God, I want to see Him. It's pointless to believe in something without proof, and Kṛṣṇa Consciousness and meditation are methods where you can actually obtain GOD perception. You can actually see God, and hear Him, play with Him. It might sound crazy, but He is actually there, actually with you.

There are many yogic Paths—Raja, Jnana, Hatha, Kriya, Karma, Bhakti—which are *all* acclaimed by the MASTERS of each method.

SWAMI BHAKTIVEDANTA is as his title says, a BHAKTI Yogi following the path of DEVOTION. By serving GOD through each thought, word, and DEED, and by chanting of HIS Holy Names, the devotee quickly develops God-consciousness. By chanting

Hare Kṛṣṇa, Hare Kṛṣṇa
Kṛṣṇa Kṛṣṇa, Hare Hare
Hare Rāma, Hare Rāma
Rāma Rāma, Hare Hare

one inevitably arrives at KṚṢṆA Consciousness. (The proof of the pudding is in the eating!)

I request that you take advantage of this book *KṚṢṆA,* and enter into its understanding. I also request that you make an appointment to meet your God now, through the self liberating process of YOGA (UNION) and GIVE PEACE A CHANCE.

ALL YOU NEED IS LOVE (KRISHNA) HARI BOL.

George Harrison 31/3/70

Apple Corps Ltd 3 Savile Row London W1 Gerrard 2772/3993 Telex Apcore London

# Foreword

It is a wonder that the average Westerner has never heard of Kṛṣṇa. Every culture has its cherished myths, its heroes, its messiahs and its gods, but Kṛṣṇa transcends our small world of cultural relativities. Knowledge of Kṛṣṇa is a transcultural (or shall we say "transcendental") phenomenon, all-consuming in its relevance and universal in its appeal. Kṛṣṇa is not the product of some fertile religious or poetic imagination appearing within the spiritual mélange of historical Hinduism. Rather, Kṛṣṇa is the Supreme Truth (*paraṁ satyam*), the cause of all causes (*sarva-kāraṇa-kāraṇam*) and, most importantly, the ultimate or supreme person (*puruṣottama*).

The Ultimate Principle is a *Person?* This may discomfit the Westerner seeking refuge from the wrathful bearded old man of Judeo-Christian monotheism. But Śrī Kṛṣṇa, "the Supreme Personality of Godhead," is not like that. He is a blissful, eternal, transcendental youth whose overwhelming bodily beauty, sublime personal attributes and extraordinary activities inspire devotional ecstasy and divine intoxication in those to whom He reveals Himself.

The traditional source of knowledge of Kṛṣṇa, and ultimately of all physical and metaphysical knowledge, is the Vedic and Vedāntic scriptures of ancient and medieval India. It is the divine sage Vyāsadeva who is accredited by orthodox Vedic historiography with exclusive authorship of the original Vedic texts. The Vedic histories recount that after this vastly learned sage completed the huge task of compiling Vedic wisdom, he felt an undefinable dissatisfaction within himself. In the midst of Vyāsa's despondency, his own spiritual preceptor, the illustrious saint Nārada Muni, revealed the root cause of his unhappiness: Vyāsa, while defining, explaining and promoting various paths of material and spiritual upliftment, had neglected to indicate distinctly the ultimate goal of the spiritual quest—realization of pure *bhakti* (selfless devotion) for the Supreme Personality of Godhead, Śrī Kṛṣṇa. Since *kṛṣṇa-bhakti* is inspired by hearing about Kṛṣṇa's sublime transcendental attributes and activities, Nārada advised Vyāsa to compile a literature dedicated to Kṛṣṇa Himself:

> Learned circles have positively concluded that the infallible purpose of advancement of knowledge . . . culminates in the transcendental descriptions of the Lord. . . . Please, therefore, describe the Almighty Lord's activities which you have learned by your vast knowledge of the *Vedas*, for that will satisfy the hankerings of great learned men and at the same time mitigate the miseries of the mass of common people who are always suffering from material pangs. Indeed, there is no other way to get out of such miseries.
>
> (*Śrīmad-Bhāgavatam* 1.5.22, 40)

In pursuance of Nārada's order, Vyāsa, after deep meditation, wrote the glorious *Bhāgavata* (*Śrīmad-Bhāgavatam* or *Bhāgavata Purāṇa*), "the literary incarnation of God."

> This *Śrīmad-Bhāgavatam* is the literary incarnation of God, and it is compiled by Śrīla Vyāsadeva, the incarnation of God. It is meant for the ultimate good of all people, and it is all-successful, all-blissful and all-perfect.
>
> (*Śrīmad-Bhāgavatam* 1.3.40)

A vast and encyclopedic work, the *Bhāgavatam* surveys a broad spectrum of knowledge in metaphysics, ontology, cosmology, epistemology, social dynamics, political science and psychology. Ultimately, it offers the cream of Vedic truth. The nineteenth-century American transcendentalist Ralph Waldo Emerson once exalted the *Bhāgavatam* as a book to be read "on one's knees."

On the summit of this monolithic literature rests the effulgent jewel of its Tenth Canto, dedicated exclusively to delineating the divine attributes and activities of Śrī Kṛṣṇa, performed when He descended to earth in a past age. This work, *Kṛṣṇa, the Supreme Personality of Godhead*, is a fluid summary study of this celebrated Tenth Canto.

Now, the question arises, "Why does Kṛṣṇa descend and from where?" Kṛṣṇa descends from the transcendental world (Vaikuṇṭha), where He eternally resides on His planet, Goloka. In this supraterrestrial abode, Kṛṣṇa perpetually enjoys blissful "pastimes" (*līlā*) in the company of His innumerable pure devotees, who relish a variety of eternal relationships with Him. But whenever civilized religious life degenerates in human society, Kṛṣṇa descends to rectify the situation, as He tells Arjuna in *Bhagavad-gītā* (4.7–8):

> Whenever and wherever there is a decline in religious practice, O descendant of Bharata, and a predominant rise in irreligion—at

> that time I descend Myself. To deliver the pious and to annihilate the miscreants, as well as to reestablish the principles of religion, I advent Myself millennium after millennium.

To ameliorate one such state of affairs, Śrī Kṛṣṇa descended five thousand years ago in the land of Bharata-varṣa (India). This state of affairs, involving the increasing militarism of irreligious and sinister kings, climaxed in the famous Battle of Kurukṣetra, in which Kṛṣṇa played a decisive role. The history of this battle fills the major portion of the great epic *Mahābhārata.*

There is another, even more significant reason for Kṛṣṇa's appearance. Kṛṣṇa descended and displayed His transcendental pastimes in the mundane realm to attract and invite the souls confined within the material world to return to their eternal home in the spiritual world. When He appeared, He fully manifested the spiritual realm, in all its transcendental splendor, on the material plane. Accompanied by His eternal associates, He performed inconceivable, extraordinary pastimes, which, by their overpowering transcendental sublimity, attract the minds of all sentient beings.

It is these pastimes which Vyāsa recorded in the Tenth Canto of the *Bhāgavatam.* It is said that by hearing of such transcendental pastimes one comes into direct spiritual contact with Kṛṣṇa. Such aural connection with Kṛṣṇa purifies the heart, provokes *kṛṣṇa-bhakti* and elevates one to perfection:

> Śrī Kṛṣṇa, the Personality of Godhead, who is the Paramātmā [Supersoul] in everyone's heart and the benefactor of the truthful devotee, cleanses desire for material enjoyment from the heart of the devotee who has developed the urge to hear His messages, which are in themselves virtuous when properly heard and chanted.
>
> Simply by hearing this Vedic literature [*Bhāgavatam*], the feeling for loving devotional service to Lord Kṛṣṇa, the Supreme Personality of Godhead, sprouts up at once to extinguish the fire of lamentation, illusion and fearfulness.
>
> (*Śrīmad-Bhāgavatam* 1.2.17/1.7.7)

Until fairly recent times, characterized by the accelerating influence of Western culture, India's spiritual culture was almost totally obsessed with *kṛṣṇa-līlā.* Even now, episodes from Kṛṣṇa's pastimes are ceaselessly recited, enacted, sung and danced in every available medium of cultural expression. Holy festivals in honor of Lord Kṛṣṇa's birth and activities are observed with great pomp and festivity throughout the year by young and old, educated and illiterate, rich and poor, in all Indian cities and villages. In addition, many of the greatest literary masterpieces of the last several centuries in India—the Sanskrit *Gīta-Govinda* of Jayadeva, the Hindi poems of Bilvamaṅgala (Suradāsa) and Mīrābhāī, the Bengali poems of Vidyāpati and Caṇḍīdāsa, the Sanskrit dramas of Rūpa Gosvāmī—were composed in glorification of Kṛṣṇa as the mischievous and captivating child and as the paramour of the *gopīs* (cowherd maidens).

*Kṛṣṇa, the Supreme Personality of Godhead* is the most comprehensive exposition of the pastimes of Kṛṣṇa now available in the English-speaking world. Each of the trilogy's ninety stories reveals one episode from the life of Śrī Kṛṣṇa in a highly readable short-story format. *Kṛṣṇa* is the product of the scholarly and devotional effort of His Divine Grace A. C. Bhaktivedanta Swami Prabhupāda, the world's most distinguished teacher of Vedic religious and philosophical thought. Śrīla Prabhupāda is a disciplic descendant of Śrī Caitanya Mahāprabhu, whose *saṅkīrtana* movement of the sixteenth century inspired a massive revival of *kṛṣṇa-bhakti* that has, in turn, played a significant role in molding the religious consciousness of modern India. In this book, *Kṛṣṇa*, Śrīla Prabhupāda provides a flowing commentary that will help the Western reader understand concepts that may be foreign to his own cultural and intellectual milieu. The author's insightful comments, gracefully interwoven with the main fabric of the stories, facilitates the flow of the narrative, supplying important background information where needed.

This important work will be many things to many readers. It will serve as a valuable textbook for students of Asian religions, philosophies and cultures because it offers the kind of penetrating, multidimensional view into Indian culture and thought not usually found in secondary historical and anthropological sources. In *Kṛṣṇa*, students of Indian art, literature, music and dance will discover a fountainhead of themes that for centuries have nourished and enriched the classical Vedic arts. *Kṛṣṇa* will provide students of world literature a rare opportunity to explore one of the classics of Indian devotional literature in a readable and easily accessible English edition. Philosophers and theologians will encounter in *Kṛṣṇa* an inexhaustible source of ideas concerning the ultimate nature of reality and the science of the Absolute Truth. Those who enjoy reading narratives of any kind will find *Kṛṣṇa* a unique and refreshing change of pace from ordinary literature. But from a careful reading of *Kṛṣṇa*, those who will perhaps derive the most are those seeking a factual and scientific basis for spiritual life. The text will lure such a reader from the banal and commonplace and beckon him to take part in a miraculous journey. What he sees at first may strike him as alien and incomprehensible. But, as our pilgrim gradually crosses beyond all ethno- and ego-centric confines, he will find himself entering a transcendental realm beyond space and time, a realm where everything is seen in the light of the Supreme Absolute, who is an eternal transcendental youth, the ultimate object of knowledge and the supreme goal of life.

# Preface

*nivṛtta-tarṣair upagīyamānād*
*bhavauṣadhāc chrotramano'bhirāmāt*
*ka uttama-śloka-guṇānuvādāt*
*pumān virajyeta vinā paśughnāt*
*(Śrīmad-Bhāgavatam 10.1.4)*

In these Western countries, when someone sees the cover of a book like *Kṛṣṇa,* he immediately asks, "Who is Kṛṣṇa? Who is the girl with Kṛṣṇa?" etc.

The immediate answer is that Kṛṣṇa is the Supreme Personality of Godhead. How is that? Because He conforms in exact detail to descriptions of the Supreme Being, the Godhead. In other words, Kṛṣṇa is the Godhead because He is all-attractive. Outside the principle of all-attraction, there is no meaning to the word Godhead. How is it one can be all-attractive? First of all, if one is very wealthy, if he has great riches, he becomes attractive to the people in general. Similarly, if someone is very powerful, he also becomes attractive, and if someone is very famous, he also becomes attractive, and if someone is very beautiful or wise or unattached to all kinds of possessions, he also becomes attractive. So from practical experience we can observe that one is attractive due to 1) wealth, 2) power, 3) fame, 4) beauty, 5) wisdom, and 6) renunciation. One who is in possession of all six of these opulences at the same time, who possesses them to an unlimited degree, is understood to be the Supreme Personality of Godhead. These opulences of the Godhead are delineated by Parāśara Muni, a great Vedic authority.

We have seen many rich persons, many powerful persons, many famous persons, many beautiful persons, many learned and scholarly persons, and persons in the renounced order of life unattached to material possessions.

But we have never seen any one person who is unlimitedly and simultaneously wealthy, powerful, famous, beautiful, wise and unattached, like Kṛṣṇa, in the history of humanity. Kṛṣṇa, the Supreme Personality of Godhead, is an historical person who appeared on this earth 5,000 years ago. He stayed on this earth for 125 years and played exactly like a human being, but His activities were unparalleled. From the very moment of His appearance to the moment of His disappearance, every one of His activities is unparalleled in the history of the world, and therefore anyone who knows what we mean by Godhead will accept Kṛṣṇa as the Supreme Personality of Godhead. No one is equal to the Godhead, and no one is greater than Him. That is the import of the familiar saying, "God is great."

There are various classes of men in the world who speak of God in different ways, but according to Vedic literatures and according to the great *ācāryas,* the authorized persons versed in the knowledge of God, in all ages, like *ācāryas* Śaṅkara, Rāmānuja, Madhva, Viṣṇusvāmī, Lord Caitanya and all their followers by disciplic succession, all unanimously agree that Kṛṣṇa is the Supreme Personality of Godhead. As far as we, the followers of Vedic civilization, are concerned, we accept the Vedic history of the whole universe, which consists of different planetary systems called Svargalokas, or the higher planetary system, Martyalokas, or the intermediary planetary system, and Pātālalokas, or the lower planetary system. The modern historians of this earth cannot supply historical evidences of events that occurred before 5,000 years ago, and the anthropologists say that 40,000 years ago Homo sapiens had not appeared on this planet because evolution had not reached that point. But the Vedic histories, the *Purāṇas* and *Mahābhārata,* relate human histories which extend millions and billions of years into the past.

For example, from these literatures we are given the histories of Kṛṣṇa's appearances and disappearances millions and billions of years ago. In the Fourth Chapter of the *Bhagavad-gītā* Kṛṣṇa tells Arjuna that both He and Arjuna had had many births before and that He (Kṛṣṇa) could remember all of them and that Arjuna could not. This illustrates the difference between the knowledge of Kṛṣṇa and that of Arjuna. Arjuna might have been a very great warrior, a well-cultured member of the Kuru dynasty, but after all, he was an ordinary human being, whereas Kṛṣṇa, the Supreme Personality of Godhead, is the possessor of unlimited knowledge. Because He possesses unlimited knowledge, Kṛṣṇa has a memory that is boundless.

Kṛṣṇa's knowledge is so perfect that He remembers all the incidences of His appearances some millions and billions of years in the past, but Arjuna's memory and knowledge are limited by time and space, for he is an ordinary human being. In the Fourth Chapter Kṛṣṇa states that He can remember instructing the lessons of the *Bhagavad-gītā* some millions of years ago to the sun-god, Vivasvān.

Nowadays it is the fashion of the atheistic class of men to try to become God by following some mystic process. Generally the atheists claim to be God by dint of their imagination or their meditational prowess. Kṛṣṇa is not that kind of God. He does not become God by manufacturing some mystic process of meditation, nor does He become God by undergoing the severe austerities of the mystic yogic exercises. Properly speaking, He never *becomes* God because He is the Godhead in all circumstances.

Within the prison of His maternal uncle Kaṁsa, where His father and mother were confined, Kṛṣṇa appeared outside His mother's body as the four-handed Viṣṇu-Nārāyaṇa. Then He turned Himself into a baby and told His father to carry Him to the house of Nanda Mahārāja and his wife Yaśodā. When Kṛṣṇa was just a small baby the gigantic demoness Pūtanā attempted to kill Him, but when He sucked her breast He pulled out her life. That is the difference between the real Godhead and a God manufactured in the mystic factory. Kṛṣṇa had no chance to practice the mystic *yoga* process, yet He manifested Himself as the Supreme Personality of Godhead at every step, from infancy to childhood, from childhood to boyhood, and from boyhood to young manhood. In this book *Kṛṣṇa,* all of His activities as a human being are described. Although Kṛṣṇa plays like a human being, He always maintains His identity as the Supreme Personality of Godhead.

Since Kṛṣṇa is all-attractive, one should know that all his desires should be focused on Kṛṣṇa. In the *Bhagavad-gītā* it is said that the individual person is the proprietor or master of the body, but Kṛṣṇa, who is the Supersoul present in everyone's heart, is the supreme proprietor and supreme master of each and every individual body. As such, if we concentrate our loving propensities upon Kṛṣṇa only, then immediately universal love, unity and tranquility will be automatically realized. When one waters the root of a tree, he automatically waters the branches, twigs, leaves and flowers; when one supplies food to the stomach through the mouth, he satisfies all the various parts of the body.

The art of focusing one's attention on the Supreme and giving one's love to Him is called Kṛṣṇa consciousness. We have inaugurated the Kṛṣṇa consciousness movement so that everyone can satisfy his propensity for loving others simply by directing his love towards Kṛṣṇa. The whole world is very much anxious to satisfy the dormant propensity of love for others, but the inventions of various methods like socialism, communism, altruism, humanitarianism, nationalism, and whatever else may be manufactured for the peace and prosperity of the world, are all useless and frustrating because of our gross ignorance of the art of loving Kṛṣṇa. Generally people think that by advancing the cause of moral principles and religious rites, they will be happy. Others may think that happiness can be achieved by economic development, and yet others think that simply by sense gratification they will be happy. But the real fact is that people can only be happy by loving Kṛṣṇa.

Kṛṣṇa can perfectly reciprocate one's loving propensities in different relationships called mellows or *rasas.* Basically there are twelve loving relationships. One can love Kṛṣṇa as the supreme unknown, as the supreme master, the supreme friend, the supreme child, the supreme lover. These are the five basic love *rasas.* One can also love Kṛṣṇa indirectly in seven different relationships, which are apparently different from the five primary relationships. All in all, however, if one simply reposes his dormant loving propensity in Kṛṣṇa, then his life becomes successful. This is not a fiction but is a fact that can be realized by practical application. One can directly perceive the effects that love for Kṛṣṇa has on his life.

In the Ninth Chapter of the *Bhagavad-gītā* this science of Kṛṣṇa consciousness is called the king of all knowledge, the king of all confidential things, and the supreme science of transcendental realization. Yet we can directly experience the results of this science of Kṛṣṇa consciousness because it is very easy to practice and is very pleasurable. Whatever percentage of Kṛṣṇa consciousness we can perform will become an eternal asset to our life, for it is imperishable in all circumstances. It has now been actually proved that today's confused and frustrated younger generation in the Western countries can directly perceive the results of channeling the loving propensity toward Kṛṣṇa alone.

It is said that although one executes severe austerities, penances and sacrifices in his life, if he fails to awaken his dormant love for Kṛṣṇa, then all his penances are to be considered useless. On the other hand, if one has awakened his dormant love for Kṛṣṇa, then what is the use in executing austerities and penances unnecessarily?

The Kṛṣṇa consciousness movement is the unique gift of Lord Caitanya to the fallen souls of this age. It is a very simple method which has actually been carried out during the last four years in the Western countries, and there is no doubt that this movement can satisfy the dormant loving propensities of humanity. This book *Kṛṣṇa* is another presentation to help the Kṛṣṇa consciousness movement in the Western world. This transcendental literature is published in two parts with profuse illustrations.

People love to read various kinds of fiction to spend their time and energy. Now this tendency can be directed to Kṛṣṇa. The result will be the imperishable satisfaction of the soul, both individually and collectively.

It is said in the *Bhagavad-gītā* that even a little effort expended on the path of Kṛṣṇa consciousness can save one from the greatest danger. Hundreds of thousands of examples can be cited of people who have escaped the greatest dangers of life due to a slight advancement in Kṛṣṇa consciousness. We therefore request everyone to take advantage of this great transcendental literature. One will find that by reading one page after another, an immense treasure of knowledge in art, science, literature, philosophy and religion will be revealed, and ultimately, by reading this one book, *Kṛṣṇa,* love of Godhead will fructify.

My grateful acknowledgement is due to Śrīmān George Harrison, now chanting Hare Kṛṣṇa, for his liberal contribution of $19,000 to meet the entire cost of printing this volume. May Kṛṣṇa bestow upon this nice boy further advancement in Kṛṣṇa consciousness.

And at last my ever-willing blessings are bestowed upon Śrīmān Śyāmasundaradāsa Adhikārī, Śrīmān Brahmānandadāsa Brahmacārī, Śrīmān Hayagrīvadāsa Adhikārī, Śrīman Satsvarūpadāsa Adhikārī, Śrīmatī Devahūti Devī, Śrīmatī Jadurāṇī Dāsī, Śrīmān Muralīdharadāsa Brahmacārī, Śrīmān Bhāradvājadāsa Adhikārī, and Śrīmān Pradyumnadāsa Adhikārī, etc., for their hard labor in different ways to make this publication a great success.

Hare Kṛṣṇa.

*Advent Day of Śrīla*
*Bhaktisiddhānta Sarasvatī*

*February 26th, 1970*
*ISKCON Headquarters*
*3764 Watseka Avenue*
*Los Angeles, California*

# Introduction

*Kṛṣṇa! Kṛṣṇa! Kṛṣṇa! Kṛṣṇa! Kṛṣṇa! Kṛṣṇa! Kṛṣṇa! he!*
*Kṛṣṇa! Kṛṣṇa! Kṛṣṇa! Kṛṣṇa! Kṛṣṇa! Kṛṣṇa! Kṛṣṇa! he!*
*Kṛṣṇa! Kṛṣṇa! Kṛṣṇa! Kṛṣṇa! Kṛṣṇa! Kṛṣṇa! rakṣa mām!*
*Kṛṣṇa! Kṛṣṇa! Kṛṣṇa! Kṛṣṇa! Kṛṣṇa! Kṛṣṇa! pāhi mām!*
*Rāma! Rāghava! Rāma! Rāghava! Rāma! Rāghava! rakṣa mām!*
*Kṛṣṇa! Keśava! Kṛṣṇa! Keśava! Kṛṣṇa! Keśava! pāhi mām!*

*Caitanya-caritāmṛta (Madhya 7.96)*

While attempting to write this book, *Kṛṣṇa,* let me first offer my respectful obeisances unto my spiritual master, Om Viṣṇupāda 108 Śrī Śrīmad Bhaktisiddhānta Sarasvatī Gosvāmī Mahārāja Prabhupāda. Then let me offer my respectful obeisances to the ocean of mercy, Lord Śrī Kṛṣṇa Caitanya Mahāprabhu. He is the Supreme Personality of Godhead, Kṛṣṇa Himself, appearing in the role of a devotee just to distribute the highest principles of devotional service. Lord Caitanya began His preaching from the country known as Gauḍadeśa (West Bengal). And as I belong to the Mādhva-Gauḍīya-sampradāya, I must therefore offer my respectful obeisances to our disciplic succession. This Mādhva-Gauḍīya-sampradāya is also known as Brahma-sampradāya because the disciplic succession originally began from Brahmā. Brahmā instructed the sage Nārada, Nārada instructed Vyāsadeva, and Vyāsadeva instructed Madhva Muni or Madhvācārya. Mādhavendra Purī, the originator of Mādhva-Gauḍīya-sampradāya, belonged to the Madhvācārya disciplic succession; he had many renowned disciples both in the *sannyāsa* (renounced) and household orders of life, disciples such as Nityānanda Prabhu, Advaita Prabhu and Īśvara Purī. Īśvara Purī happened to be the spiritual master of Lord Caitanya Mahāprabhu. So let us offer our respectful obeisances to Īśvara Purī, Nityānanda Prabhu, Śrī Advaita Ācārya Prabhu, Śrīvāsa Paṇḍit and Śrī Gadādhara Paṇḍit. Next, let us offer our respectful obeisances to Svarūpa-Dāmodara, who acted as the private secretary to Lord Caitanya Mahāprabhu; and let us offer our respectful obeisances to Śrī Vāsudeva Datta and the constant attendant of Lord Caitanya, Śrī Govinda, and the constant friend of Lord Caitanya, Mukunda, and also to Murāri Gupta. And let us offer our respectful obeisances to the six Gosvāmīs of Vṛndāvana, Śrī Rūpa Gosvāmī, Śrī Sanātana Gosvāmī, Śrī Raghunātha Bhaṭṭa Gosvāmī, Śrī Gopāla Bhaṭṭa Gosvāmī, Śrī Jīva Gosvāmī and Śrī Raghunātha Dāsa Gosvāmī.

Kṛṣṇa Himself has explained in the *Bhagavad-gītā* that He is the Supreme Personality of Godhead. Whenever there are discrepancies in the regulative principles of man's religious life and a prominence of irreligious activities, He appears on this earthly planet. In other words, when Lord Śrī Kṛṣṇa appeared, there was a necessity of minimizing the load of sinful activities accumulated on this planet, or in this universe. For affairs of the material creation, Lord Mahā-Viṣṇu, the plenary portion of Kṛṣṇa, is in charge.

When the Lord descends, the incarnation emanates from Viṣṇu. Mahā-Viṣṇu is the original cause of material creation, and from Him Garbhodakaśāyi-Viṣṇu expands, and then Kṣīrodakaśāyi-Viṣṇu. Generally, all the incarnations appearing within this material universe are plenary expansions from Kṣīrodakaśāyi-Viṣṇu. Therefore, the business of minimizing the overload of sinful activities on this earth does not belong to the Supreme Personality of Godhead, Kṛṣṇa Himself. But when Kṛṣṇa appears, all the Viṣṇu expansions also join with Him. Kṛṣṇa's different expansions, namely Nārāyaṇa, the quadrupal expansion of Vāsudeva, Saṅkarṣaṇa, Pradyumna and Aniruddha, as well as the partial plenary expansion of Matsya or the incarnation of fish, and other *yuga-avatāras* (incarnations for the millennium), and the *manvantara-avatāras*, the incarnations of Manus—all combine together and appear with the body of Kṛṣṇa, the Supreme Personality of Godhead. Kṛṣṇa is the complete whole, and all plenary expansions and incarnations always live with Him.

When Kṛṣṇa appeared, Lord Viṣṇu was also with Him. Kṛṣṇa actually appears to demonstrate His Vṛndāvana pastimes and to attract the fortunate conditioned souls and invite them back home, back to Godhead. The killing of the demons was simultaneous to His Vṛndāvana activities and was carried out only by the Viṣṇu portion of Kṛṣṇa.

In the *Bhagavad-gītā,* Eighth Chapter, 20th verse, it is stated that there is another eternal nature, the spiritual sky, which is transcendental to this manifested and nonmanifested matter. The manifested world can be seen in the form of many stars and planetary systems, such as the sun, moon, etc., but beyond this there is a nonmanifested portion which is not approachable to anyone in this body. And beyond that nonmanifested matter there is the spiritual kingdom. That kingdom is described in the *Bhagavad-gītā* as supreme and eternal. It is never annihilated. This material nature is subjected to repeated creation and annihilation. But that part, the spiritual nature, remains as it is, eternally.

The supreme abode of the Personality of Godhead, Kṛṣṇa, is also described in the *Brahma-saṁhitā* as the abode of *cintāmaṇi.* That abode of Lord Kṛṣṇa known as Goloka Vṛndāvana is full of palaces made of touchstone. There the trees are called desire trees, and the cows are called *surabhi.* The Lord is served there by hundreds and thousands of goddesses of fortune. His name is Govinda, the Primeval Lord, and He is the cause of all causes. There the Lord plays His flute, His eyes are like lotus petals, and the color of His body is like that of a beautiful cloud. On His head is a peacock feather. He is so attractive that He excels thousands of cupids. Lord Kṛṣṇa gives only a little hint in the *Gītā* of His personal abode which is the supermost planet in the spiritual kingdom. But in the *Śrīmad-Bhāgavatam,* Kṛṣṇa actually appears with all His paraphernalia and demonstrates His activities in Vṛndāvana, then at Mathurā, and then at Dvārakā. The subject matter of this book will gradually reveal all these activities.

The family in which Kṛṣṇa appeared is called the Yadu dynasty. This Yadu dynasty belongs to the family descending from Soma, the god in the moon planet. There are two different *kṣatriya* families of the royal order, one descending from the king of the moon planet and the other descending from the king of the sun planet. Whenever the Supreme Personality of Godhead appears, He generally appears in a *kṣatriya* family because He has to establish religious principles or the life of righteousness. The *kṣatriya* family is the protector of the human race, according to the Vedic system. When the Supreme Personality of Godhead appeared as Lord Rāmacandra, He appeared in the family descending from the sun-god, known as Raghu-vaṁśa; and when He appeared as Lord Kṛṣṇa, He did so in the family of Yadu-vaṁśa. There is a long list of the kings of the Yadu-vaṁśa in the Ninth Canto, 24th chapter of *Śrīmad-Bhāgavatam.* All of them were great powerful kings. Kṛṣṇa's father's name was Vasudeva, son of Śūrasena, descending from the Yadu dynasty. Actually, the Supreme Personality of Godhead does not belong to any dynasty of this material world, but the family in which the Supreme Personality of Godhead appears becomes famous, by His grace. For example, sandalwood is produced in the states of Malaya. Sandalwood has its own qualifications apart from Malaya, but because, accidently, this wood is mainly produced in the states of Malaya, it is known as Malayan sandalwood. Similarly, Kṛṣṇa the Supreme Personality of Godhead belongs to everyone, but just as the sun rises from the east, although there are other directions from which it could rise, so, by His own choice, the Lord appears in a particular family, and that family becomes famous.

When Kṛṣṇa appears, all His plenary expansions also appear with Him. Kṛṣṇa appeared along with Balarāma (Baladeva), who is known as His elder brother. Balarāma is the origin of Saṅkarṣaṇa, of the quadrupal expansion. Balarāma is also the plenary expansion of Kṛṣṇa. In this book, the attempt will be made to show how Kṛṣṇa appeared in the family of the Yadu dynasty and how He displayed His transcendental characteristics. This is very vividly described in the *Śrīmad-Bhāgavatam*—specifically, the Tenth Canto—and the basis of this book will be *Śrīmad-Bhāgavatam.*

The pastimes of the Lord are generally heard and relished by liberated souls. Those who are conditioned souls are interested in reading fictional stories of the material activities of some common man. Narrations describing the transcendental activities of the Lord are found in *Śrīmad-Bhāgavatam* and other *Purāṇas.* But, the conditioned souls still prefer to study ordinary narrations. They are not so interested in studying the narrations of the pastimes of the Lord, Kṛṣṇa. And yet, the descriptions of the pastimes of Lord Kṛṣṇa are so attractive that they are relishable for all classes of men. There are three classes of men in this world. One class consists of liberated souls, another consists of those who are trying to be liberated, and the third consists of materialistic men. Whether one is liberated or is trying to be liberated, or is even grossly materialistic, the pastimes of Lord Kṛṣṇa are worth studying.

Liberated souls have no interest in materialistic activities. The impersonalist theory that after liberation one becomes inactive and needs hear nothing does not prove that a liberated person is actually inactive. A living soul cannot be inactive. He is either active in the conditioned state or in the liberated state. A diseased person, for example, is also active, but his activities are all painful. The same person, when freed from the diseased condition, is still active, but in the healthy condition the activities are full of pleasure. Similarly, the impersonalists manage to get freed from the diseased conditional activities, but they have no information of activities in the healthy condition. Those who are actually liberated and in full knowledge take to hearing the activities of Kṛṣṇa; such engagement is pure spiritual activity.

It is essential for persons who are actually liberated to hear about the pastimes of Kṛṣṇa. That is the supreme relishable subject matter for one in the liberated state. Also, if persons who are trying to be liberated hear such narrations as *Bhagavad-gītā* and *Śrīmad-Bhāgavatam,* then their path of liberation becomes very clear. *Bhagavad-gītā* is the preliminary study of *Śrīmad-Bhāgavatam.* By studying the *Gītā,* one becomes fully conscious of the position of Lord Kṛṣṇa; and when he is situated at the lotus feet of Kṛṣṇa, he understands the narrations of Kṛṣṇa as described in the *Śrīmad-Bhāgavatam.* Lord Caitanya has therefore advised His followers that their business is to propagate *Kṛṣṇa-kathā.*

*Kṛṣṇa-kathā* means narrations about Kṛṣṇa. There are two *Kṛṣṇa-kathās:* narrations *spoken by Kṛṣṇa* and narrations *spoken about Kṛṣṇa. Bhagavad-gītā* is the narration or the philosophy or the science of God, spoken by Kṛṣṇa Himself. *Śrīmad-Bhāgavatam* is the narration about the activities and transcendental pastimes of Kṛṣṇa. Both are *Kṛṣṇa-kathā.* It is the order of Lord Caitanya that *Kṛṣṇa-kathā* should be spread all over the world, because if the conditioned souls, suffering under the pangs of material existence, take to *Kṛṣṇa-kathā,* then their path of liberation will be open and clear. The purpose of presenting this book is primarily to induce people to understand Kṛṣṇa or *Kṛṣṇa-kathā,* because thereby they can become freed from material bondage.

This *Kṛṣṇa-kathā* will also be very much appealing to the most materialistic persons because Kṛṣṇa's pastimes with the *gopīs* (cowherd girls) are exactly like the loving affairs between young girls and boys within this material world. Actually, the sex feeling found in human society is not unnatural because this same sex feeling is there in the original Personality of Godhead. The pleasure potency is called Śrīmatī Rādhārāṇī. The attraction of loving affairs on the basis of sex feeling is the original feature of the Supreme Personality of Godhead, and we, the conditioned souls, being part and parcel of the Supreme, have such feelings also, but they are experienced within a perverted, minute condition. Therefore, when those who are after sex life in this material world hear about Kṛṣṇa's pastimes with the *gopīs,* they will relish transcendental pleasure, although it appears to be materialistic. The advantage will be that they will gradually be elevated to the spiritual platform. In the *Bhāgavatam* it is stated that if one hears the pastimes of Lord Kṛṣṇa with the gopīs *from authorities with submission,* then he will be promoted to the platform of transcendental loving service to the Lord, and the material disease of lust within his heart will be completely vanquished. In other words, it will counteract the material sex life.

Kṛṣṇa will be appealing to the liberated souls and to persons who are trying to be liberated, as well as to the gross, conditioned materialist.

According to the statement of Mahārāja Parīkṣit, who heard about Kṛṣṇa from Śukadeva Gosvāmī, *Kṛṣṇa-kathā* is equally applicable to every human being, in whatever condition of life he is in. Everyone will appreciate it to the highest magnitude. But Mahārāja Parīkṣit also warned that persons who are simply engaged in killing animals and in killing themselves may not be very much attracted to *Kṛṣṇa-kathā*. In other words, ordinary persons who are following the regulative moral principles of scriptures, no matter in what condition they are found, will certainly be attracted, but not persons who are killing themselves. The exact word used in the *Śrīmad-Bhāgavatam* is *paśughna,* which means killing animals or killing oneself. Persons who are not self-realized and who are not interested in spiritual realization are killing themselves; they are committing suicide. Because this human form of life is especially meant for self-realization, by neglecting this important part of his activities, one simply wastes his time like the animals. So he is *paśughna*. The other meaning of the word refers to those who are actually killing animals. This means persons who are animal eaters (even dog eaters), and they are all engaged in killing animals in so many ways, such as hunting, opening slaughterhouses, etc. Such persons cannot be interested in *Kṛṣṇa-kathā*.

King Parīkṣit was especially interested in hearing *Kṛṣṇa-kathā* because he knew that his forefathers and particularly his grandfather, Arjuna, were victorious in the great battle of Kurukṣetra only because of Kṛṣṇa. We may also take this material world as a battlefield of Kurukṣetra. Everyone is struggling hard for existence in this battlefield, and at every step there is danger. According to Mahārāja Parīkṣit, the battlefield of Kurukṣetra was just like a vast ocean full of dangerous animals. His grandfather Arjuna had to fight with such great heroes as Bhīṣma, Droṇa, Karṇa, and many others who were not ordinary fighters. Such warriors have been compared to the *timiṅgila* fish in the ocean. The *timiṅgila* fish can very easily swallow up big whales. The great fighters on the battlefield of Kurukṣetra could swallow many, many Arjunas very easily, but simply due to Kṛṣṇa's mercy, Arjuna was able to kill all of them. Just as one can cross with no exertion over the little pit of water contained in the hoofprint of a calf, so Arjuna, by the grace of Kṛṣṇa, was able to very easily jump over the ocean of the battle of Kurukṣetra.

Mahārāja Parīkṣit very much appreciated Kṛṣṇa's activities for many other reasons. Not only was his grandfather saved by Kṛṣṇa, but he himself also was saved by Kṛṣṇa. At the end of the battle of Kurukṣetra, all the members of the Kuru dynasty, both the sons and grandsons on the side of Dhṛtarāṣṭra, as well as those on the side of the Pāṇḍavas, died in the fighting. Except the five Pāṇḍava brothers, everyone died on the battlefield of Kurukṣetra. Mahārāja Parīkṣit was at that time within the womb of his mother. His father, Abhimanyu, the son of Arjuna, also died on the battlefield of Kurukṣetra, and so Mahārāja Parīkṣit was a posthumous child. When he was in the womb of his mother, a *brahmāstra* weapon was released by Aśvatthāmā to kill the child. When Parīkṣit Mahārāja's mother, Uttarā, approached Kṛṣṇa, Kṛṣṇa, seeing the danger of abortion, entered her womb as the Supersoul and saved Mahārāja Parīkṣit. Mahārāja Parīkṣit's other name is Viṣṇurāta because he was saved by Lord Viṣṇu Himself while still within the womb.

Thus everyone, in any condition of life, should be interested in hearing about Kṛṣṇa and His activities because He is the Supreme Absolute Truth, the Personality of Godhead. He is all-pervading; He is living within everyone's heart, and He is living as His universal form. And yet, as described in the *Bhagavad-gītā,* He appears as He is in the human society just to invite everyone to His transcendental abode, back to home, back to Godhead. Everyone should be interested in knowing about Kṛṣṇa, and this book is presented with this purpose: that people may know about Kṛṣṇa and be perfectly benefitted in this human form of life.

In the Ninth Canto of *Śrīmad-Bhāgavatam,* Śrī Baladeva is described as the son of Rohiṇī, a wife of Vasudeva. Vasudeva, the father of Kṛṣṇa, had sixteen wives, and one of them was Rohiṇī, the mother of Balarāma. But Balarāma is also described as the son of Devakī, so how could He be the son of both Devakī and Rohiṇī? This was one of the questions put by Mahārāja Parīkṣit to Śukadeva Gosvāmī, and it will be answered in due course. Mahārāja Parīkṣit also asked Śukadeva Gosvāmī why Śrī Kṛṣṇa, just after His appearance as the son of Vasudeva, was immediately carried to the house of Nanda Mahārāja in Vṛndāvana, Gokula. He also wanted to know what the activities of Lord Kṛṣṇa were while He was in Vṛndāvana and while He was in Mathurā. Besides that, he was especially inquisitive to know why Kṛṣṇa killed His maternal uncle, Kaṁsa. Kaṁsa, being the brother of His mother, was a very intimate superior to Kṛṣṇa, so how was it that He killed Kaṁsa? Also, he asked how many years Lord Kṛṣṇa remained in human society, how many years He reigned over the kingdom of Dvārakā, and how many wives He accepted there. A *kṣatriya* king is generally accustomed to accept more than one wife; therefore Mahārāja Parīkṣit also inquired about His number of wives. The subject matter of this book is Śukadeva Gosvāmī's answering of these and other questions asked by Mahārāja Parīkṣit.

The position of Mahārāja Parīkṣit and Śukadeva Gosvāmī is unique.

Mahārāja Parīkṣit is the right person to hear about the transcendental pastimes of Kṛṣṇa, and Śukadeva Gosvāmī is the right person to describe them. If such a fortunate combination is made possible, then *Kṛṣṇa-kathā* immediately becomes revealed, and people may benefit to the highest possible degree from such a conversation.

This narration was presented by Śukadeva Gosvāmī when Mahārāja Parīkṣit was prepared to give up his body, fasting on the bank of the Ganges. In order to assure Śukadeva Gosvāmī that by hearing *Kṛṣṇa-kathā* he would not feel tired, Mahārāja Parīkṣit expressed himself very frankly: "Hunger and thirst may give trouble to ordinary persons or to me, but the topics of Kṛṣṇa are so nice that one can continue to hear about them without feeling tired because such hearing situates one in the transcendental position." It is understood that one must be very fortunate to hear about *Kṛṣṇa-kathā* seriously, like Mahārāja Parīkṣit. He was especially intent on the subject matter because he was expecting death at any moment. Every one of us should be conscious of death at every moment. This life is not at all assured; at any time one can die. It does not matter whether one is a young man or an old man. So before death takes place, we must be *fully* Kṛṣṇa conscious.

At the point of his death, King Parīkṣit was hearing *Śrīmad-Bhāgavatam* from Śukadeva Gosvāmī. When King Parīkṣit expressed his untiring desire to hear about Kṛṣṇa, Śukadeva Gosvāmī was very pleased. Śukadeva was the greatest of all *Bhāgavata* reciters, and thus he began to speak about Kṛṣṇa's pastimes, which destroy all inauspiciousness in this age of Kali. Śukadeva Gosvāmī thanked the King for his eagerness to hear about Kṛṣṇa, and he encouraged him by saying, "My dear King, your intelligence is very keen because you are so eager to hear about the pastimes of Kṛṣṇa." He informed Mahārāja Parīkṣit that hearing and chanting of the pastimes of Kṛṣṇa are so auspicious that the process purifies the three varieties of men involved: he who recites the transcendental topics of Kṛṣṇa, he who hears such topics, and he who inquires about Him. These pastimes are just like the Ganges water which flows from the toe of Lord Viṣṇu: they purify the three worlds, the upper, middle and lower planetary systems.

# 1 / Advent of Lord Kṛṣṇa

Once the world was overburdened by the unnecessary defense force of different kings, who were actually demons, but were posing themselves as the royal order. At that time, the whole world became perturbed, and the predominating deity of this earth, known as Bhūmi, went to see Lord Brahmā to tell of her calamities due to the demoniac kings. Bhūmi assumed the shape of a cow and presented herself before Lord Brahmā with tears in her eyes. She was bereaved and was weeping just to invoke the Lord's compassion. She related the calamitous position of the earth, and after hearing this, Lord Brahmā became much aggrieved, and he at once started for the ocean of milk, where Lord Viṣṇu resides. Lord Brahmā was accompanied by all the demigods headed by Lord Śiva, and Bhūmi also followed. Arriving on the shore of the milk ocean, Lord Brahmā began to pacify the Lord Viṣṇu who formerly saved the earthly planet by assuming the transcendental form of a boar.

In the Vedic *mantras*, there is a particular type of prayer called *Puruṣa-sūkta*. Generally, the demigods offer their obeisances unto Viṣṇu, the Supreme Personality of Godhead, by chanting the *Puruṣa-sūkta*. It is understood herein that the predominating deity of every planet can see the supreme lord of this universe, Brahmā, whenever there is some disturbance in his planet. And Brahmā can approach the Supreme Lord Viṣṇu, not by seeing Him directly, but by standing on the shore of the ocean of milk. There is a planet within this universe called *Śvetadvīpa,* and on that planet there is an ocean of milk. It is understood from various Vedic literatures that just as there is the ocean of salt water within this planet, there are various kinds of oceans in other planets. Somewhere there is an ocean of milk, somewhere there is an ocean of oil, and somewhere there is an ocean of liquor and many other types of oceans. *Puruṣa-sūkta* is the standard prayer which the demigods recite to appease the Supreme Personality of Godhead, Kṣīrodakaśāyī-Viṣṇu. Because He is lying on the ocean of milk, He is called Kṣīrodakaśāyī-Viṣṇu. He is the Supreme Personality of Godhead, through whom all the incarnations within this universe appear.

After all the demigods offered the *Puruṣa-sūkta* prayer to the Supreme Personality of Godhead, they apparently heard no response. Then Lord Brahmā personally sat in meditation, and there was a message-transmission from Lord Viṣṇu to Brahmā. Brahmā then broadcast the message to the demigods. That is the system of receiving Vedic knowledge. The Vedic knowledge is received first by Brahmā from the Supreme Personality of Godhead, through the medium of the heart. As stated in the beginning of *Śrīmad-Bhāgavatam, tene brahma hṛdā:* the transcendental knowledge of the *Vedas* was transmitted to Lord Brahmā through the heart. Here also, in the same way, only Brahmā could understand the message transmitted by Lord Viṣṇu, and he broadcast it to the demigods for their immediate action. The message was: the Supreme Personality of Godhead will appear on the earth very soon along with His supreme powerful potencies, and as long as He remains on the earth planet to execute His mission of annihilating the demons and establishing the devotees, the demigods should also remain there to assist Him. They should all immediately take birth in the family of the Yadu dynasty, wherein the Lord will also appear in due course of time.

The Supreme Personality of Godhead Himself, Kṛṣṇa, personally appeared as the son of Vasudeva. Before He appeared, all the demigods, along with their wives, appeared in different pious families in the world just to assist the Lord in executing His mission. The exact word used here is *tatpriyārtham,* which means the demigods should appear on the earth in order to please the Lord. In other words, any living entity who lives only to satisfy the Lord is a demigod. The demigods were further informed that the plenary portion of Lord Kṛṣṇa, Ananta, who is maintaining the universal planets by extending his millions of hoods, would also appear on earth before Lord Kṛṣṇa's appearance. They were also informed that the external potency of Viṣṇu *(māyā),* with whom all the conditioned souls are enamoured, would also appear just to execute the purpose of the Supreme Lord.

After instructing and pacifying all the demigods, as well as Bhūmi, with sweet words, Lord Brahmā, the father of all *prajāpatis,* or progenitors of universal population, departed for his own abode, the highest material planet, called Brahmaloka.

The leader of the Yadu dynasty, King Śūrasena, was ruling over the country known as Mathurā (the district of Mathurā) as well as the district known as Śūrasena. On account of the rule of King Śūrasena, Mathurā became the capital city of all the kings of the Yadus. Mathurā was also made the capital of the kings of the Yadu dynasty because the Yadus were a very pious family and knew that Mathurā is the place where Lord Śrī Kṛṣṇa lives eternally, just as He also lives in Dvārakā.

Once upon a time, Vasudeva, the son of Śūrasena, just after marrying Devakī, was going home on his chariot with his newly wedded wife. The father of Devakī, known as Devaka, had contributed a sufficient dowry because he was very affectionate toward his daughter. He had contributed hundreds of chariots completely decorated with gold equipment. At that time, Kaṁsa, the son of Ugrasena, in order to please his sister, Devakī, had voluntarily taken the reins of the horses of Vasudeva's chariot and was driving. According to the custom of the Vedic civilization, when a girl is married, the brother takes the sister and brother-in-law to their home. Because the newly married girl may feel too much separation from her father's family, the brother goes with her until she reaches her father-in-law's house. The full dowry contributed by Devaka was as follows: 400 elephants fully decorated with golden garlands, 15,000 decorated horses, and 1800 chariots. He also arranged for two hundred beautiful girls to follow his daughter. The *kṣatriya* system of marriage, still current in India, dictates that when a *kṣatriya* is married, a few dozen of the bride's young girl friends (in addition to the bride) go to the house of the king. The followers of the queen are called maidservants, but actually they act as friends of the queen. This practice is prevalent from time immemorial, traceable at least to the time before the advent of Lord Kṛṣṇa 5,000 years ago. So Vasudeva brought home another two hundred beautiful girls along with his wife.

While the bride and bridegroom were passing along on the chariot, there were different kinds of musical instruments playing to indicate the auspicious moment. There were conchshells, bugles, drums and kettledrums; combined together, they were vibrating a nice concert. The procession was passing very pleasingly, and Kaṁsa was driving the chariot, when suddenly there was a miraculous sound vibrated from the sky which especially announced to Kaṁsa: "Kaṁsa: you are such a fool. You are driving the chariot of your sister and your brother-in-law, but you do not know that the eighth child of this sister will kill you."

Kaṁsa was the son of Ugrasena, of the Bhoja dynasty. It is said that Kaṁsa was the most demonic of all the Bhoja dynasty kings. Immediately after hearing the prophecy from the sky, he caught hold of Devakī's hair and was just about to kill her with his sword. Vasudeva was astonished at Kaṁsa's behavior, and in order to pacify the cruel, shameless brother-in-law, he began to speak as follows, with great reason and evidence. He said, "My dear brother-in-law Kaṁsa, you are the most famous king of the Bhoja dynasty, and people know that you are the greatest warrior and a valiant king. How is it that you are so infuriated that you are prepared to kill a woman who is your own sister at this auspicious time of her marriage? Why should you be so much afraid of death? Death is already born along with your birth. From the very day you took your birth, you began to die. Suppose you are twenty-five years old; that means you have already died twenty-five years. Every moment, every second, you are dying. Why then should you be so much afraid of death? Final death is inevitable. You may die either today or in a hundred years; you cannot avoid death. Why should you be so much afraid? Actually, death means annihilation of the present body. As soon as the present body stops functioning and mixes with the five elements of material nature, the living entity within the body accepts another body, according to his present action and reaction. It is just as when a man walks on the street; he puts forward his foot, and when he is confident that his foot is situated on sound ground, he lifts the other foot. In this way, one after another, the body changes and the soul transmigrates. See how the plantworms change from one twig to another so carefully! Similarly, the living entity changes his body as soon as the higher authorities decide on his next body. As long as a living entity is conditioned within this material world, he must take material bodies one after another. His next particular body is offered by the laws of nature, according to the actions and reactions of this life.

"This body is exactly like one of the bodies which we always see in dreams. During our dream of sleep, we create so many bodies according to mental creation. We have seen gold and we have also seen a mountain, so in a dream we can see a golden mountain by combining the two ideas. Sometimes in dreams, we see that we have a body which is flying in the sky, and at that time we completely forget our present body. Similarly, these bodies are changing. When you have one body, you forget the past body. During a dream, we may make contact with so many new kinds of bodies, but when we are awake we forget them all. And actually these material bodies are the creations of our mental activities. But at the present moment we do not recollect our past bodies.

"The nature of the mind is flickering. Sometimes it accepts something, and immediately it rejects the same thing. Accepting and rejecting is the process of the mind in contact with the five objects of sense gratification:

form, taste, smell, sound, and touch. In its speculative way, the mind comes in touch with the objects of sense gratification, and when the living entity desires a particular type of body, he gets it. Therefore, the body is an offering by the laws of material nature. The living entity accepts a body and comes out again into the material world to enjoy or suffer according to the construction of the body. Unless we have a particular type of body, we cannot enjoy or suffer according to our mental proclivities inherited from the previous life. The particular type of body is actually offered to us according to our mental condition at the time of death.

"The luminous planets like the sun, moon or the stars reflect themselves in different types of reservoirs, like water, oil or ghee. The reflection moves according to the movement of the reservoir. The reflection of the moon is on the water, and the moving water makes the moon also appear to be moving, but actually the moon is not moving. Similarly, by mental concoction, the living entity attains different kinds of bodies, although actually he has no connection with such bodies. But on account of illusion, being enchanted by the influence of *māyā,* the living entity thinks that he belongs to a particular type of body. That is the way of conditioned life. Suppose a living entity is now in a human form of body. He thinks that he belongs to the human community, or a particular country or particular place. He identifies himself in that way and unnecessarily prepares for another body which is not required by him. Such desires and mental concoctions are the cause of different types of body. The covering influence of material nature is so strong that the living entity is satisfied in whatever body he gets, and he identifies with that body with great pleasure. Therefore, I beg to request you not to be overwhelmed by the dictation of your mind and body."

Vasudeva thus requested Kaṁsa not to be envious of his newly married sister. One should not be envious of anyone because envy is the cause of fear both in this world and in the next when one is before Yamarāja (the lord of punishment after death). Vasudeva appealed to Kaṁsa on behalf of Devakī, stating that she was his younger sister. He also appealed at an auspicious moment, at the time of marriage. A younger sister or brother are supposed to be protected as one's children. "The position is overall so delicate," Vasudeva reasoned, "that if you kill her, it will go against your high reputation."

Vasudeva tried to pacify Kaṁsa by good instruction as well as by philosophical discrimination, but Kaṁsa was not to be pacified because his association was demoniac. Because of his demoniac associations, he was always a demon, although born in a very high royal family. A demon never cares for any good instruction. He is just like a determined thief: one can give him moral instruction, but it will not be effective. Similarly, those who are demoniac or atheistic by nature can hardly assimilate any good instruction, however authorized it may be. That is the difference between demigod and demon. Those who can accept good instruction and try to live their lives in that way are called demigods, and those who are unable to take such good instruction are called demons. Failing in his attempt to pacify Kaṁsa, Vasudeva wondered how he would protect his wife Devakī. When there is imminent danger, an intelligent person should try to avoid the dangerous position as far as possible. But if, in spite of endeavoring by all intelligence, one fails to avoid the dangerous position, there is no fault on his part. One should try his best to execute his duties, but if the attempt fails, he is not at fault.

Vasudeva thought of his wife as follows: "For the present let me save the life of Devakī, then later on, if there are children, I shall see how to save them." He further thought, "If in the future I get a child who can kill Kaṁsa–just as Kaṁsa is thinking–then both Devakī and the child will be saved because the law of Providence is inconceivable. But now, some way or other, let me save the life of Devakī."

There is no certainty how a living entity contacts a certain type of body, just as there is no certainty how the blazing fire comes in contact with a certain type of wood in the forest. When there is a forest fire, it is experienced that the blazing fire sometimes leaps over one tree and catches another by the influence of the wind. Similarly, a living entity may be very careful and fearful in the matter of executing his duties, but it is still very difficult for him to know what type of body he is going to get in the next life. Mahārāja Bharata was very faithfully executing the duties of self-realization, but by chance he contacted temporary affection for a deer, and he had to accept his next life in the body of a deer.

Vasudeva, after deliberating on how to save his wife, began to speak to Kaṁsa with great respect, although Kaṁsa was the most sinful man. Sometimes it happens that a most virtuous person like Vasudeva has to flatter a person like Kaṁsa, a most vicious person. That is the way of all diplomatic transactions. Although Vasudeva was deeply aggrieved, he presented himself outwardly as cheerful. He addressed the shameless Kaṁsa in that way because he was so atrocious. Vasudeva said to Kaṁsa, "My dear brother-in-law, please consider that you have no danger from your sister. You are awaiting some danger because you have heard a prophetic voice in the sky. But the danger is to come from the sons of your sister, who are not present now. And who knows? There may or may not be sons in the future.

Considering all this, you are safe for the present. Nor is there cause of fear from your sister. If there are any sons born of her, I promise that I shall present all of them to you for necessary action."

Kaṁsa knew the value of Vasudeva's word of honor, and he was convinced by his argument. For the time being, he desisted from the heinous killing of his sister. Thus Vasudeva was pleased and praised the decision of Kaṁsa. In this way, he returned to his home.

After due course of time, Vasudeva and Devakī gave birth to eight male children, as well as one daughter. When the first son was born, Vasudeva kept his word of honor and immediately brought the child before Kaṁsa. It is said that Vasudeva was very much elevated and famous for his word of honor, and he wanted to maintain this fame. Although it was very painful for Vasudeva to hand over the newly born child, Kaṁsa was very glad to receive him. But he became a little compassionate with the behavior of Vasudeva. This event is very exemplary. For a great soul like Vasudeva, there is nothing considered to be painful in the course of discharging one's duty. A learned person like Vasudeva carries out his duties without hesitation. On the other hand, a demon like Kaṁsa never hesitates in committing any abominable action. It is said, therefore, that a saintly person can tolerate all kinds of miserable conditions of life, a learned man can discharge his duties without awaiting favorable circumstances, a heinous person like Kaṁsa can act in any sinful way, and a devotee can sacrifice everything to satisfy the Supreme Personality of Godhead.

Kaṁsa became satisfied by the action of Vasudeva. He was surprised to see Vasudeva keeping his promise, and being compassionate upon him and pleased, he began to speak as follows: "My dear Vasudeva, you need not present this child to me. I am not in danger from this child. I have heard that the eighth child born of you and Devakī will kill me. Why should I accept this child unnecessarily? You can take him back."

When Vasudeva was returning home with his first-born child, although he was pleased by the behavior of Kaṁsa, he could not believe in him because he knew that Kaṁsa was uncontrolled. An atheistic person cannot be firm in his word of honor. One who cannot control the senses cannot be steady in his determination. The great politician, Cāṇakya Paṇḍit, said, "Never put your trust in a diplomat or in a woman." Those who are addicted to unrestricted sense gratification can never be truthful, nor can they be trusted with any faith.

At that time the great sage Nārada came to Kaṁsa. He was informed of Kaṁsa's becoming compassionate to Vasudeva and returning his first-born child. Nārada was very anxious to accelerate the descent of Lord Kṛṣṇa as soon as possible. He therefore informed Kaṁsa that personalities like Nanda Mahārāja and all the cowherd men and girls and the wives of the cowherd men in Vṛndāvana, and, on the other side, Vasudeva, his father Śūrasena and all his relatives born in the family of Vṛṣṇi of the Yadu Dynasty, were preparing for the appearance of the Lord. Nārada warned Kaṁsa to be careful of the friends and well-wishers and all the demigods taking birth in those families. Kaṁsa and his friends and advisors were all demons. Demons are always afraid of demigods. After being thus informed by Nārada about the appearance of the demigods in different families, Kaṁsa at once became alert. He understood that since the demigods had already appeared, Lord Viṣṇu must be coming soon. He at once arrested both his brother-in-law Vasudeva and Devakī and put them behind prison bars.

Within the prison, shackled in iron chains, Vasudeva and Devakī gave birth to a male child year after year, and Kaṁsa, thinking each of the babies to be the incarnation of Viṣṇu, killed them one after another. He was particularly afraid of the eighth child, but after the visit of Nārada, he came to the conclusion that any child might be Kṛṣṇa. Therefore it was better to kill all the babies who took birth of Devakī and Vasudeva.

This action of Kaṁsa is not very difficult to understand. There are many instances in the history of the world of persons in the royal order who have killed father, brother, or a whole family and friends for the satisfaction of their ambitions. There is nothing astonishing about this, for the demoniac can kill anyone for their nefarious ambitions.

Kaṁsa was made aware of his previous birth by the grace of Nārada. He learned that in his previous birth he was a demon of the name Kālanemi and that he was killed by Viṣṇu. Having taken his birth in the Bhoja family, he decided to become the deadly enemy of the Yadu dynasty; Kṛṣṇa was going to take birth in that family, and Kaṁsa was very much afraid that he would be killed by Kṛṣṇa, just as he was killed in his last birth.

He first of all imprisoned his father Ugrasena because he was the chief king among the Yadu, Bhoja, and Andhaka dynasties, and he also occupied the kingdom of Śūrasena, Vasudeva's father. He declared himself the king of all such places.

*Thus ends the Bhaktivedanta purport of the First Chapter of* Kṛṣṇa, *"Advent of Lord Kṛṣṇa."*

# 2 / Prayers by the Demigods for Lord Kṛṣṇa in the Womb

King Kaṁsa not only occupied the kingdoms of the Yadu, Bhoja, and Andhaka dynasties and the kingdom of Śūrasena, but he also made alliances with all the other demoniac kings, as follows: the demon Pralamba, demon Baka, demon Cāṇūra, demon Tṛṇāvarta, demon Aghāsura, demon Muṣṭika, demon Ariṣṭa, demon Dvivida, demon Pūtanā, demon Keśī and demon Dhenuka. At that time, Jarāsandha was the king of Magadha province (known at present as Behar state). Thus by his diplomatic policy, Kaṁsa consolidated the most powerful kingdom of his time, under the protection of Jarāsandha. He made further alliances with such kings as Bāṇāsura and Bhaumāsura, until he was the strongest. Then he began to behave most inimically towards the Yadu dynasty into which Kṛṣṇa was to take His birth.

Being harassed by Kaṁsa, the kings of the Yadu, Bhoja and Andhaka dynasties began to take shelter in different states such as the state of the Kurus, the state of the Pañcālas and the states known as Kekaya, Śālva, Vidarbha, Niṣadha, Videha and Kośala. Kaṁsa broke the solidarity of the Yadu Kingdom, as well as the Bhoja and Andhaka. He made his position the most solid within the vast tract of land known at that time as Bhāratavarṣa.

When Kaṁsa killed the six babies of Devakī and Vasudeva one after another, many friends and relatives of Kaṁsa approached him and requested him to discontinue these heinous activities. But all of them became worshipers of Kaṁsa.

When Devakī became pregnant for the seventh time, a plenary expansion of Kṛṣṇa known as Ananta appeared within her womb. Devakī was overwhelmed both with jubilation and lamentation. She was joyful, for she could understand that Lord Viṣṇu had taken shelter within her womb, but at the same time she was sorry that as soon as her child would come out,

Kaṁsa would kill Him. At that time, the Supreme Personality of Godhead, Kṛṣṇa, being compassionate upon the fearful condition of the Yadus, due to atrocities committed by Kaṁsa, ordered the appearance of His *Yogamāyā,* or His internal potency. Kṛṣṇa is the Lord of the universe, but He is especially the Lord of the Yadu dynasty.

This *Yogamāyā* is the principal potency of the Personality of Godhead. In the *Vedas* it is stated that the Lord, the Supreme Personality of Godhead, has multipotencies. *Parāsya śaktir vividhaiva śrūyate.* All the different potencies are acting externally and internally, and *Yogamāyā* is the chief of all potencies. He ordered the appearance of *Yogamāyā* in the land of Vrajabhūmi, in Vṛndāvana, which is always decorated and full with beautiful cows. In Vṛndāvana, Rohiṇī, one of the wives of Vasudeva, was residing at the house of King Nanda and Queen Yaśodā. Not only Rohiṇī, but many others in the Yadu dynasty were scattered all over the country due to their fear of the atrocities of Kaṁsa. Some of them were even living in the caves of the mountains.

The Lord thus informed *Yogamāyā:* "Under the imprisonment of Kaṁsa are Devakī and Vasudeva, and at the present moment, My plenary expansion, Śeṣa, is within the womb of Devakī. You can arrange the transfer of Śeṣa from the womb of Devakī to the womb of Rohiṇī. After this arrangement, I am personally going to appear in the womb of Devakī with My full potencies. Then I shall appear as the son of Devakī and Vasudeva. And you shall appear as the daughter of Nanda and Yaśodā in Vṛndāvana.

"Since you will appear as My contemporary sister, people within the world will worship you with all kinds of valuable presentations: incense, candles, flowers and offerings of sacrifice. You shall quickly satisfy their desires for sense gratification. People who are after materialistic affection will worship you under the different forms of your expansions, which will be named Durgā, Bhadrakālī, Vijayā, Vaiṣṇavī, Kumudā, Caṇḍikā, Kṛṣṇā, Mādhavī, Kanyakā, Māyā, Nārāyaṇī, Īśānī, Śāradā and Ambikā."

Kṛṣṇa and *Yogamāyā* appeared as brother and sister—the Supreme Powerful and the supreme power. Although there is no clear distinction between the Powerful and the power, power is always subordinate to the Powerful. Those who are materialistic are worshippers of the power, but those who are transcendentalists are worshippers of the Powerful. Kṛṣṇa is the Supreme Powerful, and Durgā is the supreme power within the material world. Actually people in the Vedic culture worship both the Powerful and the power. There are many hundreds of thousands of temples of Viṣṇu and Devī, and sometimes they are worshipped simultaneously. The worshipper of the power, Durgā, or the external energy of Kṛṣṇa, may achieve all kinds of material success very easily, but anyone who wants to be elevated transcendentally must engage in worshipping the Powerful in Kṛṣṇa consciousness.

The Lord also declared to *Yogamāyā* that His plenary expansion, Ananta Śeṣa, was within the womb of Devakī. On account of being forcibly attracted to the womb of Rohiṇī, He would be known as Saṅkarṣaṇa and would be the source of all spiritual power or *bala*, by which one could be able to attain the highest bliss of life which is called *ramaṇa*. Therefore the plenary portion Ananta would be known after His appearance either as Saṅkarṣaṇa or Balarāma.

In the *Upaniṣads* it is stated, *Nāyam ātma bala hinena labhya.* The purport is that one cannot attain the Supreme or any form of self-realization without being sufficiently favored by Balarāma. *Bala* does not mean physical strength. No one can attain spiritual perfection by physical strength. One must have the spiritual strength which is infused by Balarāma or Saṅkarṣaṇa. *Ananta* or *Śeṣa* is the power which sustains all the planets in their different positions. Materially this sustaining power is known as the law of gravitation, but actually it is the display of the potency of Saṅkarṣaṇa. Balarāma or Saṅkarṣaṇa is spiritual power, or the original spiritual master. Therefore Lord Nityānanda Prabhu, who is also the incarnation of Balarāma, is the original spiritual master. And the spiritual master is the representative of Balarāma, the Supreme Personality of Godhead, who supplies spiritual strength. In the *Caitanya-caritāmṛta* it is confirmed that the spiritual master is the manifestation of the mercy of Kṛṣṇa.

When *Yogamāyā* was thus ordered by the Supreme Personality of Godhead, she circumambulated the Lord and then appeared within this material world according to His order. When the Supreme Powerful Personality of Godhead transferred Lord Śeṣa from the womb of Devakī to the womb of Rohiṇī, both of them were under the spell of *Yogamāyā,* which is also called *yoga-nidrā.* When this was done, people understood that Devakī's seventh pregnancy was a miscarriage. Thus although Balarāma appeared as the son of Devakī, He was transferred to the womb of Rohiṇī to appear as her son. After this arrangement, the Supreme Personality of Godhead, Kṛṣṇa, who is always ready to place His full potencies in His unalloyed devotees, entered as the Lord of the whole creation within the mind of Vasudeva. It is understood in this connection that Lord Kṛṣṇa first of all situated Himself in the unalloyed heart of Devakī. He was not put into the womb of Devakī by seminal discharge. The Supreme Personality of Godhead, by His inconceivable potency, can appear in any way. It is not necessary for Him to appear in the ordinary way by seminal injection within the womb of a woman.

When Vasudeva was sustaining the form of the Supreme Personality of Godhead within his heart, he appeared just like the glowing sun whose shining rays are always unbearable and scorching to the common man. The form of the Lord situated in the pure unalloyed heart of Vasudeva is not different from the original form of Kṛṣṇa. The appearance of the form of Kṛṣṇa anywhere, and specifically within the heart, is called *dhāma. Dhāma* does not only refer to Kṛṣṇa's form, but His name, His form, His quality and His paraphernalia. Everything becomes manifest simultaneously.

Thus the eternal form of the Supreme Personality of Godhead with full potencies was transferred from the mind of Vasudeva to the mind of Devakī, exactly as the setting sun's rays are transferred to the full moon rising in the east.

Kṛṣṇa, the Supreme Personality of Godhead, entered the body of Devakī from the body of Vasudeva. He was beyond the conditions of the ordinary living entity. When Kṛṣṇa is there, it is to be understood that all His plenary expansions, such as Nārāyaṇa, and incarnations like Lord Nṛsiṁha, Varāha, etc., are with Him, and they are not subject to the conditions of material existence. In this way, Devakī became the residence of the Supreme Personality of Godhead who is one without a second and the cause of all creation. Devakī became the residence of the Absolute Truth, but because she was within the house of Kaṁsa, she looked just like a suppressed fire, or like misused education. When fire is covered by the walls of a pot or is kept in a jug, the illuminating rays of the fire cannot be very much appreciated. Similarly, misused knowledge, which does not benefit the people in general, is not very much appreciated. So Devakī was kept within the prison walls of Kaṁsa's palace, and no one could see her transcendental beauty which resulted from her conceiving the Supreme Personality of Godhead.

Kaṁsa, however, saw the transcendental beauty of his sister Devakī, and he at once concluded that the Supreme Personality of Godhead had taken shelter in her womb. She had never before looked so wonderfully beautiful. He could distinctly understand that there was something wonderful within the womb of Devakī. In this way, Kaṁsa became perturbed. He was sure that the Supreme Personality of Godhead would kill him in the future and that He had now come. Kaṁsa began to think: "What is to be done with Devakī? Surely she has Viṣṇu or Kṛṣṇa within her womb, so it is certain that Kṛṣṇa has come to execute the mission of the demigods. And even if I immediately kill Devakī, His mission cannot be frustrated." Kaṁsa knew very well that no one can frustrate the purpose of Viṣṇu. Any intelligent man can understand that the laws of God cannot be violated. His purpose will be served in spite of all impediments offered by the demons. Kaṁsa thought: "If I kill Devakī at the present moment, Viṣṇu will enforce His supreme will more vehemently. To kill Devakī just now would be a most abominable act. No one desires to kill his reputation, even in an awkward situation; if I kill Devakī now, my reputation will be spoiled. Devakī is a woman, and she is under my shelter; she is pregnant, and if I kill her, immediately all my reputation, the result of pious activities and duration of life, will be finished."

He also further deliberated: "A person who is too cruel, even in this lifetime is as good as dead. No one likes a cruel person during his lifetime, and after his death, people curse him. On account of his self-identification with the body, he must be degraded and pushed into the darkest region of hell." Kaṁsa thus meditated on all the pros and cons of killing Devakī at that time.

Kaṁsa finally decided not to kill Devakī right away but to wait for the inevitable future. But his mind became absorbed in animosity against the Personality of Godhead. He patiently waited for the deliverance of the child, expecting to kill Him, as he had done previously with the other babies of Devakī. Thus being merged in the ocean of animosity against the Personality of Godhead, he began to think of Kṛṣṇa and Viṣṇu while sitting, while sleeping, while walking, while eating, while working—in all the situations of his life. His mind became so much absorbed with the thought of the Supreme Personality of Godhead that indirectly he could see only Kṛṣṇa or Viṣṇu around him. Unfortunately, although his mind was so absorbed in the thought of Viṣṇu, he is not recognized as a devotee because he was thinking of Kṛṣṇa as an enemy. The state of mind of a great devotee is also to be always absorbed in Kṛṣṇa, but a devotee thinks of Him favorably, not unfavorably. To think of Kṛṣṇa favorably is Kṛṣṇa consciousness, but to think of Kṛṣṇa unfavorably is not Kṛṣṇa consciousness.

At this time Lord Brahmā and Lord Śiva, accompanied by great sages like Nārada and followed by many other demigods, invisibly appeared in the house of Kaṁsa. They began to pray for the Supreme Personality of Godhead in select prayers which are very pleasing to the devotees and which award fulfillment of their desires. The first words they spoke acclaimed that the Lord is true to His vow. As stated in the *Bhagavad-gītā*,

Kṛṣṇa descends in this material world just to protect the pious and destroy the impious. That is His vow. The demigods could understand that the Lord had taken His residence within the womb of Devakī in order to fulfill this vow. The demigods were very glad that the Lord was appearing to fulfill His mission, and they addressed Him as *satyam param,* or the Supreme Absolute Truth.

Everyone is searching after the truth. That is the philosophical way of life. The demigods give information that the Supreme Absolute Truth is Kṛṣṇa. One who becomes fully Kṛṣṇa conscious can attain the Absolute Truth. Kṛṣṇa is the Absolute Truth. Relative truth is not truth in all the three phases of eternal time. Time is divided into past, present and future. Kṛṣṇa is Truth always, past, present and future. In the material world everything is being controlled by supreme time, in the course of past, present and future. But before the creation, Kṛṣṇa was existing, and when there is creation, everything is resting in Kṛṣṇa, and when this creation is finished, Kṛṣṇa will remain. Therefore, He is Absolute Truth in all circumstances. If there is any truth within this material world, it emanates from the Supreme Truth, Kṛṣṇa. If there is any opulence within this material world, the cause of the opulence is Kṛṣṇa. If there is any reputation within this material world, the cause of the reputation is Kṛṣṇa. If there is any strength within this material world, the cause of such strength is Kṛṣṇa. If there is any wisdom and education within this material world, the cause of such wisdom and education is Kṛṣṇa. Therefore Kṛṣṇa is the source of all relative truths.

This material world is composed of five principal elements: earth, water, fire, air and ether, and all such elements are emanations from Kṛṣṇa. The material scientists accept these primary five elements as the cause of material manifestation, but the elements in their gross and subtle states are produced by Kṛṣṇa. The living entities who are working within this material world are also products of His marginal potency. In the Seventh Chapter of the *Bhagavad-gītā,* it is clearly stated that the whole manifestation is a combination of two kinds of energies of Kṛṣṇa, the superior energy and the inferior energy. The living entities are the superior energy, and the dead material elements are His inferior energy. In its dormant stage, everything remains in Kṛṣṇa.

The demigods continued to offer their respectful prayers unto the supreme form of the Personality of Godhead, Kṛṣṇa, by analytical study of the material manifestation. What is this material manifestation? It is just like a tree. A tree stands on the ground. Similarly, the tree of the material manifestation is standing on the ground of material nature. This material manifestation is compared with a tree because a tree is ultimately cut off in due course of time. A tree is called *vṛkṣa. Vṛkṣa* means that thing which will be ultimately cut off. Therefore, this tree of the material manifestation cannot be accepted as the Ultimate Truth. The influence of time is on the material manifestation, but Kṛṣṇa's body is eternal. He existed before the material manifestation, He is existing while the material manifestation is continuing, and when it will be dissolved, He will continue to exist.

The *Kaṭha Upaniṣad* also cites this example of the tree of material manifestation standing on the ground of material nature. This tree has two kinds of fruits, distress and happiness. Those who are living on the tree of the body are just like two birds. One bird is the localized aspect of Kṛṣṇa known as the Paramātmā, and the other bird is the living entity. The living entity is eating the fruits of this material manifestation. Sometimes he eats the fruit of happiness, and sometimes he eats the fruit of distress. But the other bird is not interested in eating the fruit of distress or happiness because he is self-satisfied. The *Kaṭha Upaniṣad* states that one bird on the tree of the body is eating the fruits, and the other bird is simply witnessing. The roots of this tree extend in three directions. That means the root of the tree is the three modes of material nature: goodness, passion and ignorance. Just as the tree's root expands, so, by association of the modes of material nature (goodness, passion and ignorance), one expands his duration of material existence. The taste of the fruits are of four kinds: religiosity, economic development, sense gratification and ultimately, liberation. According to the different associations in the three modes of material nature, the living entities are tasting different kinds of religiosity, different kinds of economic development, different kinds of sense gratification and different kinds of liberation. Practically all material work is performed in ignorance, but because there are three qualities, sometimes the quality of ignorance is covered with goodness or passion. The taste of these material fruits is accepted through five senses. The five sense organs through which knowledge is acquired are subjected to six kinds of whips: lamentation, illusion, infirmity, death, hunger and thirst. This material body, or the material manifestation, is covered by seven layers: skin, muscle, flesh, marrow, bone, fat and semina. The branches of the tree are eight: earth, water, fire, air, ether, mind, intelligence and ego. There are nine gates in this body: the two eyes, two nostrils, two ears, one mouth, one genital, one rectum. And there are ten kinds of internal air passing within the body: *prāṇa, apāna, udāna, vyāna, samāna,* etc. The two birds seated in this tree, as explained above, are the living entity and the localized Supreme Personality of Godhead.

The root cause of the material manifestation described here is the Supreme Personality of Godhead. The Supreme Personality of Godhead expands Himself and takes charge of the three qualities of the material world. Viṣṇu takes charge of the modes of goodness, Brahmā takes charge of the modes of passion, and Lord Śiva takes charge of the modes of ignorance. Brahmā, by the modes of passion, creates this manifestation, Lord Viṣṇu maintains this manifestation by the modes of goodness, and Lord Śiva annihilates it by the modes of ignorance. The whole creation ultimately rests in the Supreme Lord. He is the cause of creation, maintenance and dissolution. And when the whole manifestation is dissolved, in its subtle form as the energy of the Lord, it rests within the body of the Supreme Lord.

"At the present," the demigods prayed, "the Supreme Lord Kṛṣṇa is appearing just for the maintenance of this manifestation." Actually the Supreme Cause is one, but, being deluded by the three modes of material nature, less intelligent persons see that the material world is manifested through different causes. Those who are intelligent can see that the cause is one, Kṛṣṇa. As it is stated in the *Brahma-saṁhitā: sarva-kāraṇa-kāraṇam.* Kṛṣṇa, the Supreme Personality of Godhead, is the cause of all causes. Brahmā is the deputed agent for creation, Viṣṇu is the expansion of Kṛṣṇa for maintenance, and Lord Śiva is the expansion of Kṛṣṇa for dissolution.

"Our dear Lord," the demigods prayed, "it is very difficult to understand Your eternal form of personality. People in general are unable to understand Your actual form; therefore You are personally descending to exhibit Your original eternal form. Somehow people can understand the different incarnations of Your Lordship, but they are puzzled to understand the eternal form of Kṛṣṇa with two hands, moving among human beings exactly like one of them. This eternal form of Your Lordship is ever increasing in transcendental pleasure for the devotees. But for the nondevotees, this form is very dangerous." As stated in the *Bhagavad-gītā,* Kṛṣṇa is very pleasing to the *sādhu.* It is said, *paritrāṇāya sādhūnām.* But this form is very dangerous for the demons because Kṛṣṇa also descends to kill the demons. He is, therefore, simultaneously pleasing to the devotees and dangerous to the demons.

"Our dear lotus-eyed Lord, You are the source of pure goodness. There are many great sages who simply by *samādhi,* or transcendentally meditating upon Your lotus feet and thus being absorbed in Your thought, have easily transformed the great ocean of nescience created by the material nature to no more than water in a calf's hoofprint." The purpose of meditation is to focus the mind upon the Personality of Godhead, beginning from

His lotus feet. Simply by meditation on the lotus feet of the Lord, great sages cross over this vast ocean of material existence without difficulty.

"O self-illuminated one, the great saintly persons who have crossed over the ocean of nescience, by the help of the transcendental boat of Your lotus feet, have not taken away that boat. It is still lying on this side." The demigods are using a nice simile. If one takes a boat to cross over a river, the boat also goes with one to the other side of the river. And so when one reaches the destination, how can the same boat be available to those who are still on the other side? To answer this difficulty, the demigods say in their prayer that the boat is not taken away. The devotees still remaining on the other side are able to pass over the ocean of material nature because the pure devotees do not take the boat with them when they cross over. When one simply approaches the boat, the whole ocean of material nescience is reduced to the size of water in a calf's hoofprint. Therefore, the devotees do not need to take a boat to the other side; they simply cross the ocean immediately. Because the great saintly persons are compassionate toward all conditioned souls, the boat is still lying at the lotus feet of the Lord. One can meditate upon His feet at any time, and by so doing, one can cross over the great ocean of material existence.

Meditation means concentration upon the lotus feet of the Lord. Lotus feet indicate the Supreme Personality of Godhead. Those who are impersonalists do not recognize the lotus feet of the Lord, and therefore their object of meditation is something impersonal. The demigods express their mature verdict that persons who are interested in meditating on something void or impersonal cannot cross over the ocean of nescience. Such persons are simply imagining that they have become liberated. "O lotus-eyed Lord! Their intelligence is contaminated because they fail to meditate upon the lotus feet of Your Lordship." As a result of this neglectful activity, the impersonalists fall down again into the material way of conditioned life, although they may temporarily rise up to the point of impersonal realization. Impersonalists, after undergoing severe austerities and penances, merge themselves into the Brahman effulgence or impersonal Brahman existence. But their minds are not free from material contamination; they have simply tried to negate the material ways of thinking. That does not mean that they have become liberated. Thus they fall down. In the *Bhagavad-gītā* it is stated that the impersonalist has to undergo great tribulation in realizing the ultimate goal. At the beginning of the *Śrīmad-Bhāgavatam,* it is also stated that without devotional service to the Supreme Personality of Godhead, one cannot achieve liberation from the bondage of fruitive activities. The statement of Lord Kṛṣṇa is there in the *Bhagavad-gītā,* and in the *Śrīmad-Bhāgavatam* the statement of the great sage Nārada is there, and here also the demigods confirm it. "Persons who have not taken to devotional service are understood to have come short of the ultimate purpose of knowledge and are not favored by Your grace." The impersonalists simply *think* that they are liberated, but actually they have no feeling for the Personality of Godhead. They think that when Kṛṣṇa comes into the material world, he accepts a material body. They therefore overlook the transcendental body of Kṛṣṇa. This is also confirmed in the *Bhagavad-gītā. Avajānanti māṁ mūḍhāḥ.* In spite of conquering material lust and rising up to the point of liberation, the impersonalists fall down. If they are engaged just in knowing things for the sake of knowledge and do not take to the devotional service of the Lord, they cannot achieve the desired result. Their achievement is the trouble they take, and that is all. It is clearly stated in the *Bhagavad-gītā* that to realize Brahman identification is not all. Brahman identification may help one become joyful without material attachment or detachment and to achieve the platform of equanimity, but after this stage, one has to take to devotional service. When one takes to devotional service after being elevated to the platform of Brahman realization, he is then admitted into the spiritual kingdom for permanent residence in association with the Supreme Personality of Godhead. That is the result of devotional service. Those who are devotees of the Supreme Personality of Godhead never fall down like the impersonalists. Even if the devotees fall down, they remain affectionately attached to their Lordship. They can meet all kinds of obstacles on the path of devotional service, and freely, without any fear, they can surmount such obstacles. Because of their surrender, they are certain that Kṛṣṇa will always protect them. As it is promised by Kṛṣṇa in the *Bhagavad-gītā:* "My devotees are never vanquished."

"Our dear Lord, You have appeared in Your original unalloyed form, the eternal form of goodness, for the welfare of all living entities within this material world. Taking advantage of Your appearance, all of them can now very easily understand the nature and form of the Supreme Personality of Godhead. Persons who belong to the four divisions of the social order (the *brahmacārīs,* the *gṛhasthas,* the *vānaprasthas* and the *sannyāsīs*) can all take advantage of Your appearance.

"Dear Lord, husband of the goddess of fortune, devotees who are dovetailed in Your service do not fall down from their high position like the impersonalists. Being protected by You, the devotees are able to traverse over the heads of many of *māyā's* commanders-in-chief, who can always put stumbling blocks on the path of liberation. My dear Lord, You appear in Your transcendental form for the benefit of the living entities so that they can see You face to face and offer their worshipful sacrifices by ritualistic performance of the *Vedas,* mystic meditation and devotional service as recommended in the scriptures. Dear Lord, if You did not appear in Your eternal transcendental form, full of bliss and knowledge—which can eradicate all kinds of speculative ignorance about Your position—then all people would simply speculate about You according to their respective modes of material nature."

The appearance of Kṛṣṇa is the answer to all imaginative iconography of the Supreme Personality of Godhead. Everyone imagines the form of the Supreme Personality of Godhead according to his mode of material nature. In the *Brahma-saṁhitā* it is said that the Lord is the oldest person. Therefore a section of religionists imagine that God must be very old, and therefore they depict a form of the Lord like a very old man. But in the same *Brahma-saṁhitā,* that is contradicted; although He is the oldest of all living entities, He has His eternal form as a fresh youth. The exact words used in this connection in the *Śrīmad-Bhāgavatam* are *vijñānam ajñānabhid āpamārjanam. Vijñānam* means transcendental knowledge of the Supreme Personality. *Vijñānam* is also experienced knowledge. Transcendental knowledge has to be accepted by the descending process of disciplic succession as Brahmā presents the knowledge of Kṛṣṇa in the *Brahma-saṁhitā. Brahma-saṁhitā* is *vijñānam* as realized by Brahmā's transcendental experience, and in that way he presented the form and the pastimes of Kṛṣṇa in the transcendental abode. *Ajñānabhid* means that which can match all kinds of speculation. In ignorance, people are imagining the form of the Lord; sometimes He has no form and sometimes He has form, according to their different imaginations. But the presentation of Kṛṣṇa in the *Brahma-saṁhitā* is *vijñānam*—scientific, experienced knowledge given by Lord Brahmā and accepted by Lord Caitanya. There is no doubt about it. Śrī Kṛṣṇa's form, Śrī Kṛṣṇa's flute, Kṛṣṇa's color—everything is reality. Here it is said that this *vijñānam* is always defeating all kinds of speculative knowledge. "Therefore, without Your appearing as Kṛṣṇa, as You are, neither *ajñānabhid* (nescience of speculative knowledge) nor *vijñānam* would be realized. *Ajñānabhid āpamārjanam*—by Your appearance the speculative knowledge of ignorance will be vanquished and the real experienced knowledge of authorities like Lord Brahmā will be established. Men influenced by the three modes of material nature imagine their own God according to the modes of material nature. In this way God is presented in various ways, but Your appearance will establish what the real form of God is."

The highest blunder committed by the impersonalist is to think that when the incarnation of God comes, He accepts the form of matter in the modes of goodness. Actually the form of Kṛṣṇa or Nārāyaṇa is transcendental to any material idea. Even the greatest impersonalist, Śaṅkarācārya, has admitted that *nārāyaṇaḥ paro'vyaktāt:* the material creation is caused by the *avyakta* impersonal manifestation of matter or the nonphenomenal total reservation of matter, and Kṛṣṇa is transcendental to that material conception. That is expressed in the *Śrīmad-Bhāgavatam* as *śuddha-sattva,* or transcendental. He does not belong to the material mode of goodness, and He is above the position of material goodness. He belongs to the transcendental eternal status of bliss and knowledge.

"Dear Lord, when You appear in Your different incarnations, You take different names and forms according to different situations. Lord Kṛṣṇa is Your name because You are all attractive; You are called Śyāmasundara because of Your transcendental beauty. *Śyāma* means blackish, yet they say that You are more beautiful than thousands of cupids. *Kandarpa-koṭi-kamanīya.* Although You appear in a color which is compared to the blackish cloud, because You are transcendental Absolute, Your beauty is many many times more attractive than the delicate body of Cupid. Sometimes You are called Giridhārī because You lifted the hill known as Govardhana. You are sometimes called Nandanandana or Vāsudeva or Devakīnandana because You appear as the son of Mahārāja Nanda or Devakī or Vasudeva. Impersonalists think that Your many names or forms are according to a particular type of work and quality because they accept You from the position of a material observer.

"Our dear Lord, the way of understanding is not to study Your absolute nature, form and activities by mental speculation. One must engage himself in devotional service; then one can understand Your absolute nature, transcendental form, name and quality. Actually only a person who has a little taste for the service of Your lotus feet can understand Your transcendental nature or form and quality. Others may go on speculating for millions of years, but it is not possible for them to understand even a single part of Your actual position." In other words, the Supreme Personality of Godhead, Kṛṣṇa, cannot be understood by the nondevotees because there is a curtain of *Yogamāyā* which covers Kṛṣṇa's actual features. As confirmed in the *Bhagavad-gītā, nāhaṁ prakāśaḥ sarvasya.* The Lord says, "I am not exposed to anyone and everyone." When Kṛṣṇa came, He was actually present on the battlefield of Kurukṣetra, and everyone saw Him. But not everyone could understand that He was the Supreme Personality of

Godhead. Still, everyone who died in His presence attained complete liberation from material bondage and was transferred to the spiritual world.

"O Lord, the impersonalists or nondevotees cannot understand that Your name is identical with Your form." Since the Lord is Absolute, there is no difference between His name and His actual form. In the material world there is a difference between form and name. The mango fruit is different from the name of the mango. One cannot taste the mango fruit simply by chanting, "Mango, mango, mango." But the devotee who knows that there is no difference between the name and the form of the Lord chants Hare Kṛṣṇa, Hare Kṛṣṇa, Kṛṣṇa Kṛṣṇa, Hare Hare, Hare Rāma, Hare Rāma, Rāma Rāma, Hare Hare, and realizes that he is always in Kṛṣṇa's company.

For persons who are not very advanced in absolute knowledge of the Supreme, Lord Kṛṣṇa exhibits His transcendental pastimes. They can simply think of the pastimes of the Lord and get the full benefit. Since there is no difference between the transcendental name and form of the Lord, there is no difference between the transcendental pastimes and the form of the Lord. For those who are less intelligent (like women, laborers or the mercantile class), the great sage Vyāsadeva wrote *Mahābhārata.* In the *Mahābhārata,* Kṛṣṇa is present in His different activities. *Mahābhārata* is history, and simply by studying, hearing and memorizing the transcendental activities of Kṛṣṇa, the less intelligent can also gradually rise to the standard of pure devotees.

The pure devotees, who are always absorbed in the thought of the transcendental lotus feet of Kṛṣṇa and who are always engaged in devotional service in full Kṛṣṇa consciousness, are never to be considered to be in the material world. Śrī Rūpa Gosvāmī has explained that those who are always engaged in Kṛṣṇa consciousness, by body, mind and activities, are to be considered liberated even within this body. This is also confirmed in the *Bhagavad-gītā:* those who are engaged in the devotional service of the Lord have already transcended the material position.

Kṛṣṇa appears to give a chance both to the devotees and nondevotees for realization of the ultimate goal of life. The devotees get the direct chance to see Him and worship Him. Those who are not on that platform get the chance to become acquainted with His activities and thus become elevated to the same position.

"O dear Lord," the demigods continued, "You are unborn; therefore we do not find any reason for Your appearance other than for Your pleasurable pastimes." Although the reason for the appearance of the Lord is stated in the *Bhagavad-gītā* (He descends just to give protection to the devotee and vanquish the nondevotee), actually He descends for His pleasure-meeting with the devotees, not really to vanquish the nondevotees. The nondevotees can be vanquished simply by material nature. "The action and reaction of the external energy of material nature (creation, maintenance and annihilation) are being carried on automatically. But simply by taking shelter of Your holy name—because Your holy name and Your personality are nondifferent—the devotees are sufficiently protected." The protection of the devotees and the annihilation of the nondevotees are actually not the business of the Supreme Personality of Godhead when He descends. They are just for His transcendental pleasure. There cannot be any other reason for His appearance.

"Our dear Lord, You are appearing as the best of the Yadu dynasty, and we are offering our respectful humble obeisance unto Your lotus feet. Before this appearance, You also appeared as the fish incarnation, the horse incarnation, the tortoise incarnation, the swan incarnation, as King Rāmacandra, as Paraśurāma, and as many other incarnations. You appeared just to protect the devotees, and we request You in Your present appearance as the Supreme Personality of Godhead Himself to give us similar protection all over the three worlds and remove all obstacles for the peaceful execution of our lives.

"Dear mother Devakī, within your womb is the Supreme Personality of Godhead, appearing along with all His plenary extensions. He is the original Personality of Godhead appearing for our welfare. Therefore you should not be afraid of your brother, the King of Bhoja. Your son Lord Kṛṣṇa, who is the original Personality of Godhead, will appear for the protection of the pious Yadu dynasty. The Lord is appearing not only alone but accompanied by His immediate plenary portion, Balarāma."

Devakī was very much afraid of her brother Kaṁsa because he had already killed so many of her children. She used to remain very anxious about Kṛṣṇa. In the *Viṣṇu Purāṇa* it is stated that in order to pacify Devakī, all the demigods, along with their wives, used to always visit her to encourage her not to be afraid that her son would be killed by Kaṁsa. Kṛṣṇa, who was within her womb, was to appear not only to diminish the burden of the world but specifically to protect the interest of the Yadu dynasty, and certainly to protect Devakī and Vasudeva.

*Thus ends the Bhaktivedanta purport of the Second Chapter of* Kṛṣṇa, *"Prayers by the Demigods for Lord Kṛṣṇa in the Womb."*

# 3 / Birth of Lord Kṛṣṇa

As stated in the *Bhagavad-gītā,* the Lord says that His appearance, birth, and activities are all transcendental, and one who understands them factually becomes immediately eligible to be transferred to the spiritual world. The Lord's appearance or birth is not like that of an ordinary man who is forced to accept a material body according to his past deeds. The Lord's appearance is explained in the Second Chapter: He appears out of His own sweet pleasure. When the time was mature for the appearance of the Lord, the constellations became very auspicious. The astrological influence of the star known as Rohiṇī was also predominant because this star is considered to be very auspicious. Rohiṇī is under the direct supervision of Brahmā. According to the astrological conclusion, besides the proper situation of the stars, there are auspicious and inauspicious moments due to the different situations of the different planetary systems. At the time of Kṛṣṇa's birth, the planetary systems were automatically adjusted so that everything became auspicious.

At that time, in all directions, east, west, south, north, everywhere, there was an atmosphere of peace and prosperity. There were auspicious stars visible in the sky, and on the surface in all towns and villages or pasturing grounds and within the minds of everyone there were signs of good fortune. The rivers were flowing full of waters, and lakes were beautifully decorated with lotus flowers. The forests were full with beautiful birds and peacocks. All the birds within the forests began to sing with sweet voices, and the peacocks began to dance along with their consorts. The wind blew very pleasantly, carrying the aroma of different flowers, and the sensation of bodily touch was very pleasing. At home, the *brāhmaṇas,* who were accustomed to offer sacrifices in the fire, found their homes very pleasant for offerings. Due to disturbances created by the demoniac kings, the sacrificial fire altar had been almost stopped in the houses of *brāhmaṇas,* but now they could find the opportunity to start the fire peacefully. Being forbidden to offer sacrifices, the *brāhmaṇas* were very distressed in mind, intelligence and activities, but just on the point of Kṛṣṇa's appearance, automatically their minds became full of joy because they could hear loud vibrations in the sky of transcendental sounds proclaiming the appearance of the Supreme Personality of Godhead.

The denizens of the Gandharva and Kinnara planets began to sing, and the denizens of Siddhaloka and the planets of the Cāraṇas began to offer prayers in the service of the Personality of Godhead. In the heavenly planets, the angels along with their wives, accompanied by the Apsaras, began to dance.

The great sages and the demigods, being pleased, began to shower flowers. At the seashore, there was the sound of mild waves, and above the sea there were clouds in the sky which began to thunder very pleasingly.

When things were adjusted like this, Lord Viṣṇu, who is residing within the heart of every living entity, appeared in the darkness of night as the Supreme Personality of Godhead before Devakī, who also appeared as one of the demigoddesses. The appearance of Lord Viṣṇu at that time could be compared with the full moon in the sky as it rises on the eastern horizon. The objection may be raised that, since Lord Kṛṣṇa appeared on the eighth day of the waning moon, there could be no rising of the full moon. In answer to this it may be said that Lord Kṛṣṇa appeared in the dynasty which is in the hierarchy of the moon; therefore, although the moon was incomplete on that night, because of the Lord's appearance in the dynasty wherein the moon is himself the original person, the moon was in an overjoyous condition, so by the grace of Kṛṣṇa he could appear just as a full moon.

In an astronomical treatise by the name *Khamānikya,* the constellations at the time of the appearance of Lord Kṛṣṇa are very nicely described. It is confirmed that the child born at that auspicious moment was the Supreme Brahman or the Absolute Truth.

Vasudeva saw that wonderful child born as a baby with four hands, holding conchshell, club, disc, and lotus flower, decorated with the mark of Śrīvatsa, wearing the jeweled necklace of *kaustubha* stone, dressed in yellow silk, appearing dazzling like a bright blackish cloud, wearing a helmet bedecked with the *vaidūrya* stone, valuable bracelets, earrings and similar other ornaments all over His body and an abundance of hair on His head. Due to the extraordinary features of the child, Vasudeva was struck with wonder. How could a newly born child be so decorated? He could therefore understand that Lord Kṛṣṇa had now appeared, and he became overpowered by the occasion. Vasudeva very humbly wondered that although he was an ordinary living entity conditioned by material nature and was externally imprisoned by Kaṁsa, the all-pervading Personality of Godhead, Viṣṇu or Kṛṣṇa, was appearing as a child in his home, exactly in His original position. No earthly child is born with four hands decorated with ornaments and nice clothing, fully equipped with all the signs of the Supreme Personality of Godhead. Over and over again, Vasudeva glanced at his child, and he considered how to celebrate this auspicious moment: "Generally, when a male child is born," he thought, "people observe the occasion with jubilant celebrations, and in my home, although I am imprisoned, the Supreme Personality of Godhead has taken birth. How many millions of millions of times should I be prepared to observe this auspicious ceremony!"

When Vasudeva, who is also called Ānakadundubhi, was looking at his newborn baby, he was so happy that he wanted to give many thousands of cows in charity to the *brāhmaṇas.* According to the Vedic system, whenever there is an auspicious ceremony in the *kṣatriya* king's palace, the king gives many things in charity. Cows decorated with golden ornaments are delivered to the *brāhmaṇas* and sages. Vasudeva wanted to perform a charitable ceremony to celebrate Kṛṣṇa's appearance, but because he was shackled within the walls of Kaṁsa's prison, this was not possible. Instead, within his mind he gave thousands of cows to the *brāhmaṇas.*

When Vasudeva was convinced that the newborn child was the Supreme Personality of Godhead Himself, he bowed down with folded hands and began to offer Him prayers. At that time Vasudeva was in the transcendental position, and he became completely free from all fear of Kaṁsa. The newborn baby was also flashing His effulgence within the room in which He appeared.

Vasudeva then began to offer his prayers. "My dear Lord, I can understand who You are. You are the Supreme Personality of Godhead, the Supersoul of all living entities and the Absolute Truth. You have appeared in Your own eternal form which is directly perceived by us. I understand that because I am afraid of Kaṁsa, You have appeared just to deliver me from that fear. You do not belong to this material world; You are the same person who brings about the cosmic manifestation simply by glancing over material nature."

One may argue that the Supreme Personality of Godhead, who creates the whole cosmic manifestation simply by His glance, cannot come within the womb of Devakī, the wife of Vasudeva. To eradicate this argument, Vasudeva said, "My dear Lord, it is not a very wonderful thing that You appear within the womb of Devakī because the creation was also made in that way. You were lying in the Causal Ocean as Mahā-Viṣṇu, and by Your breathing process, innumerable universes came into existence. Then You entered into each of the universes as Garbhodakaśāyī Viṣṇu. Then again You expanded Yourself as Kṣīrodakaśāyī Viṣṇu and entered into the hearts of all living entities and entered even within the atoms. Therefore Your entrance in the womb of Devakī is understandable in the same way. You appear to have entered, but You are simultaneously all-pervading. We can understand Your entrance and nonentrance from material examples. The total material energy remains intact even after being divided into sixteen elements. The material body is nothing but the combination of the five gross elements—namely earth, water, fire, air and ether. Whenever there is a material body, it appears that such elements are newly created, but actually the elements are always existing outside of the body. Similarly, although You appear as a child in the womb of Devakī, You are also existing outside. You are always in Your abode, but still You can simultaneously expand Yourself into millions of forms.

"One has to understand Your appearance with great intelligence because the material energy is also emanating from You. You are the original source of the material energy, just as the sun is the source of the sunshine. The sunshine cannot cover the sun globe, nor can the material energy—being an emanation from You—cover You. You appear to be in the three modes of material energy, but actually the three modes of material energy cannot cover You. This is understood by the highly intellectual philosophers. In other words, although You appear to be within the material energy, You are never covered by it."

We hear from the Vedic version that the Supreme Brahman exhibits His effulgence, and therefore everything becomes illuminated. We can understand from *Brahma-saṁhitā* that the *brahmajyoti,* or the Brahman effulgence, emanates from the body of the Supreme Lord. And from the Brahman effulgence, all creation takes place. It is further stated in the *Bhagavad-gītā* that the Lord is also the support of the Brahman effulgence. Originally He is the root cause of everything. But persons who are less intelligent think that when the Supreme Personality of Godhead comes within this material world, He accepts the material qualities. Such conclusions are not very mature, but are made by the less intelligent.

The Supreme Personality of Godhead is directly and indirectly existing everywhere; He is outside this material creation, and He is also within it. He is within this material creation not only as Garbhodakaśāyī Viṣṇu; He is also within the atom. Existence is due to His presence. Nothing can be separated from His existence. In the Vedic injunction we find that the Supreme Soul or the root cause of everything has to be searched out because nothing exists independent of the Supreme Soul. Therefore the material manifestation is also a transformation of His potency. Both inert matter and the living force—soul—are emanations from Him. Only the foolish conclude that when the Supreme Lord appears He accepts the conditions of matter. Even if He appears to have accepted the material body, He is still not subjected to any material condition. Kṛṣṇa has therefore appeared and defeated all imperfect conclusions about the appearance and disappearance of the Supreme Personality of Godhead.

"My Lord, Your appearance, existence and disappearance are beyond the influence of the material qualities. Because Your Lordship is the controller of everything and the resting place of the Supreme Brahman, there is nothing inconceivable or contradictory in You. As You have said, material nature works under Your superintendence. It is just like government officers working under the orders of the chief executive. The influence of subordinate activities cannot affect You. The Supreme Brahman and all phenomena are existing within You, and all the activities of material nature are controlled by Your Lordship.

"You are called *śuklam. Śuklam* or 'whiteness' is the symbolic representation of the Absolute Truth because it is unaffected by the material qualities. Lord Brahmā is called *rakta,* or red, because Brahmā represents the qualities of passion for creation. Darkness is entrusted to Lord Śiva because he annihilates the cosmos. The creation, annihilation and maintenance of this cosmic manifestation is conducted by Your potencies, yet You are always unaffected by those qualities. As confirmed in the *Vedas, Harir hi nirguṇaḥ sākṣāt:* the Supreme Personality of Godhead is always free from all material qualities. It is also said that the qualities of passion and ignorance are nonexistent in the person of the Supreme Lord.

"My Lord, You are the supreme controller, the Personality of Godhead, the supreme great, maintaining the order of this cosmic manifestation. And in spite of Your being the supreme controller, You have so kindly appeared in my home. The purpose of Your appearance is to kill the followers of the demonic rulers of the world who are in the dress of royal princes but are actually demons. I am sure that You will kill all of them and their followers and soldiers.

"I understand that You have appeared to kill the uncivilized Kaṁsa and his followers. But knowing that You were to appear to kill him and his followers, he has already killed so many of Your predecessors, elder brothers. Now he is simply awaiting the news of Your birth. As soon as he hears about it, he will immediately appear with all kinds of weapons to kill You."

After this prayer of Vasudeva, Devakī, the mother of Kṛṣṇa, offered her prayers. She was very frightened because of her brother's atrocities. Devakī said "My dear Lord, Your eternal forms, like Nārāyaṇa, Lord Rāma, Śeṣa, Varāha, Nṛsiṁha, Vāmana, Baladeva, and millions of similar incarnations emanating from Viṣṇu, are described in the Vedic literature as original. You are original because all Your forms as incarnations are outside of this material creation. Your form was existing before this cosmic manifestation was created. Your forms are eternal and all-pervading. They are self-effulgent, changeless and uncontaminated by the material qualities. Such eternal forms are ever-cognizant and full of bliss; they are situated in transcendental goodness and are always engaged in different pastimes. You are not limited to a particular form only; all such transcendental eternal forms are self-sufficient. I can understand that You are the Supreme Lord Viṣṇu.

"After many millions of years, when Lord Brahmā comes to the end of his life, the annihilation of the cosmic manifestation takes place. At that time the five elements—namely earth, water, fire, air and ether—enter into the *mahat-tattva.* The *mahat-tattva* again enters, by the force of time, into the nonmanifested total material energy; the total material energy enters into the energetic *pradhāna,* and the *pradhāna* enters into You. Therefore after the annihilation of the whole cosmic manifestation, You alone remain with Your transcendental name, form, quality and paraphernalia.

"My Lord, I offer my respectful obeisances unto You because You are the director of the unmanifested total energy, and the ultimate reservoir of the material nature. My Lord, the whole cosmic manifestation is under the influence of time, beginning from the moment up to the duration of the year. All act under Your direction. You are the original director of everything and the reservoir of all potent energies.

"Therefore my Lord, I request You to save me from the cruel hands of the son of Ugrasena, Kaṁsa. I am praying to Your Lordship to please rescue me from this fearful condition because You are always ready to give protection to Your servitors." The Lord has confirmed this statement in the *Bhagavad-gītā* by assuring Arjuna, "You may declare to the world, My devotee shall never be vanquished."

While thus praying to the Lord for rescue, mother Devakī expressed her motherly affection: "I understand that this transcendental form is generally perceived in meditation by the great sages, but I am still afraid because as soon as Kaṁsa understands that You have appeared, he might harm You. So I request that for the time being You become invisible to our material eyes." In other words, she requested the Lord to assume the form of an ordinary child. "My only cause of fear from my brother Kaṁsa is due to Your appearance. My Lord Madhusūdana, Kaṁsa may know that You are already born. Therefore I request You to conceal this four-armed form of Your Lordship which holds the four symbols of Viṣṇu—namely the conchshell, the disc, the club and the lotus flower. My dear Lord, at the end of the annihilation of the cosmic manifestation, You put the whole universe within Your abdomen; still by Your unalloyed mercy You have appeared in my womb. I am surprised that You imitate the activities of ordinary human beings just to please Your devotee."

On hearing the prayers of Devakī, the Lord replied, "My dear mother, in the millennium of Svāyambhuva Manu, My father Vasudeva was living as one of the *Prajāpatis,* and his name at that time was Sutapā, and you were his wife named Pṛśni. At that time, when Lord Brahmā was desiring to increase the population, he requested you to generate offspring. You controlled your senses and performed severe austerities. By practicing the breathing exercise of the *yoga* system, both you and your husband could tolerate all the influences of the material laws: the rainy season, the onslaught of the wind, and the scorching heat of the sunshine. You also executed all religious principles. In this way you were able to cleanse your heart and control the influence of material law. In executing your austerity, you used to eat only the leaves of the trees which fell to the ground. Then with steady mind and controlled sex drive, you worshiped Me, desiring some wonderful benediction from Me. Both of you practiced severe austerities for 12,000 years, by the calculation of the demigods. During that time, your mind was always absorbed in Me. When you were executing devotional service and always thinking of Me within your heart, I was very much pleased with you. O sinless mother, your heart is therefore always pure. At that time also I appeared before you in this form just to fulfill your desire, and I asked you to ask whatever you desired. At that time you wished to have Me born as your son. Although you saw Me personally, instead of asking for your complete liberation from the material bondage, under the influence of My energy, you asked Me to become your son."

In other words, the Lord selected His mother and father—namely Pṛśni and Sutapā—specifically to appear in the material world. Whenever the Lord comes as a human being, He must have someone as a mother and father, so He selected Pṛśni and Sutapā perpetually as His mother and father. And on account of this, both Pṛśni and Sutapā could not ask the Lord for liberation. Liberation is not so important as the transcendental loving service of the Lord. The Lord could have awarded Pṛśni and Sutapā immediate liberation, but He preferred to keep them within this material world for His different appearances, as will be explained in the following verses. On receiving the benediction from the Lord to become His father and mother, both Pṛśni and Sutapā returned from the activities of austerity and lived as husband and wife in order to beget a child who was the Supreme Lord Himself.

In due course of time Pṛśni became pregnant and gave birth to the child. The Lord spoke to Devakī and Vasudeva: "At that time My name was Pṛśnigarbha. In the next millennium also you took birth as Aditi and Kaśyapa, and I became your child of the name Upendra. At that time My form was just like a dwarf, and for this reason I was known as Vāmanadeva. I gave you the benediction that I would take birth as your son three times. The first time I was known as Pṛśnigarbha, born of Pṛśni and Sutapā, the next birth I was Upendra born of Aditi and Kaśyapa, and now for the third time I am born as Kṛṣṇa from you, Devakī and Vasudeva. I appeared in this Viṣṇu form just to convince you that I am the same Supreme Personality of Godhead again taken birth. I could have appeared just like an ordinary child, but in that way you would not believe that I, the Supreme Personality of Godhead, have taken birth in your womb. My dear father and mother, you have therefore raised Me many times as your child, with great affection and love, and I am therefore very pleased and obliged to you. And I assure you that this time you shall go back to home, back to Godhead, on account of your perfection in your mission. I know you are very concerned about Me and afraid of Kaṁsa. Therefore I order you to take me immediately to Gokula and replace Me with the daughter who has just been born to Yaśodā."

Having spoken thus in the presence of His father and mother, the Lord turned Himself into an ordinary child and remained silent.

Being ordered by the Supreme Personality of Godhead, Vasudeva attempted to take his son from the delivery room, and exactly at that time, a daughter was born of Nanda and Yaśodā. She was *Yogamāyā*, the internal potency of the Lord. By the influence of this internal potency, *Yogamāyā*, all the residents of Kaṁsa's palace, especially the doorkeepers, were overwhelmed with deep sleep, and all the palace doors opened, although they were barred and shackled with iron chains. The night was very dark, but as soon as Vasudeva took Kṛṣṇa on his lap and went out, he could see everything just as in the sunlight.

In the *Caitanya-caritāmṛta* it is said that Kṛṣṇa is just like sunlight, and wherever there is Kṛṣṇa, the illusory energy, which is compared to darkness, cannot remain. When Vasudeva was carrying Kṛṣṇa, the darkness of the night disappeared. All the prison doors automatically opened. At the same time there was a thunder in the sky and severe rainfall. While Vasudeva was carrying his son Kṛṣṇa in the falling rain, Lord Śeṣa in the shape of a serpent spread his hood over the head of Vasudeva so that he would not be hampered by the rainfall. Vasudeva came onto the bank of the Yamunā and saw that the water of the Yamunā was roaring with waves and that the whole span was full of foam. Still, in that furious feature, the river gave passage to Vasudeva to cross, just as the great Indian Ocean gave a path to Lord Rāma when He was bridging over the gulf. In this way Vasudeva crossed the River Yamunā. On the other side, he went to the place of Nanda Mahārāja situated in Gokula, where he saw that all the cowherd men were fast asleep. He took the opportunity of silently entering into the house of Yaśodā, and without difficulty he replaced his son, taking away the baby girl newly born in the house of Yaśodā. Then, after entering the house very silently and exchanging the boy with the girl, he again returned to the prison of Kaṁsa and silently put the girl on the lap of Devakī. He again clamped the shackles on himself so that Kaṁsa could not recognize that so many things had happened.

Mother Yaśodā understood that a child was born of her, but because she was very tired from the labor of childbirth, she was fast asleep. When she awoke, she could not remember whether she had given birth to a male or female child.

*Thus ends the Bhaktivedanta purport of the Third Chapter of* Kṛṣṇa, *"Birth of Lord Kṛṣṇa."*

# 4 / Kaṁsa Begins His Persecutions

After Vasudeva adjusted all the doors and gates, the gatekeepers awoke and heard the newborn child crying. Kaṁsa was waiting to hear the news of the child's birth, and the gatekeepers immediately approached him and informed him that the child was born. At that time, Kaṁsa got up from his bed very quickly and exclaimed, "Now the cruel death of my life is born!" Kaṁsa became perplexed now that his death was approaching, and his hair stood on end. Immediately he proceeded toward the place where the child was born.

Devakī, on seeing her brother approaching, prayed in a very meek attitude to Kaṁsa: "My dear brother, please do not kill this female child. I promise that this child will be the wife of your son; therefore don't kill her. You are not to be killed by any female child. That was the omen. You are to be killed by a male child, so please do not kill her. My dear brother, you have killed so many of my children who were just born, shining as the sun. That is not your fault. You have been advised by demoniac friends to kill my children. But now I beg you to excuse this girl. Let her live as my daughter."

Kaṁsa was so cruel that he did not listen to the beautiful prayers of his sister Devakī. He forcibly grabbed the newborn child to rebuke his sister and attempted to dash her on the stone mercilessly. This is a graphic example of a cruel brother who could sacrifice all relationships for the sake of personal gratification. But immediately the child slipped out of his hands, went up in the sky and appeared with eight arms as the younger sister of Viṣṇu. She was decorated with a nice dress and flower garlands and ornaments; in her eight hands she held a bow, lancet, arrows, bell, conchshell, disc, club and shield.

Seeing the appearance of the child (who was actually the goddess Durgā), all the demigods from different planets like Siddhaloka, Cāraṇaloka, Gandharvaloka, Apsaraloka, Kinnaraloka, and Uragaloka presented her articles and began to offer their respective prayers. From above, the goddess addressed Kaṁsa: "You rascal, how can you kill me? The child who will kill you is already born before me somewhere within this world. Don't be so cruel to your poor sister." After this appearance, the goddess Durgā became known by various names in various parts of the world.

After hearing these words, Kaṁsa became very much overwhelmed with fear. Out of pity, he immediately released Vasudeva and Devakī from the bondage of their shackles and very politely began to address them. He said, "My dear sister and brother-in-law, I have acted just like a demon in killing my own nephews. I have given up all consideration of our intimate relationship. I do not know what will be the result of these acts of mine. Probably I shall be sent to the hell where killers of the *brāhmaṇas* go. I am surprised, however, that the celestial prophecy has not come true. False propaganda is not found only in the human society. Now it appears that even the celestial denizens speak lies. Because I believed in the words of the celestial denizens, I have committed so many sins by killing the children of my sister. My dear Vasudeva and Devakī, you are both very great souls. I have nothing to instruct you, but still I request that you not be sorry for the death of your children. Every one of us is under the control of superior power, and that superior power does not allow us to remain together. We are bound to be separated from our friends and relatives in due course of time. But we must know for certain that even after the disappearance of the different material bodies, the soul remains intact eternally. For example, there are many pots made of earthly clay, and they are prepared and also broken. But in spite of this, the earth remains as it is perpetually. Similarly, the bodies of the soul under different conditions are made and destroyed, but the spirit soul remains eternally. So there is nothing to lament over. Everyone should understand that this material body is different from the spirit soul, and so long as one does not come to that understanding, he is sure to accept the processes of transmigration from one body to another. My dear sister Devakī, you are so gentle and kind. Please excuse me—don't be aggrieved by the death of your children, which I have caused. Actually this was not done by me because all these are predestined activities. One has to act according to the predestined plan, even unwillingly. People misunderstand that with the end of the body, the self dies, or they think that one can kill another living entity. All these misconceptions oblige one to accept the conditions of material existence. In other words, as long as one is not firmly convinced of the eternality of the soul, one is subjected to the tribulation of being killer and killed. My dear sister Devakī and brother-in-law Vasudeva, kindly excuse the atrocities I have committed against you. I am very poor-hearted, and you are so great-hearted, so take compassion upon me and excuse me."

While Kaṁsa was speaking to his brother-in-law and sister, tears flowed from his eyes and he fell down at their feet. Believing the words of Durgādevī, whom he had tried to kill, Kaṁsa immediately released his brother-in-law and sister. He personally unlocked the iron shackles and very sympathetically showed his friendship, just like a family member,

When Devakī saw her brother so repentent, she also became pacified and forgot all his atrocious activities against her children. Vasudeva also, forgetting all past incidents, spoke smilingly with his brother-in-law. Vasudeva told Kaṁsa, "My dear fortunate brother-in-law, what you are saying about the material body and the soul is correct. Every living entity is born ignorant, understanding this material body to be his self. This conception of life is due to ignorance, and on the basis of this ignorance we create enmity or friendship. Lamentation, jubilation, fearfulness, envy, greed, illusion and madness are different features of our material concept of life. A person influenced like this engages in enmity due only to the material body. Being engaged in such activities, we forget our eternal relationship with the Supreme Personality of Godhead."

Vasudeva took the opportunity of Kaṁsa's benevolence and informed him that his atheistic activities were also due to this misconception of life —namely taking the material body to be the self. When Vasudeva talked with Kaṁsa in such an illuminating way, Kaṁsa became very pleased, and his guilt for killing his nephews subdued. With the permission of his sister Devakī and brother-in-law Vasudeva, he returned to his home with a relieved mind.

But the next day Kaṁsa called all his counsellors together and narrated to them all the incidents that had happened the night before. All the counsellors of Kaṁsa were demons and eternal enemies of the demigods, so they became depressed upon hearing their master speak of the night's events. And although they were not very much experienced or learned, they began to give instructions to Kaṁsa as follows: "Dear sir, let us now make arrangements to kill all children who were born within the last ten days in all towns, countries, villages and pasturing grounds. Let us execute this plan indiscriminately. We think that the demigods cannot do anything against us if we perform these atrocities. They are always afraid of fighting with us, and even if they wish to check our activities, they will not dare to do so. Because of the immeasurable strength of your bow, they fear you. Indeed, we have practical experience that whenever you stood to fight with them and began to shower your arrows on them, they immediately began to flee in all directions just to save their lives. Many of the demigods were unable to fight with you, and they immediately surrendered themselves unto you by opening their turbans and the flag on their heads. With folded hands they begged you to spare them and said, 'My lord, we are all afraid of your strength. Please release us from this dangerous fight.' We have also seen many times that you would never kill such surrendered fighters when they were all fearful, their bows, arrows and chariots broken, forgetful of their military activities and unable to fight with you. So actually we have nothing to fear from these demigods. They are very proud of being great fighters in peacetime outside of the warfield, but actually they cannot show any talent or military power on the warfield. Although Lord Viṣṇu, Lord Siva and Lord Brahmā are always ready to help the demigods headed by Indra, we have no reason to be afraid of them. As far as Lord Viṣṇu is concerned, He has already hidden Himself within the hearts of all living entities, and He cannot come out. As far as Lord Śiva is concerned, he has renounced all activities; he has already entered into the forest. And Lord Brahmā is always engaged in different types of austerities and meditation. And what to speak of Indra–he is a straw in comparison to your strength. Therefore we have nothing to fear from all these demigods. But we must not neglect them because the demigods are our determined enemies. We must be careful to protect ourselves. To root them out from their very existence, we should just engage ourselves in your service and be always ready for your command."

The demons continued to say: "If there is some disease in the body which is neglected, it becomes incurable. Similarly, when one is not careful about restraining the senses and lets them loose, it is very difficult to control them at all. Therefore, we must always be very careful of the demigods before they get too strong to be subdued. The foundation of strength of the demigods is Lord Viṣṇu, because the ultimate goal of all religious principles is to satisfy Him. The Vedic injunctions, the *brāhmaṇas,* the cows, austerities, sacrifices, performances of charity and distribution of wealth are all for the satisfaction of Lord Viṣṇu. So let us immediately begin by killing all the *brāhmaṇas* who are in charge of the Vedic knowledge and the great sages who are in charge of sacrificial ritualistic performances. Let us kill all the cows which are the source of butter which is so necessary for performing sacrifices. Please give us your permission to kill all these creatures."

Actually the limbs of the transcendental body of Lord Viṣṇu are the *brāhmaṇas,* the cows, Vedic knowledge, austerity, truthfulness, sense and mind control, faithfulness, charity, tolerance and performance of sacrifices. Lord Viṣṇu is situated in everyone's heart and is the leader of all demigods, including Lord Śiva and Lord Brahmā. "We think that to kill Lord Viṣṇu is to persecute the great sages and *brāhmaṇas*," said the ministers.

Thus being advised by the demonic ministers, Kaṁsa, who was from the very beginning the greatest rascal, decided to persecute the *brāhmaṇas* and Vaiṣṇavas, being entrapped by the shackles of all-devouring, eternal time. He ordered the demons to harass all kinds of saintly persons, and then he entered his house. The adherents of Kaṁsa were all influenced by the modes of passion as well as illusioned by the modes of ignorance, and their only business was to create enmity with saintly persons. Such activities can only reduce the duration of life. The demons accelerated the process and invited their deaths as soon as possible. The result of persecuting saintly persons is not only untimely death. The act is so offensive that the actor also gradually loses his beauty, his fame and his religious principles, and his promotion to higher planets is also checked. Driven by various kinds of mental concoctions, the demons diminish all kinds of welfare. An offense at the lotus feet of the devotees and *brāhmaṇas* is a greater offense than that committed at the lotus feet of the Supreme Personality of Godhead. Thus a godless civilization becomes the source of all calamities.

*Thus ends the Bhaktivedanta purport of the Fourth Chapter of* Kṛṣṇa, *"Kaṁsa Begins His Persecutions."*

# 5 / Meeting of Nanda and Vasudeva

Although Kṛṣṇa was the real son of Vasudeva and Devakī, because of Kaṁsa's atrocious activities Vasudeva could not enjoy the birth ceremony of his son. But Nanda Mahārāja, the foster father, celebrated the birth ceremony of Kṛṣṇa very joyfully. The next day, it was declared that a male child was born of Yaśodā. According to Vedic custom, Nanda Mahārāja called for learned astrologers and *brāhmaṇas* to perform the birth ceremony. After the birth of a child, the astrologers calculate the moment of the birth and make a horoscope of the child's future life. Another ceremony takes place after the birth of the child: the family members take baths, cleanse themselves and decorate themselves with ornaments and garlands; then they come before the child and the astrologer to hear of the future life of the child. Nanda Mahārāja and other members of the family dressed and sat down in front of the birth place. All the *brāhmaṇas* who were assembled there on this occasion chanted auspicious *mantras,* according to the rituals, while the astrologers performed the birth ceremony. All the demigods are also worshiped on this occasion, as well as the forefathers of the family. Nanda Mahārāja distributed 200,000 well decorated, dressed and ornamented cows to the *brāhmaṇas.* He not only gave cows in charity, but hills of grains, decorated with golden-bordered garments and many ornaments.

In the material world we possess riches and wealth in many ways, but sometimes not in very honest and pious ways, because that is the nature of accumulating wealth. According to Vedic injunction, therefore, such wealth should be purified by giving cows and gold in charity to the *brāhmaṇas.* A newborn child is also purified by giving grains in charity to the *brāhmaṇas.* In this material world it is to be understood that we are always living in a contaminated state. We therefore have to purify the duration of our lives, our possession of wealth and ourselves. The duration of life is purified by taking daily bath and cleansing the body inside and outside and accepting the ten kinds of purificatory processes. By austerities, by worship of the Lord, and by distribution of charity, we can purify the possession of wealth. We can purify ourselves by studying the *Vedas,* by striving for self-realization and by understanding the Supreme Absolute Truth. It is therefore stated in the Vedic literature that by birth everyone is born a *śūdra,* and by accepting the purificatory process one becomes twice-born. By studies of the *Vedas* one can become *vipra,* which is the preliminary qualification for becoming a *brāhmaṇa.* When one understands the Absolute Truth in perfection, he is called a *brāhmaṇa.* And when the *brāhmaṇa* reaches further perfection, he becomes a Vaiṣṇava or a devotee.

In that ceremony, all the *brāhmaṇas* assembled began to chant different kinds of Vedic *mantras* to invoke all good fortune for the child. There are different kinds of chanting known as *sūta, māgadha, vandī,* and *virudāvalī.* Along with this chanting of *mantras* and songs, bugles and kettledrums sounded outside the house. On this occasion, the joyous vibrations could be heard in all the pasturing grounds and all the houses. Within and outside of the houses there were varieties of artistic paintings, done with rice pulp, and scented water was sprinkled everywhere, even on the roads and streets. Ceilings and roofs were decorated with different kinds of flags, festoons and green leaves. The gates were made of green leaves and flowers. All the cows, bulls and calves were smeared with a mixture of oil and turmeric and painted with minerals like red oxide, yellow clay and manganese. They wore garlands of peacock feathers, and were covered with nice colored dresses and gold necklaces.

When all the ecstatic cowherd men heard that Nanda Mahārāja, father of Kṛṣṇa, was celebrating the birth ceremony of his son, they became spontaneously joyful. They dressed themselves with very costly garments and ornamented their bodies with different kinds of earrings and necklaces and wore great turbans on their heads. After dressing themselves in this gorgeous way, they took various kinds of presentations and thus approached the house of Nanda Mahārāja.

As soon as they heard that mother Yaśodā had given birth to a child, all the cowherd women became overwhelmed with joy, and they also dressed themselves with various kinds of costly garments and ornaments and smeared scented cosmetics on their bodies.

As the dust on the lotus flower exhibits the exquisite beauty of the flower, all the *gopīs* (cowherd girls) applied the dust of *kuṅkuma* on their lotus-like faces. These beautiful *gopīs* took their different presentations and very soon reached the house of Mahārāja Nanda. Overburdened with their heavy hips and swollen breasts, the *gopīs* could not proceed very quickly towards the house of Nanda Mahārāja, but out of ecstatic love for Kṛṣṇa they began to proceed as quickly as possible. Their ears were decorated with pearl rings, their necks were decorated with jewel padlocks, their lips and eyes were decorated with different kinds of lipstick and ointment, and their hands were decorated with nice golden bangles. As they were very hastily passing over the stone road, the flower garlands which were decorating their bodies fell to the ground, and it appeared that a shower of flowers was falling from the sky. From the movement of the different kinds of ornaments on their bodies, they were looking still more beautiful. In this way, they all reached the house of Nanda-Yaśodā and blessed the child: "Dear child, You live long just to protect us." While they were blessing child Kṛṣṇa in this way, they offered a mixture of turmeric powder with oil, yogurt, milk and water. They not only sprinkled this mixture on the body of child Kṛṣṇa but on all other persons who were present there. Also on that auspicious occasion, there were different bands of expert musicians playing.

When the cowherd men saw the pastimes of the cowherd women, they became very joyful, and in response they also began to throw yogurt, milk, clarified butter and water upon the bodies of the *gopīs.* Then both parties began to throw butter on each other's bodies. Nanda Mahārāja was also very happy to see the pastimes of the cowherd men and women, and he became very liberal in giving charity to the different singers who were assembled there. Some singers were reciting great verses from the *Upaniṣads* and *Purāṇas,* some were glorifying the family ancestors, and some were singing very sweet songs. There were also many learned *brāhmaṇas* present, and Nanda Mahārāja, being very satisfied on this occasion, began to give them different kinds of garments, ornaments, and cows in charity.

It is very important to note in this connection how wealthy the inhabitants of Vṛndāvana were simply by raising cows. All the cowherd men belonged to the *vaiśya* community, and their business was to protect the cows and cultivate crops. By their dress and ornaments and by their behavior, it appears that although they were in a small village, they still were rich in material possessions. They possessed such an abundance of various kinds of milk products that they were throwing butter lavishly on each other's bodies without restriction. Their wealth was in milk, yogurt, clarified butter and many other milk products, and by trading their agricultural products, they were rich in various kinds of jewelry, ornaments and costly dresses. Not only did they possess all these things, but they could give them away in charity, as did Nanda Mahārāja.

Thus Nanda Mahārāja, the foster father of Lord Kṛṣṇa, began to satisfy the desires of all the men assembled there. He respectively received them and gave them in charity whatever they desired. The learned *brāhmaṇas,* who had no other source of income, were completely dependent on the *vaiśya* and *kṣatriya* communities for their maintenance, and they received gifts on such festive occasions as birthdays, marriages, etc. While Nanda Mahārāja was worshiping Lord Viṣṇu on this occasion and was trying to satisfy all the people there, his only desire was that the newborn child Kṛṣṇa would be happy. Nanda Mahārāja had no knowledge that this child was the origin of Viṣṇu, but he was praying to Lord Viṣṇu to protect Him.

Rohiṇīdevī, mother of Balarāma, was the most fortunate wife of Vasudeva. She was away from her husband, yet just to congratulate Mahārāja Nanda on the occasion of the birth ceremony of his son, Kṛṣṇa, she dressed herself very nicely. Wearing a garland, a necklace and other bodily ornaments, she appeared on the scene and moved hither and thither. According to the Vedic system, a woman whose husband is not at home does not dress herself very nicely. But although Rohiṇī's husband was away, she still dressed herself on this occasion.

From the opulence of the birth ceremony of Kṛṣṇa, it is very clear that at that time Vṛndāvana was rich in every respect. Because Lord Kṛṣṇa took birth in the house of King Nanda and mother Yaśodā, the goddess of fortune was obliged to manifest her opulences in Vṛndāvana. It appeared that Vṛndāvana had already become a site for the pastimes of the goddess of fortune.

After the birth ceremony, Nanda Mahārāja decided to go to Mathurā to pay the annual tax to the government of Kaṁsa. Before leaving, he called for the able cowherd men of the village and asked them to take care of Vṛndāvana in his absence. When Nanda Mahārāja arrived in Mathurā, Vasudeva got the news and was very eager to congratulate his friend. He immediately went to the place where Nanda Mahārāja was staying. When Vasudeva saw Nanda, he felt that he had regained his life. Nanda, overwhelmed with joy, immediately stood up and embraced Vasudeva. Vasudeva was received very warmly and offered a nice place to sit. At that time Vasudeva was anxious about his two sons who had been put under the protection of Nanda without Nanda's knowledge. With great anxiety, Vasudeva inquired about them. Both Balarāma and Kṛṣṇa were the sons of Vasudeva. Balarāma was transferred to the womb of Rohiṇī, Vasudeva's own wife, but Rohiṇī was kept under the protection of Nanda Mahārāja. Kṛṣṇa was personally delivered to Yaśodā and exchanged with her daughter. Nanda Mahārāja knew that Balarāma was the son of Vasudeva, although he did not know that Kṛṣṇa was also Vasudeva's son. But Vasudeva was aware of this fact and inquired very eagerly about Kṛṣṇa and Balarāma.

Vasudeva then addressed him, "My dear brother, you were old enough and very anxious to beget a son, and yet you had none. Now by the grace of the Lord you are fortunate to have a very nice son. I think that this incident is very auspicious for you. Dear friend, I was imprisoned by Kaṁsa, and now I am released; therefore this is another birth for me. I had no hope of seeing you again, but by God's grace I can see you." Vasudeva then expressed his anxiety about Kṛṣṇa. Kṛṣṇa was sent incognito to the bed of mother Yaśodā, and after very pompously celebrating His birth ceremony, Nanda went to Mathurā. So Vasudeva was very pleased and said, "This is a new birth for me." He never expected that Kṛṣṇa would live because all his other sons were killed by Kaṁsa.

Vasudeva continued, "My dear friend, it is very difficult for us to live together. Although we have our family and relatives, sons and daughters, by nature's way we are generally separated from one another. The reason for this is that every living entity appears on this earth under different pressures of fruitive activities; although they assemble together, there is no certainty of their remaining together for a long time. According to one's fruitive activities, one has to act differently and thereby be separated. For example, many plants and creepers are floating on the waves of the ocean. Sometimes they come together and sometimes they separate forever: one plant goes one way and another plant goes another. Similarly, our family assembly may be very nice while we are living together, but after some time, in the course of the waves of time, we are separated."

The purport of this expression by Vasudeva is this: although he had eight sons born in the womb of Devakī, unfortunately they were all gone. He could not even keep his one son Kṛṣṇa with him. Vasudeva was feeling His separation, but he could not express the real fact. "Please tell me about the welfare of Vṛndāvana," he said. "You have many animals—are they happy? Are they getting sufficient grass and water? Please also let me know whether the place where you are now living is undisturbed and peaceful." This inquiry was made by Vasudeva because he was very anxious about Kṛṣṇa's safety. He knew that Kaṁsa and his followers were trying to kill Kṛṣṇa by sending various kinds of demons. They had already resolved that all children born within ten days of the birthday of Kṛṣṇa should be killed. Because Vasudeva was so anxious about Kṛṣṇa, he inquired about the safety of His residence. He also inquired about Balarāma and His mother Rohiṇī, who were entrusted to the care of Nanda Mahārāja. Vasudeva also reminded Nanda Mahārāja that Balarāma did not know His real father. "He knows you as His father. And now you have another child, Kṛṣṇa, and I think you are taking very nice care for both of Them." It is also significant that Vasudeva inquired about the welfare of Nanda Mahārāja's animals. The animals, and especially the cows, were protected exactly in the manner of one's children. Vasudeva was a *kṣatriya,* and Nanda Mahārāja was a *vaiśya.* It is the duty of the *kṣatriya* to give protection to the citizens of mankind, and it is the duty of the *vaiśyas* to give protection to the cows. The cows are as important as the citizens. Just as the human citizens should be given all kinds of protection, so the cows also should be given full protection.

Vasudeva continued to say that the maintenance of religious principles, economic development and the satisfactory execution of meeting the demands of the senses depend on cooperation among relatives, nations and all humanity. Therefore, it is everyone's duty to see that his fellow citizens and the cows are not put into difficulty. One should see to the peace and comfort of his fellow man and the animals. The development of religious principles, economic development and sense gratification can then be achieved without difficulty. Vasudeva expressed his sorrow due to not being able to give protection to his own sons born of Devakī. He was thinking that religious principles, economic development and the satisfaction of his senses were therefore all lost.

On hearing this, Nanda Mahārāja replied, "My dear Vasudeva, I know that you are very much aggrieved because the cruel king Kaṁsa has killed all your sons born of Devakī. Although the last child was a daughter, Kaṁsa could not kill her, and she has entered into the celestial planets. My dear friend, do not be aggrieved; we are all being controlled by our past unseen activities. Everyone is subjected to his past deeds, and one who is conversant with the philosophy of *karma* and its reaction is a man in knowledge. Such a person will not be aggrieved at any incident, happy or miserable."

Vasudeva then replied, "My dear Nanda, if you have already paid the government taxes, then return soon to your place, because I think that there may be some disturbances in Gokula."

After the friendly conversation between Nanda Mahārāja and Vasudeva, Vasudeva returned to his home. The cowherd men headed by Nanda Mahārāja, who had come to Mathurā to pay their taxes, also returned.

*Thus ends the Bhaktivedanta purport of the Fifth Chapter of* Kṛṣṇa, *"Meeting of Nanda and Vasudeva."*

# 6 / Pūtanā Killed

While Nanda Mahārāja was returning home, he considered Vasudeva's warning that there might be some disturbance in Gokula. Certainly the advice was friendly and not false. So Nanda thought, "There is some truth in it." Therefore, out of fear, he began to take shelter of the Supreme Personality of Godhead. It is quite natural for a devotee in danger to think of Kṛṣṇa because he has no other shelter. When a child is in danger, he takes shelter of his mother or father. Similarly, a devotee is always under the shelter of the Supreme Personality of Godhead, but when he specifically sees some danger, he remembers the Lord very rapidly.

After consulting with his demonic ministers, Kaṁsa instructed a witch named Pūtanā, who knew the black art of killing small children by ghastly sinful methods, to kill all kinds of children in the cities, villages and pasturing grounds. Such witches can play their black art only where there is no chanting or hearing of the holy name of Kṛṣṇa. It is said that wherever the chanting of the holy name of Kṛṣṇa is done, even negligently, all bad elements–witches, ghosts, and dangerous calamities–immediately disappear. And this is certainly true of the place where the chanting of the holy name of Kṛṣṇa is done seriously–especially in Vṛndāvana when the Supreme Lord was personally present. Therefore, the doubts of Nanda Mahārāja were certainly based on affection for Kṛṣṇa. Actually there was no danger from the activities of Pūtanā, despite her powers. Such witches are called *khecarī*, which means they can fly in the sky. This black art of witchcraft is still practiced by some women in the remote northwestern side of India. They can transfer themselves from one place to another on the branch of an uprooted tree. Pūtanā knew this witchcraft, and therefore she is described in the *Bhāgavatam* as *khecarī*.

Pūtanā entered the county of Gokula, the residential quarter of Nanda Mahārāja, without permission. Dressing herself just like a beautiful woman, she entered the house of mother Yaśodā. She appeared very beautiful with raised hips, nicely swollen breasts, earrings, and flowers in her hair. She looked especially beautiful on account of her thin waist. She was glancing at everyone with very attractive looks and smiling face, and all the residents of Vṛndāvana were captivated. The innocent cowherd women thought that she was a goddess of fortune appearing in Vṛndāvana with a lotus flower in her hand. It seemed to them that she had personally come to see Kṛṣṇa, who is her husband. Because of her exquisite beauty, no one checked her movement, and therefore she freely entered the house of Nanda Mahārāja. Pūtanā, the killer of many, many children, found baby Kṛṣṇa lying on a small bed, and she could at once perceive that the baby was hiding His unparalleled potencies. Pūtanā thought, "This child is so powerful that He can destroy the whole universe immediately."

Pūtanā's understanding is very significant. The Supreme Personality of Godhead, Kṛṣṇa, is situated in everyone's heart. It is stated in the *Bhagavad-gītā* that He gives one necessary intelligence, and He also causes one to forget. Pūtanā was immediately aware that the child whom she was observing in the house of Nanda Mahārāja was the Supreme Personality of Godhead Himself. He was lying there as a small baby, but that does not mean that He was less powerful. The materialistic theory that God-worship is anthropomorphic is not correct. No living being can become God by undergoing meditation or austerities. God is always God. Kṛṣṇa as the child-baby is as complete as He is as a full-fledged youth. The Māyāvādī theory holds that the living entity was formerly God but has now become overwhelmed by the influence of *māyā*. Therefore they say that presently he is not God, but when the influence of *māyā* is taken away, then he again becomes God. This theory cannot be applied to the minute living entities. The living entities are minute parts and parcels of the Supreme Personality of Godhead; they are minute particles or sparks of the supreme fire, but are not the original fire, or Kṛṣṇa. Kṛṣṇa is the Supreme Personality of Godhead, even from the beginning of His appearance in the house of Vasudeva and Devakī.

Kṛṣṇa showed the nature of a small baby and closed His eyes, as if to avoid the face of Pūtanā. This closing of the eyes is interpreted and studied in different ways by the devotees. Some say that Kṛṣṇa closed His eyes because He did not like to see the face of Pūtanā, who had killed so many children and who had now come to kill Him. Others say that something extraordinary was being dictated to her, and in order to give her assurance, Kṛṣṇa closed His eyes so that she would not be frightened. And yet others interpret in this way: Kṛṣṇa appeared to kill the demons and give protection to the devotees, as it is stated in the *Bhagavad-gītā: paritrāṇāya sādhūnāṁ vināśāya ca duṣkṛtām.* The first demon to be killed was a woman. According to Vedic rules, the killing of a woman, a *brāhmaṇa,* cows, or of a child, is forbidden. Kṛṣṇa was obliged to kill the demon Pūtanā, and because the killing of a woman is forbidden according to Vedic Śāstra, He could not help but close His eyes. Another interpretation is that Kṛṣṇa closed His eyes because He simply took Pūtanā to be His nurse. Pūtanā came to Kṛṣṇa just to offer her breast for the Lord to suck. Kṛṣṇa is so merciful that even though He knew Pūtanā was there to kill Him, He took her as His nurse or mother.

There are seven kinds of mothers according to Vedic injunction: the real mother, the wife of a teacher or spiritual master, the wife of a king, the wife of a *brāhmaṇa,* the cow, the nurse, and the mother earth. Because Pūtanā came to take Kṛṣṇa on her lap and offer her breast's milk to be sucked by Him, she was accepted by Kṛṣṇa as one of His mothers. That is considered to be another reason He closed His eyes: He had to kill a nurse or mother. But His killing of His mother or nurse was no different from His love for His real mother or foster mother Yaśodā. We further understand from Vedic information that Pūtanā was also treated as a mother and given the same facility as Yaśodā. As Yaśodā was given liberation from the material world, so Pūtanā was also given liberation. When the baby Kṛṣṇa closed His eyes, Pūtanā took Him on her lap. She did not know that she was holding death personified. If a person mistakes a snake for a rope, he dies. Similarly, Pūtanā killed so many babies before meeting Kṛṣṇa, but now she was accepting the snake that would kill her immediately.

When Pūtanā was taking baby Kṛṣṇa on her lap, both Yaśodā and Rohiṇī were present, but they did not forbid her because she was so beautifully dressed and because she showed motherly affection towards Kṛṣṇa. They could not understand that she was a sword within a decorated case. Pūtanā had smeared a very powerful poison on her breasts, and immediately after taking the baby on her lap, she pushed her breastly nipple within His mouth. She was hoping that as soon as He would suck her breast, He would die. But baby Kṛṣṇa very quickly took the nipple in anger. He sucked the milk-poison along with the life air of the demon. In other words, Kṛṣṇa simultaneously sucked the milk from her breast and killed her by sucking out her life. Kṛṣṇa is so merciful that because the demon Pūtanā came to offer her breast-milk to Him, He fulfilled her desire and accepted her activity as motherly. But to stop her from further nefarious activities, He immediately killed her. And because the demon was killed by Kṛṣṇa, she got liberation. When Kṛṣṇa sucked out her very breath, Pūtanā fell down on the ground, spread her arms and legs and began to cry, "Oh child, leave me, leave me!" She was crying loudly and perspiring, and her whole body became wet.

As she died, screaming, there was a tremendous vibration both on the earth and in the sky, in all directions, and people thought that thunderbolts were falling. Thus the nightmare of the Pūtanā witch was over, and she assumed her real feature as a great demon. She opened her fierce mouth and spread her arms and legs all over. She fell exactly as Vṛtrāsura when struck by the thunderbolt of Indra. The long hair on her head was scattered all over her body. Her fallen body extended up to twelve miles and smashed all the trees to pieces, and everyone was struck with wonder upon seeing this gigantic body. Her teeth appeared just like ploughed roads, and her nostrils appeared just like mountain caves. Her breasts appeared like small hills, and her hair was a vast reddish bush. Her eye sockets appeared like blind wells, and her two thighs appeared like two banks of a river; her two hands appeared like two strongly constructed bridges, and her abdomen seemed like a dried-up lake. All the cowherd men and women became struck with awe and wonder upon seeing this. And the tumultuous sound of her falling shocked their brains and ears and made their hearts beat strongly.

When the *gopīs* saw little Kṛṣṇa fearlessly playing on Pūtanā's lap, they very quickly came and picked Him up. Mother Yaśodā, Rohiṇī, and other elderly *gopīs* immediately performed the auspicious rituals by taking the tail of a cow and circumambulating His body. The child was completely washed with the urine of a cow, and the dust created by the hooves of the cows was thrown all over His body. This was all just to save little Kṛṣṇa from future inauspicious accidents. This incident gives us a clear indication of how important the cow is to the family, society and to living beings in general. The transcendental body of Kṛṣṇa did not require any protection, but to instruct us on the importance of the cow, the Lord was smeared over with cow dung, washed with the urine of a cow, and sprinkled with the dust upraised by the walking of the cows.

After this purificatory process, the *gopīs,* headed by mother Yaśodā and Rohiṇī, chanted twelve names of Viṣṇu to give Kṛṣṇa's body full protection from all evil influences. They washed their hands and feet and sipped water three times, as is the custom before chanting *mantra.* They chanted as follows: "My dear Kṛṣṇa, may the Lord who is known as Maṇimān protect Your thighs; may Lord Viṣṇu who is known as Yajña protect Your legs; may Lord Acyuta protect Your arms; may Lord Hayagrīva protect Your abdomen; may Lord Keśava protect Your heart; may Lord Viṣṇu protect

Your arms; may Lord Urukrama protect Your face; may Lord Īśvara protect Your head; may Lord Cakradhara protect Your front; may Lord Gadādhara protect Your back; may Lord Madhusūdana who carries a bow in His hand protect Your eyesight; may Lord Viṣṇu with His conchshell protect Your left side; may the Personality of Godhead Upendra protect You from above, and may Lord Tārkṣya protect You from below the earth; may Lord Haladhara protect You from all sides; may the Personality of Godhead known as Hṛṣīkeśa protect all Your senses; may Lord Nārāyaṇa protect Your breath; and may the Lord of Śvetadvīpa, Nārāyaṇa, protect Your heart; may Lord Yogeśvara protect Your mind; may Lord Pṛśnigarbha protect Your intelligence, and may the Supreme Personality of Godhead protect Your soul. While You are playing, may Lord Govinda protect You from all sides, and when You are sleeping, may Lord Mādhava protect You from all danger; when You are working may the Lord of Vaikuṇṭha protect You from falling down; when You are sitting, may the Lord of Vaikuṇṭha give You all protection; and while You are eating, may the Lord of all sacrifices give You all protection."

Thus mother Yaśodā began to chant different names of Viṣṇu to protect the child Kṛṣṇa's different bodily parts. Mother Yaśodā was firmly convinced that she should protect her child from different kinds of evil spirits and ghosts—namely Ḍākinīs, Yātudhānīs, Kūṣmāṇḍās, Yakṣas, Rākṣasas, Vināyakas, Koṭarā, Revatī, Jyeṣṭhā, Pūtanā, Mātṛkās, Unmādas and similar other evil spirits who cause persons to forget their own existence and give trouble to the life-air and the senses. Sometimes they appear in dreams and cause much perturbation; sometimes they appear as old women and suck the blood of small children. But all such ghosts and evil spirits cannot remain where there is chanting of the holy name of God. Mother Yaśodā was firmly convinced of the Vedic injunctions about the importance of cows and the holy name of Viṣṇu; therefore she took all shelter in the cows and the name of Viṣṇu just to protect her child Kṛṣṇa. She recited all the holy names of Viṣṇu so that He might save the child. Vedic culture has taken advantage of keeping cows and chanting the holy name of Viṣṇu since the beginning of history, and persons who are still following the Vedic ways, especially the householders, keep at least one dozen cows and worship the Deity of Lord Viṣṇu, who is installed in their house.

The elderly *gopīs* of Vṛndāvana were so absorbed in affection for Kṛṣṇa that they wanted to save Him, although there was no need to, for He had already protected Himself. They could not understand that Kṛṣṇa was the Supreme Personality of Godhead playing as a child. After performing the formalities to protect the child, mother Yaśodā took Kṛṣṇa and let Him suck her own breast. When the child was protected by Viṣṇu *mantra,* mother Yaśodā felt that He was safe. In the meantime, all the cowherd men who went to Mathurā to pay tax returned home and were struck with wonder at seeing the gigantic dead body of Pūtanā.

Nanda Mahārāja recalled the prophecy of Vasudeva and considered him a great sage and mystic *yogī;* otherwise, how could he have foretold an incident that happened during his absence from Vṛndāvana. After this, all the residents of Vraja cut the gigantic body of Pūtanā into pieces and piled it up with wood for burning. When all the limbs of Pūtanā's body were burning, the smoke emanating from the fire created a good aroma. This aroma was due to her being killed by Kṛṣṇa. This means that the demon Pūtanā was washed of all her sinful activities and attained a celestial body. Here is an example of how the Supreme Personality of Godhead is all good: Pūtanā came to kill Kṛṣṇa, but because He sucked her milk, she was immediately purified, and her dead body attained a transcendental quality. Her only business was to kill small children; she was only fond of blood. But in spite of being envious of Kṛṣṇa, she attained salvation because she gave her milk to Him to drink. So what can be said of others who are affectionate to Kṛṣṇa in the relationship of mother or father?

The pure devotees always serve Kṛṣṇa with great love and affection, for He is the Supreme Personality of Godhead, the Supersoul of every living entity. It is concluded therefore that even a little energy expended in the service of the Lord gives one immense transcendental profit. This is explained in the *Bhagavad-gītā: svalpam apy asya dharmasya.* Devotional service in Kṛṣṇa consciousness is so sublime that even a little service to Kṛṣṇa, knowingly or unknowingly, gives one the greatest benefit. The system of worshiping Kṛṣṇa by offering flowers from a tree is also beneficial for the living entity who is confined to the bodily existence of that tree. When flowers and fruits are offered to Kṛṣṇa, the tree that bore them also receives much benefit, indirectly. The *arcanā* process, or worshiping procedure, is therefore beneficial for everyone. Kṛṣṇa is worshipable by great demigods like Brahmā and Lord Śiva, and Pūtanā was so fortunate that the same Kṛṣṇa played in her lap as a little child. The lotus feet of Kṛṣṇa, which are worshiped by great sages and devotees, were placed on the body of Pūtanā. People worship Kṛṣṇa and offer food, but automatically He sucked the milk from the body of Pūtanā. Devotees therefore pray that if simply by offering something as an enemy, Pūtanā got so much benefit, then who can measure the benefit of worshiping Kṛṣṇa in love and affection?

One should only worship Kṛṣṇa if for no other reason than so much benefit awaits the worshiper. Although Pūtanā was an evil spirit, she gained elevation just like the mother of the Supreme Personality of Godhead. It is clear that the cows and the elderly *gopīs* who offered milk to Kṛṣṇa were also elevated to the transcendental position. Kṛṣṇa can offer anyone anything, from liberation to anything materially conceivable. Therefore, there cannot be any doubt of the salvation of Pūtanā, whose bodily milk was sucked by Kṛṣṇa for such a long time. And how can there be any doubt about the salvation of the *gopīs* who were so fond of Kṛṣṇa? Undoubtedly all the *gopīs* and cowherd boys and cows who served Kṛṣṇa in Vṛndāvana with love and affection were liberated from the miserable condition of material existence.

When all the inhabitants of Vṛndāvana smelled the good aroma from the smoke of the burning Pūtanā, they inquired from each other, "Where is this good flavor coming from?" And while conversing, they came to understand that it was the fumes of the burning Pūtanā. They were very fond of Kṛṣṇa, and as soon as they heard that the demon Pūtanā was killed by Kṛṣṇa, they offered blessings to the little child out of affection. After the burning of Pūtanā, Nanda Mahārāja came home and immediately took up the child on his lap and began to smell His head. In this way, he was quite satisfied that his little child was saved from this great calamity. Śrīla Śukadeva Gosvāmī has blessed all persons who hear the narration of the killing of Pūtanā by Kṛṣṇa. They will surely attain the favor of Govinda.

*Thus ends the Bhaktivedanta purport of the Sixth Chapter of* Kṛṣṇa, *"Pūtanā Killed."*

# 7 / Salvation of Tṛṇāvarta

The Supreme Personality of Godhead, Kṛṣṇa, is always full of six opulences—namely complete wealth, complete strength, complete fame, complete knowledge, complete beauty and complete renunciation. The Lord appears in different complete, eternal forms of incarnation. The conditioned soul has immense opportunity to hear about the transcendental activities of the Lord in these different incarnations. In the *Bhagavad-gītā* it is said, *janma karma ca me divyam.* The pastimes and activities of the Lord are not material; they are beyond the material conception. But the conditioned soul can benefit by hearing such uncommon activities. Hearing is an opportunity to associate with the Lord; to hear His activities is to evolve to the transcendental nature—simply by hearing. The conditioned soul has a natural aptitude to hear something about other conditioned souls in the form of fiction, drama and novel. That inclination to hear something about others may be utilized in hearing the pastimes of the Lord. Then one can immediately evolve to his transcendental nature. Kṛṣṇa's pastimes are not only beautiful; they are also very pleasing to the mind.

If someone takes advantage of hearing the pastimes of the Lord, the material contamination of dust, accumulated in the heart due to long association with material nature, can be immediately cleansed. Lord Caitanya also instructed that simply by hearing the transcendental name of Lord Kṛṣṇa, one can cleanse the heart of all material contamination. There are different processes for self-realization, but this process of devotional service—of which hearing is the most important function—when adopted by any conditioned soul, will automatically cleanse him of the material contamination and enable him to realize his real constitutional position. Conditional life is due to this contamination only, and as soon as it is cleared off, then naturally the dormant function of the living entity—rendering service to the Lord—awakens. By developing his eternal relationship with the Supreme Lord, one becomes eligible to create friendship with the devotees. Mahārāja Parīkṣit recommended, from practical experience, that everyone try to hear about the transcendental pastimes of the Lord. This *Kṛṣṇa* treatise is meant for that purpose, and the reader may take advantage in order to attain the ultimate goal of human life.

The Lord, out of His causeless mercy, descends on this material world and displays His activities just like an ordinary man. Unfortunately the impious entities or the atheistic class of men consider Kṛṣṇa to be an ordinary man like themselves, and so they deride Him. This is condemned in the *Bhagavad-gītā* by the Lord Himself when He says, "*Avajānanti māṁ mūḍhāḥ.*" The *mūḍhas,* or the rascals, take Kṛṣṇa to be an ordinary man or a slightly more powerful man; out of their great misfortune, they cannot accept Him as the Supreme Personality of Godhead. Sometimes such unfortunate persons misrepresent themselves as incarnations of Kṛṣṇa without referring to the authorized scriptures.

When Kṛṣṇa grew up a little more, He began to turn Himself backside up; He did not merely lie down on His back. And another function was observed by Yaśodā and Nanda Mahārāja: Kṛṣṇa's first birthday. They arranged for Kṛṣṇa's birthday ceremony, which is still observed by all followers of the Vedic principles. (Kṛṣṇa's birthday ceremony is observed in India by all Hindus, irrespective of different sectarian views.) All the cowherd men and women were invited to participate, and they arrived in jubilation. A nice band played, and the people assembled enjoyed it. All the learned *brāhmaṇas* were invited, and they chanted Vedic hymns for the good fortune of Kṛṣṇa. During the chanting of the Vedic hymns and playing of the bands, Kṛṣṇa was bathed by mother Yaśodā. This bathing ceremony is technically called *abhiṣeka,* and even today this is observed in all the temples of Vṛndāvana as Janmāṣṭamī Day or the birthday anniversary of Lord Kṛṣṇa.

On this occasion, mother Yaśodā arranged to distribute a large quantity of grains, and first-class cows decorated with golden ornaments were made ready to be given in charity to the learned, respectable *brāhmaṇas.* Yaśodā took her bath and dressed herself nicely, and taking child Kṛṣṇa, duly dressed and bathed, on her lap, she sat down to hear the Vedic hymns chanted by the *brāhmaṇas.* While listening to the chanting of the Vedic hymns, the child appeared to be falling asleep, and therefore mother Yaśodā very silently laid Him down on the bed. Being engaged in receiving all the friends, relatives and residents of Vṛndāvana on that holy occasion, she forgot to feed the child milk. He was crying, being hungry, but mother Yaśodā could not hear Him cry because of the various noises. The child, however, became angry because He was hungry and His mother was not paying attention to Him. So He lifted His legs and began to kick His lotus feet just like an ordinary child. Baby Kṛṣṇa had been placed underneath a hand-driven cart, and while He was kicking His legs, He accidently touched the wheel of the cart, and it collapsed. Various kinds of utensils and brass and metal dishes had been piled up in the hand cart, and they all fell down with a great noise. The wheel of the cart separated from the axle, and the spokes of the wheel were all broken and scattered hither and thither. Mother Yaśodā and all the *gopīs,* as well as Mahārāja Nanda and the cowherd men, were astonished as to how the cart could have collapsed by itself. All the men and women who were assembled for the holy function crowded around and began to suggest how the cart might have collapsed. No one could ascertain the cause, but some small children who were entrusted to play with baby Kṛṣṇa informed the crowd that it was due to Kṛṣṇa's striking His feet against the wheel. They assured the crowd that they had seen how it happened with their own eyes, and they strongly asserted the point. Some were listening to the statement of the small children, but others said, "How can you believe the statements of these children?" The cowherd men and women could not understand that the all-powerful Personality of Godhead was lying there as a baby, and He could do anything. Both the possible and impossible were in His power. While the discussion was going on, baby Kṛṣṇa cried. Without remonstration, mother Yaśodā picked the child up on her lap and called the learned *brāhmaṇas* to chant holy Vedic hymns to counteract the evil spirits. At the same time she allowed the baby to suck her breast. If a child sucks the mother's breast nicely, it is to be understood that he is out of all danger. After this, all the stronger cowherd men put the broken cart in order, and all the scattered things were set up nicely as before. The *brāhmaṇas* thereafter began to offer oblations to the sacrificial fire with yogurt, butter, *kuśa* grass, and water. They worshiped the Supreme Personality of Godhead for the good fortune of the child.

The *brāhmaṇas* who were present at that time were all qualified because they were not envious; they never indulged in untruthfulness, they were never proud, they were nonviolent, and they never claimed any false prestige. They were all bona fide *brāhmaṇas,* and there was no reason to think that their blessing would be useless. With firm faith in the qualified *brāhmaṇas,* Nanda Mahārāja took his child on his lap and bathed Him with water mixed with various herbs while the *brāhmaṇas* chanted hymns from the *Ṛk, Yajus* and *Sāma Vedas.*

It is said that without being a qualified *brāhmaṇa,* one should not read the *mantras* of the *Vedas*. Here is the proof that the *brāhmanas* were qualified with all the brahminical symptoms. Mahārāja Nanda also had full faith in them. Therefore they were allowed to perform the ritualistic ceremonies by chanting the Vedic *mantras*. There are many different varieties of sacrifices recommended for different purposes, but the *mantras* are all to be chanted by qualified *brāhmaṇas*. And because in this age of Kali such qualified *brāhmaṇas* are not available, all Vedic ritualistic sacrifices are forbidden. Śrī Caitanya Mahāprabhu has therefore recommended only one kind of sacrifice in this age—namely *saṅkīrtana yajña*, or simply chanting the *mahāmantra*, Hare Kṛṣṇa, Hare Kṛṣṇa, Kṛṣṇa Kṛṣṇa, Hare Hare, Hare Rāma, Hare Rāma, Rāma Rāma, Hare Hare.

As the *brāhmaṇas* chanted the Vedic hymns and performed the ritualistic ceremonies for the second time, Nanda Mahārāja again gave huge quantities of grains and many cows to them. All the cows which were given in charity were covered with nice gold-embroidered garments, and their horns were bedecked with golden rings; the hooves were covered with silver plate, and they wore garlands of flowers. He gave so many cows just for the welfare of his wonderful child, and the *brāhmaṇas* in return bestowed their heartfelt blessing. And the blessings offered by the able *brāhmaṇas* were never to be baffled.

One day, shortly after this ceremony, when mother Yaśodā was patting her baby on her lap, the baby felt too heavy, and being unable to carry Him, she unwillingly placed Him on the ground. After a while, she became engaged in household affairs. At that time, one of the servants of Kaṁsa, known as Tṛṇāvarta, as instructed by Kaṁsa, appeared there in the shape of a whirlwind. He picked the child up on his shoulders and raised a great dust storm all over Vṛndāvana. Because of this, everyone's eyes became covered within a few moments, and the whole area of Vṛndāvana became densely dark so that no one could see himself or anyone else. During this great catastrophe, mother Yaśodā could not see her baby, who was taken away by the whirlwind, and she began to cry very piteously. She fell down on the ground exactly like a cow who has just lost her calf. When mother Yaśodā was so piteously crying, all the cowherd women immediately came and began to look for the baby, but they were disappointed and could not find Him. The Tṛṇāvarta demon who took baby Kṛṣṇa on his shoulder went high in the sky, but the baby assumed such a weight that suddenly he could not go any further, and he had to stop his whirlwind activities. Baby Kṛṣṇa made Himself heavy and began to weigh down the demon. The Lord caught hold of his neck. Tṛṇāvarta felt the baby to be as heavy as a big mountain, and he tried to get out of His clutches, but he was unable to do so, and his eyes popped out from their sockets. Crying very fiercely, he fell down to the ground of Vṛndāvana and died. The demon fell exactly like Tripurāsura, who was pierced by the arrow of Lord Śiva. He hit the stone ground, and His limbs were smashed. His body became visible to all the inhabitants of Vṛndāvana.

When the *gopīs* saw the demon killed and child Kṛṣṇa very happily playing on his body, they immediately picked Kṛṣṇa up with great affection. The cowherd men and women became very happy to get back their beloved child Kṛṣṇa. At that time they began to talk about how wonderful it was that the demon took away the child to devour Him but could not do so; instead he fell down dead. Some of them supported the situation: "This is proper because those who are too sinful die from their sinful reactions, and child Kṛṣṇa is pious; therefore He is saved from all kinds of fearful situations. And we too must have performed great sacrifices in our previous lives, worshiping the Supreme Personality of Godhead, giving great wealth in charity and acting philanthropically for the general welfare of men. Because of such pious activities, the child is saved from all danger."

The *gopīs* assembled there spoke among themselves: "What sort of austerities and penances we must have undergone in our previous lives! We must have worshiped the Supreme Personality of Godhead, offered different kinds of sacrifices, made charities and performed many welfare activities for the public such as growing banyan trees and excavating wells. As a result of these pious activities, we have got back our child, even though He was supposed to be dead. Now He has come back to enliven His relatives." After observing such wonderful happenings, Nanda Mahārāja began to think of the words of Vasudeva again and again.

After this incident, when Yaśodā once was nursing her child and patting Him with great affection, there streamed a profuse supply of milk from her breast, and when she opened the mouth of the child with her fingers, she suddenly saw the universal manifestation within His mouth. She saw within the mouth of Kṛṣṇa the whole sky, including the luminaries, stars in all directions, the sun, moon, fire, air, seas, islands, mountains, rivers, forests, and all other movable and immovable entities. Upon seeing this, mother Yaśodā's heart began to throb, and she murmured within herself, "How wonderful this is!" She could not express anything, but simply closed her eyes. She was absorbed in wonderful thoughts. Kṛṣṇa's showing the universal form of the Supreme Personality of Godhead, even when lying down on the lap of His mother, proves that the Supreme Personality of Godhead is always the Supreme Personality of Godhead, whether He is manifested as a child on the lap of His mother or as a charioteer on the battlefield of Kurukṣetra. The concoction of the impersonalist, that one can become God by meditation or by some artificial material activities, is herewith declared false. God is always God in any condition or status, and the living entities are always the parts and parcels of the Supreme Lord. They can never be equal to the inconceivable supernatural power of the Supreme Personality of Godhead.

*Thus ends the Bhaktivedanta purport of the Seventh Chapter of* Kṛṣṇa, *"Salvation of Tṛṇāvarta."*

# 8 / Vision of the Universal Form

After this incident, Vasudeva asked his family priest Gargamuni to visit the place of Nanda Mahārāja in order to astrologically calculate the future life of Kṛṣṇa. Gargamuni was a great saintly sage who underwent many austerities and penances and was appointed priest of the Yadu dynasty. When Gargamuni arrived at the home of Nanda Mahārāja, Nanda Mahārāja was very pleased to see him and immediately stood up with folded hands and offered his respectful obeisances. He received Gargamuni with the feeling of one who is worshiping God or the Supreme Personality of Godhead. He offered him a nice sitting place, and when he sat down, Nanda Mahārāja offered him a warm reception. Addressing him very politely, he said: "My dear *brāhmaṇa,* your appearance in a householder's place is only to enlighten. We are always engaged in household duties and are forgetting our real duty of self-realization. Your coming to our house is to give us some enlightenment about spiritual life. You have no other purpose to visit householders." Actually a saintly person or a *brāhmaṇa* has no business visiting householders who are always busy in the matter of dollars and cents. If it is asked, "Why don't the householders go to a saintly person or a *brāhmaṇa* for enlightenment?" the answer is that householders are very poor-hearted. Generally householders think that their engagement in family affairs is their prime duty and that self-realization or enlightenment in spiritual knowledge is secondary. Out of compassion only, saintly persons and *brāhmaṇas* go to householders' homes.

Nanda Mahārāja addressed Gargamuni as one of the great authorities in astrological science. The foretellings of astrological science, such as the occurrence of solar or lunar eclipses, are wonderful calculations, and by this particular science, a person can understand the future very clearly. Gargamuni was proficient in this knowledge. By this knowledge one can understand what his previous activities were, and by the result of such activities one may enjoy or suffer in this life.

Nanda Mahārāja also addressed Gargamuni as the "best of the *brāhmaṇas.*" A *brāhmaṇa* is one who is expert in the knowledge of the Supreme. Without knowledge of the Supreme Absolute, one cannot be recognized as a *brāhmaṇa.* The exact word used in this connection is *brahmavidām,* which means those who know the Supreme very well. An expert *brāhmaṇa* is able to give reformatory facilities to the sub-castes—namely the *kṣatriyas* and *vaiśyas.* The *śūdras* observe no reformatory performances. The *brāhmaṇa* is considered to be the spiritual master or priest for the *kṣatriya* and *vaiśya.* Nanda Mahārāja happened to be a *vaiśya,* and he accepted Gargamuni as a first class *brāhmaṇa.* He therefore offered his two foster sons—namely Kṛṣṇa and Balarāma—to Him to purify. He agreed that not only these boys, but all human beings just after birth should accept a qualified *brāhmaṇa* as spiritual master.

Upon this request, Gargamuni replied, "Vasudeva has sent me to see to the reformatory performances of these boys, especially Kṛṣṇa's. I am their family priest, and incidentally, it appears to me that Kṛṣṇa is the son of Devakī." By his astrological calculation, Gargamuni could understand that Kṛṣṇa was the son of Devakī but that He was being kept under the care of Nanda Mahārāja, which Nanda did not know. Indirectly he said that Kṛṣṇa, as well as Balarāma, were both sons of Vasudeva. Balarāma was known as the son of Vasudeva because His mother Rohiṇī was present there, but Nanda Mahārāja did not know about Kṛṣṇa. Gargamuni indirectly disclosed the fact that Kṛṣṇa was the son of Devakī. Gargamuni also warned Nanda Mahārāja that if he would perform the reformatory ceremony, then Kaṁsa, who was naturally very sinful, would understand that Kṛṣṇa was the son of Devakī and Vasudeva. According to astrological calculation, Devakī could not have a female child, although everyone thought that the eighth child of Devakī was female. In this way Gargamuni intimated to Nanda Mahārāja that the female child was born of Yaśodā and that Kṛṣṇa was born of Devakī, and they were exchanged. The female child, or Durgā, also informed Kaṁsa that the child who would kill him was already born somewhere else. Gargamuni stated, "If I give your child a name and if He fulfills the prophecy of the female child to Kaṁsa, then it may be that the sinful demon will come and kill this child also after the name-giving ceremony. But I do not want to become responsible for all these future calamities."

On hearing the words of Gargamuni, Nanda Mahārāja said, "If there is such danger, then it is better not to plan any gorgeous name-giving ceremony. It would be better for you to simply chant the Vedic hymns and perform the purificatory process. We belong to the twice-born caste, and I am taking this opportunity of your presence. So please perform the name-giving ceremony without external pomp." Nanda Mahārāja wanted to keep the name-giving ceremony a secret and yet take advantage of Gargamuni's performing the ceremony.

When Gargamuni was so eagerly requested by Nanda Mahārāja, he performed the name-giving ceremony as secretly as possible in the cowshed of Nanda Mahārāja. He informed Nanda Mahārāja that Balarāma, the son of Rohiṇī, would be very pleasing to his family members and relatives and therefore would be called Rāma. In the future He would be extraordinarily strong and therefore would be called Balarāma. Gargamuni said further, "Because your family and the family of the Yadus are so intimately connected and attracted, therefore His name will also be Saṅkarṣaṇa." This means that Gargamuni awarded three names to the son of Rohiṇī–namely Balarāma, Saṅkarṣaṇa, and Baladeva. But he carefully did not disclose the fact that Balarāma also appeared in the womb of Devakī and was subsequently transferred to the womb of Rohinī. Kṛṣṇa and Balarāma are real brothers, being originally sons of Devakī.

Gargamuni then informed Nanda Mahārāja, "As far as the other boy is concerned, this child has taken different bodily complexions in different *yugas* (millennia). First of all He assumed the color white, then He assumed the color red, then the color yellow and now He has assumed the color black. Besides that, He was formerly the son of Vasudeva; therefore His name should be Vāsudeva as well as Kṛṣṇa. Some people will call Him Kṛṣṇa, and some will call Him Vāsudeva. But one thing you must know: This son has had many, many other names and activities due to His different pastimes."

Gargamuni gave Nanda Mahārāja a further hint that his son will also be called Giridharī because of His uncommon pastimes of lifting Goverdhana Hill. Since he could understand everything past and future, he said, "I know everything about His activities and name, but others do not know. This child will be very pleasing to all the cowherd men and cows. Being very popular in Vṛndāvana, He will be the cause of all good fortune for you. Because of His presence, you will overcome all kinds of material calamities, despite opposing elements."

Gargamuni continued to say, "My dear King of Vraja, in His previous births, this child many times protected righteous persons from the hands of rogues and thieves whenever there was political disruption. Your child is so powerful that anyone who will become a devotee of your boy will never be troubled by enemies. Just as demigods are always protected by Lord

Viṣṇu, so the devotees of your child will always be protected by Nārāyaṇa, the Supreme Personality of Godhead. This child will grow in power, beauty, opulence–in everything–on the level of Nārāyaṇa, the Supreme Personality of Godhead. Therefore I would advise that you protect Him very carefully so that He may grow without disturbance."

Gargamuni further informed Nanda Mahārāja that because he was a great devotee of Nārāyaṇa, Lord Nārāyaṇa gave a son who is equal to Him. At the same time he indicated, "Your son will be disturbed by so many demons, so be careful and protect Him." In this way, Gargamuni convinced Nanda Mahārāja that Nārāyaṇa Himself had become his son. In various ways he described the transcendental qualities of his son. After giving this information, Gargamuni returned to his home. Nanda Mahārāja began to think of himself as the most fortunate person, and he was very satisfied to be benedicted in this way.

A short time after this incident, both Balarāma and Kṛṣṇa began to crawl on Their hands and knees. When They were crawling like that, They pleased Their mothers. The bells tied to Their waist and ankles sounded fascinating, and They would move around very pleasingly. Sometimes, just like ordinary children, They would be frightened by others and would immediately hurry to Their mothers for protection. Sometimes They would fall into the clay and mud of Vṛndāvana and would approach Their mothers smeared with clay and saffron. They were actually smeared with saffron and sandalwood pulp by Their mothers, but due to crawling over muddy clay, They would simultaneously smear Their bodies with clay. As soon as They would come crawling to their mothers, Yaśodā and Rohiṇī would take Them on their laps and, covering the lower portion of their saris, allow Them to suck their breasts. When the babies were sucking their breasts, the mothers would see small teeth coming in. Thus their joy would be intensified to see their children grow. Sometimes the naughty babies would crawl up to the cowshed, catch the tail of a calf and stand up. The calves, being disturbed, would immediately begin running here and there, and the children would be dragged over clay and cow dung. To see this fun, Yaśodā and Rohiṇī would call all their neighboring friends, the *gopīs*. Upon seeing these childhood pastimes of Lord Kṛṣṇa, the *gopīs* would be merged in transcendental bliss. In their enjoyment they would laugh very loudly.

Both Kṛṣṇa and Balarāma were so restless that Their mothers Yaśodā and Rohiṇī would try to protect Them from cows, bulls, monkeys, water, fire and birds while they were executing their household duties. Always being anxious to protect the children and to execute their duties, they were not very tranquil. In a very short time, both Kṛṣṇa and Balarāma began to stand up and slightly move on Their legs. When Kṛṣṇa and Balarāma began to walk, other friends of the same age joined Them, and together they began to give the highest transcendental pleasure to the *gopīs*, specifically to mother Yaśodā and Rohiṇī.

All the *gopī* friends of Yaśodā and Rohiṇī enjoyed the naughty childish activities of Kṛṣṇa and Balarāma in Vṛndāvana. In order to enjoy further transcendental bliss, they all assembled and went to mother Yaśodā to lodge complaints against the restless boys. When Kṛṣṇa was sitting before mother Yaśodā, all the elderly *gopīs* began to lodge complaints against Him so that Kṛṣṇa could hear. They said, "Dear Yaśodā, why don't you restrict your naughty Kṛṣṇa. He comes to our houses along with Balarāma every morning and evening, and before the milking of the cows They let loose the calves, and the calves drink all the milk of the cows. So when we go to milk the cows, we find no milk, and we have to return with empty pots. If we warn Kṛṣṇa and Balarāma about doing this, They simply smile charmingly. We cannot do anything. Also, your Kṛṣṇa and Balarāma find great pleasure in stealing our stock of yogurt and butter from wherever we keep it. When Kṛṣṇa and Balarāma are caught stealing the yogurt and butter, They say, 'Why do you charge us with stealing? Do you think that butter and yogurt are in scarcity in our house?' Sometimes They steal butter, yogurt and milk and distribute them to the monkeys. When the monkeys are well fed and do not take any more, then your boys chide, 'This milk and butter and yogurt are useless–even the monkeys won't take it.' And They break the pots and throw them hither and thither. If we keep our stock of yogurt, butter and milk in a solitary dark place, your Kṛṣṇa and Balarāma find it in the darkness by the glaring effulgence of the ornaments and jewels on Their bodies. If by chance they cannot find the hidden butter and yogurt, They go to our little babies and pinch their bodies so that they cry, and then They go away. If we keep our stock of butter and yogurt high on the ceiling, hanging on a swing, although it is beyond Their reach, They arrange to reach it by piling all kinds of wooden crates over the grinding machine. And if They cannot reach, They make a hole in the pot. We think therefore that you better take all the jeweled ornaments from the bodies of your children."

On hearing this, Yaśodā would say, "All right, I will take all the jewels from Kṛṣṇa so that He can not see the butter hidden in the darkness." Then the *gopīs* would say, "No, no, don't do this. What good will you do by taking away the jewels? We do not know what kind of boys these are, but even without ornaments They spread some kind of effulgence so that even in darkness They can see everything." Then mother Yaśodā would inform them, "All right, keep your butter and yogurt carefully so that They may not reach it." In reply to this, the *gopīs* said, "Yes, actually we do so, but because we are sometimes engaged in our household duties, these naughty boys enter our house somehow or other and spoil everything. Sometimes being unable to steal our butter and yogurt, out of anger They pass urine on the clean floor and sometimes spit on it. Just see your boy now—He is hearing this complaint. All day They simply make arrangements to steal our butter and yogurt, and now They are sitting just like very silent good boys. Just see His face." When mother Yaśodā thought to chastise her boy after hearing all the complaints, she saw His pitiable face, and smiling, she did not chastise Him.

Another day, when Kṛṣṇa and Balarāma were playing with Their friends, all the boys joined Balarāma and told mother Yaśodā that Kṛṣṇa had eaten clay. On hearing this, mother Yaśodā caught hold of Kṛṣṇa's hand and said, "My dear Kṛṣṇa, why have You eaten earth in a solitary place? Just see, all Your friends including Balarāma are complaining about You." Being afraid of His mother, Kṛṣṇa replied, "My dear mother, all these boys, including My elder brother Balarāma, are speaking lies against Me. I have never eaten clay. My elder brother Balarāma, while playing with Me today, became angry, and therefore He has joined with the other boys to complain against Me. They have all combined together to complain so you will be angry and chastise Me. If you think they are truthful, then you can look within My mouth to see whether I have taken clay or not." His mother replied, "All right, if You have actually not taken any clay, then just open Your mouth. I shall see."

When the Supreme Personality of Godhead Kṛṣṇa was so ordered by His mother, He immediately opened His mouth just like an ordinary boy. Then mother Yaśodā saw within that mouth the complete opulence of creation. She saw the entire outer space in all directions, mountains, islands, oceans, seas, planets, air, fire, moon and stars. Along with the moon and the stars she also saw the entire elements, water, sky, the extensive ethereal existence along with the total ego and the products of the senses and the controller of the senses, all the demigods, the objects of the senses like sound, smell, etc., and the three qualities of material nature. She also could perceive that within His mouth were all living entities, eternal time, material nature, spiritual nature, activity, consciousness and different forms of the whole creation. Yaśodā could find within the mouth of her child everything necessary for cosmic manifestation. She also saw, within His mouth, herself taking Kṛṣṇa on her lap and having Him sucking her breast. Upon seeing all this, she became struck with awe and began to wonder whether she were dreaming or actually seeing something extraordinary. She concluded that she was either dreaming or seeing the play of the illusory energy of the Supreme Personality of Godhead. She thought that she had become mad, mentally deranged, to see all those wonderful things. Then she thought, "It may be cosmic mystic power attained by my child, and therefore I am perplexed by such visions within His mouth. Let me offer my respectful obeisances unto the Supreme Personality of Godhead under whose energy bodily self and bodily possessions are conceived." She then said, "Let me offer my respectful obeisances unto Him, under whose illusory energy I am thinking that Nanda Mahārāja is my husband and Kṛṣṇa is my son, that all the properties of Nanda Mahārāja belong to me and that all the cowherd men and women are my subjects. All this misconception is due to the illusory energy of the Supreme Lord. So let me pray to Him that He may protect me always."

While mother Yaśodā was thinking in this high philosophical way, Lord Kṛṣṇa again expanded His internal energy just to bewilder her with maternal affection. Immediately mother Yaśodā forgot all philosophical speculation and accepted Kṛṣṇa as her own child. She took Him on her lap and became overwhelmed with maternal affection. She thus began to think, "Kṛṣṇa is not understandable to the masses through the gross process of knowledge, but He can be received through the *Upaniṣads* and the Vedānta or mystic Yoga system and Saṅkhya philosophy." Then she began to think of the Supreme Personality of Godhead as her own begotten child.

Certainly mother Yaśodā had executed many, many pious activities as a result of which she got the Absolute Truth, Supreme Personality of Godhead, as her son who sucked milk from her breast. Similarly, Nanda Mahārāja also must have performed many great sacrifices and pious activities for Lord Kṛṣṇa to become his son and address him as father. But it is surprising that Vasudeva and Devakī did not enjoy the transcendental bliss of Kṛṣṇa's childhood pastimes, although Kṛṣṇa was their real son. The childhood pastimes of Kṛṣṇa are glorified even today by many sages and saintly persons, but Vasudeva and Devakī could not enjoy such childhood pastimes personally. The reason for this was explained by Śukadeva Gosvāmī to Mahārāja Parīkṣit as follows.

When the best of the Vasus of the name Droṇa along with his wife Dharā were ordered to increase progeny by Lord Brahmā, they said unto him, "Dear father, we are seeking your benediction." Droṇa and Dharā then took benediction from Brahmā that in the future—when they would take birth again within the universe—the Supreme Lord Kṛṣṇa in His most attractive feature of childhood would absorb their whole attention. Their dealings with Kṛṣṇa would be so powerful that simply by hearing of Kṛṣṇa's childhood activities with them, anyone could very easily cross over the nescience of birth and death. Lord Brahmā agreed to give them the benediction, and as a result the same Droṇa appeared as Nanda Mahārāja in Vṛndāvana, and the same Dharā appeared as mother Yaśodā, the wife of Nanda Mahārāja.

In this way, Nanda Mahārāja and his wife, mother Yaśodā, developed their unalloyed devotion for the Supreme Personality of Godhead, having gotten Him as their son. And all the *gopīs* and cowherd men who were associates of Kṛṣṇa naturally developed their own different feelings of love for Kṛṣṇa.

Therefore, just to fulfill the benediction of Lord Brahmā, Lord Kṛṣṇa appeared along with His plenary expansion, Balarāma, and performed all kinds of childhood pastimes in order to increase the transcendental pleasure of all residents of Vṛndāvana.

*Thus ends the Bhaktivedanta purport of the Eighth Chapter of* Kṛṣṇa, *"Vision of the Universal Form."*

# 9 / Mother Yaśodā Binding Lord Kṛṣṇa

Once upon a time, seeing that her maidservant was engaged in different household duties, mother Yaśodā personally took charge of churning butter. And while she churned butter, she sang the childhood pastimes of Kṛṣṇa and enjoyed thinking of her son.

The end of her sari was tightly wrapped while she churned, and on account of her intense love for her son, milk automatically dripped from her breasts which moved as she labored very hard, churning with two hands. The bangles and bracelets on her hands tinkled as they touched each other, and her earrings and breasts shook. There were drops of perspiration on her face, and the flower garland which was on her head scattered here and there. Before this picturesque sight, Lord Kṛṣṇa appeared as a child. He felt hungry, and out of love for His mother, He wanted her to stop churning. He indicated that her first business was to let Him suck her breast and then churn butter later.

Mother Yaśodā took her son on her lap and pushed the nipples of her breasts into His mouth. And while Kṛṣṇa was sucking the milk, she was smiling, enjoying the beauty of her child's face. Suddenly, the milk which was on the oven began to boil over. Just to stop the milk from spilling, mother Yaśodā at once put Kṛṣṇa aside and went to the oven. Left in that state by His mother, Kṛṣṇa became very angry, and His lips and eyes became red in rage. He pressed His teeth and lips, and taking up a piece of stone, He immediately broke the butter pot. He took butter out of it, and with false tears in His eyes, He began to eat the butter in a secluded place.

In the meantime, mother Yaśodā returned to the churning place after setting the overflowing milk pan in order. She saw the broken pot in which the churning yogurt was kept. Since she could not find her boy, she concluded that the broken pot was His work. She began to smile as she thought, "The child is very clever. After breaking the pot He has left this place, fearing punishment." After she sought all over, she found a big wooden grinding mortar which was kept upside down, and she found her son sitting on it. He was taking butter which was hanging from the ceiling on a swing, and He was feeding it to the monkeys. She saw Kṛṣṇa looking this way and that way in fear of her because He was conscious of His naughty behavior. After seeing her son so engaged, she very silently approached Him from behind. Kṛṣṇa, however, quickly saw her coming at Him with a stick in her hand, and immediately He got down from the grinding mortar and began to flee in fear.

Mother Yaśodā chased Him to all corners, trying to capture the Supreme Personality of Godhead who is never approached even by the meditations of great *yogīs*. In other words, the Supreme Personality of Godhead, Kṛṣṇa, who is never caught by the *yogīs* and speculators, was playing just like a little child for a great devotee like mother Yaśodā. Mother Yaśodā, however, could not easily catch the fast-running child because of her thin waist and heavy body. Still she tried to follow Him as fast as possible. Her hair loosened, and the flower in her hair fell to the ground. Although she was tired, she somehow reached her naughty child and captured Him. When He was caught, Kṛṣṇa was almost on the point of crying. He smeared His hands over His eyes, which were anointed with black eye cosmetics. The child saw His mother's face while she stood over Him, and His eyes became restless from fear. Mother Yaśodā could understand that Kṛṣṇa was unnecessarily afraid, and for His benefit she wanted to allay His fears.

Being the topmost well-wisher of her child, mother Yaśodā began to think, "If the child is too fearful of me, I don't know what will happen to Him." Mother Yaśodā then threw away her stick. In order to punish Him, she thought to bind His hands with some ropes. She did not know it, but it was actually impossible for her to bind the Supreme Personality of Godhead. Mother Yaśodā was thinking that Kṛṣṇa was her tiny child; she did not know that the child had no limitation. There is no inside or outside of Him, nor beginning or end. He is unlimited and all-pervading. Indeed, He is Himself the whole cosmic manifestation. Still, mother Yaśodā was thinking of Kṛṣṇa as her child. Although He is beyond the reach of all senses, she endeavored to bind Him up to a wooden grinding mortar. But when she tried to bind Him, she found that the rope she was using was too short—by two inches. She gathered more ropes from the house and added to it, but at the end she found the same shortage. In this way, she connected all the ropes available at home, but when the final knot was added, she saw that it was still two inches too short. Mother Yaśodā was smiling, but she was astonished. How was it happening?

In attempting to bind her son, she became tired. She was perspiring, and the garland on her head fell down. Then Lord Kṛṣṇa appreciated the hard labor of His mother, and being compassionate upon her, He agreed to be bound up by the ropes. Kṛṣṇa, playing as a human child in the house of mother Yaśodā, was performing His own selected pastimes. Of course no one can control the Supreme Personality of Godhead. The pure devotee surrenders himself unto the lotus feet of the Lord, who may either protect or vanquish the devotee. But for his part, the devotee never forgets his own position of surrender. Similarly, the Lord also feels transcendental pleasure by submitting Himself to the protection of the devotee. This was exemplified by Kṛṣṇa's surrender unto His mother, Yaśodā.

Kṛṣṇa is the supreme bestower of all kinds of liberation to His devotees, but the benediction which was bestowed upon mother Yaśodā was never experienced even by Lord Brahmā or Lord Śiva or the goddess of fortune.

The Supreme Personality of Godhead, who is known as the son of Yaśodā and Nanda Mahārāja, is never so completely known to the *yogīs* and speculators. But He is easily available to His devotees. Nor is He appreciated as the supreme reservoir of all pleasure by the *yogīs* and speculators.

After binding her son, mother Yaśodā engaged herself in household affairs. At that time, bound up to the wooden mortar, Kṛṣṇa could see a pair of trees before Him which were known as *arjuna* trees. The great reservoir of pleasure, Lord Śrī Kṛṣṇa, thus thought to Himself, "Mother Yaśodā first of all left without feeding Me sufficient milk, and therefore I broke the pot of yogurt and distributed the stock butter in charity to the monkeys. Now she has bound Me up to a wooden mortar. So I shall do something more mischievous than before." And thus He thought of pulling down the two very tall *arjuna* trees.

There is a history behind the pair of *arjuna* trees. In their previous lives, the trees were born as the human sons of Kuvera, and their names were Nalakūvara and Maṇigrīva. Fortunately, they came within the vision of the Lord. In their previous lives they were cursed by the great sage Nārada in order to receive the highest benediction of seeing Lord Kṛṣṇa. This benediction-curse was bestowed upon them because of their forgetfulness due to intoxication. This story will be narrated in the next chapter.

*Thus ends the Bhaktivedanta purport of the Ninth Chapter of* Kṛṣṇa, *"Mother Yaśodā Binding Lord Kṛṣṇa."*

# 10 / Deliverance of Nalakūvara and Manigrīva

The story of the cursing of Nalakūvara and Maṇigrīva and their deliverance by Kṛṣṇa, under the all-blissful desire of the great sage Nārada, is here described.

The two great demigods, Nalakūvara and Maṇigrīva, were sons of the treasurer of the demigods, Kuvera, who was a great devotee of Lord Śiva. By the grace of Lord Śiva, Kuvera's material opulences had no limit. As a rich man's sons often become addicted to wine and women, so these two sons of Kuvera were also addicted to wine and sex. Once, these two demigods, desiring to enjoy, entered the garden of Lord Śiva in the province of Kailāsa on the bank of Mandākinī Ganges. There they drank much and engaged in hearing the sweet singing of beautiful women who accompanied them in that garden of fragrant flowers. In an intoxicated condition, they both entered the water of the Ganges, which was full with lotus flowers, and there they began to enjoy the company of the young girls exactly as the male elephant enjoys the female elephants within the water.

While they were thus enjoying themselves in the water, all of a sudden Nārada, the great sage, happened to pass that way. He could understand that the demigods Nalakūvara and Maṇigrīva were too intoxicated and could not even see that he was passing. The young girls, however, were not so intoxicated as the demigods, and they at once became ashamed at being naked before the great sage Nārada. They began to cover themselves with all haste. The two demigod-sons of Kuvera were so intoxicated that they could not appreciate the presence of the sage Nārada and therefore did not cover their bodies. On seeing the two demigods so degraded by intoxication, Nārada desired their welfare, and therefore he exhibited his causeless mercy upon them by cursing them.

Because the great sage was compassionate upon them, he wanted to finish their false enjoyment of intoxication and association with young girls and wanted them to see Lord Kṛṣṇa eye to eye. He conceived of cursing them as follows. He said that the attraction for material enjoyment is due to an increase of the mode of passion. A person in the material world, when favored by the material opulence of riches, generally becomes addicted to three things–intoxication, sex and gambling. Materially opulent men, being puffed up with the accumulation of wealth, also become so merciless that they indulge in killing animals by opening slaughterhouses. And they think that they themselves will never die. Such foolish persons, forgetting the laws of nature, become overly infatuated with the body. They forget that the material body, even though very much advanced in civilization, up to the position of the demigods, will finally be burned to ashes. And while one is living, whatever the external condition of the body may be, within there is only stool, urine and various kinds of worms. Thus being engaged in jealousy and violence to other bodies, materialists cannot understand the ultimate goal of life, and without knowing this goal of life, they generally glide down to a hellish condition. In their next birth, such foolish persons commit all kinds of sinful activities on account of this temporary body, and they are even unable to consider whether this body actually belongs to them. Generally it is said that the body belongs to the persons who feed the body. One might therefore consider whether this body belongs to one personally or to the master to whom one renders service. The master of slaves claims full right to the bodies of the slaves because the master feeds the slaves. It may be questioned then whether the body belongs to the father, who is the seed-giving master of this body, or to the mother, who develops the child's body in her womb.

Foolish persons are engaged in committing all sorts of sins due to the misconception of identifying the material body with the self. But one should be intelligent enough to understand to whom this body belongs. A foolish person indulges in killing other animals to maintain the body, but he does not consider whether this body belongs to him or to his father or mother or grandfather. Sometimes a grandfather or a father gives his daughter in charity to a person with a view of getting back the daughter's child as a son. The body may also belong to a stronger man who forces it to work for him. Sometimes the slave's body is sold to the master on the basis that the body will belong to the master. And at the end of life, the body belongs to the fire, because the body is given to the fire and burned to ashes. Or the body is thrown into the street to be eaten by the dogs and vultures.

Before committing all kinds of sins to maintain the body, one should understand to whom the body belongs. Ultimately it is concluded that the body is a product of material nature, and at the end it merges into material nature; therefore, the conclusion should be that the body belongs to material nature. One should not wrongly think that the body belongs to him. To maintain a false possession, why should one indulge in killing? Why should one kill innocent animals to maintain the body?

When a man is infatuated with the false prestige of opulence, he does not care for any moral instruction but indulges in wine, women and animal killing. In such circumstances, a poverty-stricken man is often better situated because a poor man thinks of himself in relation to other bodies. A poor man often does not wish to inflict injuries to other bodies because he can understand more readily that when he himself is injured he feels pain. As such, the great sage Nārada considered that because the demigods Nalakūvara and Maṇigrīva were so infatuated by false prestige, they should be put into a condition of life devoid of opulence.

A person who has a pinprick in his body does not wish others to be pricked by pins; a considerate man in the life of poverty does not wish others to be also put into that condition. Generally it is seen that one who has risen from a poverty-stricken life and becomes wealthy creates some charitable institution at the end of his life so that other poverty-stricken men might be benefited. In short, a compassionate poor man may consider others' pains and pleasures with empathy. A poor man may be seldom puffed with false pride, and he may be freed from all kinds of infatuation. He may remain satisfied by whatever he gets for his maintenance by the grace of the Lord.

To remain in the poverty-stricken condition is a kind of austerity. According to Vedic culture, therefore, the *brāhmaṇas,* as a matter of routine, keep themselves in a poverty-stricken condition to save themselves from the false prestige of material opulence. False prestige due to advancement of material prosperity is a great impediment for spiritual emancipation. A poverty-stricken man cannot become unnaturally fat by eating more and more. And on account of not being able to eat more than he requires, his senses are not very turbulent. When the senses are not very turbulent, he cannot become violent.

Another advantage of poverty is that a saintly person can easily enter a poor man's house, and thus the poor man can take advantage of the saintly person's association. A very opulent man does not allow anyone to enter his house; therefore, the saintly person cannot enter. According to the Vedic system, a saintly person takes the position of a mendicant so that on the plea of begging something from the householder, he can enter any house. The householder, who has usually forgotten everything about spiritual advancement because he is busy maintaining family affairs, can be benefited by the association of a saintly person. There is a great chance for the poor man to become liberated through association with a saint. Of what use are persons who are puffed up with material opulence and prestige if they are bereft of the association of saintly persons and devotees of the Supreme Personality of Godhead?

The great sage Nārada thereafter thought that it was his duty to put those demigods into a condition where they could not be falsely proud of their material opulence and prestige. Nārada was compassionate and wanted to save them from their fallen life. They were in the mode of darkness, and being therefore unable to control their senses, they were addicted to sex life. It was the duty of a saintly person like Nārada to save them from their abominable condition. In animal life, the animal has no sense to understand that he is naked. But Kuvera was the treasurer of the demigods, a very responsible man, and Nalakūvara and Maṇigrīva were two of his sons. And yet they became so animalistic and irresponsible that they could not understand, due to intoxication, that they were naked. To cover the lower part of the body is a principle of human civilization, and when a man or woman forgets this principle, they become degraded. Nārada therefore thought that the best punishment for them was to make them immovable living entities, or trees. Trees are, by nature's laws, immovable. Although trees are covered by the mode of ignorance, they cannot do harm. The great sage Nārada thought it fitting that, although the brothers, by his mercy, would be punished to become trees, they continue to keep their memory to be able to know why they were being punished. After changing the body, a living entity generally forgets his previous life, but in special cases, by the grace of the Lord, as with Nalakūvara and Maṇigrīva, one can remember.

Sage Nārada therefore contemplated that the two demigods should remain for one hundred years, in the time of the demigods, in the form of trees, and after that they would be fortunate enough to see the Supreme Personality of Godhead, face to face, by His causeless mercy. And thus they would be again promoted to the life of the demigods and great devotees of the Lord.

After this, the great sage Nārada returned to his abode known as Nārāyaṇa Āśrama, and the two demigods turned into trees, known as twin *arjuna* trees. The two demigods were favored by the causeless mercy of Nārada and given a chance to grow in Nanda's courtyard and see Lord Kṛṣṇa face to face.

Although the child Kṛṣṇa was bound up to the wooden mortar, He began to proceed towards the growing trees in order to fulfill the prophecy of His great devotee Nārada. Lord Kṛṣṇa knew that Nārada was His great devotee and that the trees standing before Him as twin *arjuna* trees were actually the sons of Kuvera. "I must now fulfill the words of My great devotee Nārada," He thought. Then He began to proceed through the passage between the two trees. Although He was able to pass through the passage, the large wooden mortar stuck horizontally between the trees. Taking advantage of this, Lord Kṛṣṇa began to pull the rope which was tied to the mortar. As soon as He pulled, with great strength, the two trees, with all branches and limbs, fell down immediately with a great sound. Out of the broken, fallen trees came two great personalities, shining like blazing fire. All sides became illuminated and beautiful by their presence. The two purified bodies immediately came before child Kṛṣṇa and bowed down to offer their respects and prayers in the following words.

"Dear Lord Kṛṣṇa, You are the original Personality of Godhead, master of all mystic powers. Learned *brāhmaṇas* know very well that this cosmic manifestation is an expansion of Your potencies which are sometimes manifest and sometimes unmanifest. You are the original provider of the life, body and senses of all living entities. You are the eternal God, Lord Viṣṇu, who is all-pervading, the principal controller of everything. You are the original source of the cosmic manifestation which is acting under the spell of the three modes of material nature—goodness, passion and ignorance. You are living as the Supersoul in all the multi-forms of living entities, and You know very well what is going on within their bodies and minds. Therefore You are the supreme director of all activities of all living entities. But although You are in the midst of everything which is under the spell of the material modes of nature, You are not affected by such contaminated qualities. No one under the jurisdiction of the material modes can understand Your transcendental qualities, which existed before the creation; therefore You are called the Supreme Brahman who is always glorified by His personal internal potencies. In this material world You can be known only by Your different incarnations. Although You assume different types of bodies, these bodies are not part of the material creation. They are always full of transcendental potencies of unlimited opulence, strength, beauty, fame, wisdom and renunciation. In the material existence, there is a difference between the body and the owner of the body, but because You appear in Your original spiritual body, there is no such difference for You. When You appear, Your uncommon activities indicate that You are the Supreme Personality of Godhead. Such uncommon activities are not possible for anyone in material existence. You are that Supreme Personality of Godhead, now appearing to cause the birth and death as well as liberation of the living entities, and You are full with all Your plenary expansions. You can bestow on everyone all kinds of benediction. O Lord! O source of all fortune and goodness, we offer our respectful obeisances unto You. You are the all-pervading Supreme Personality of Godhead, the source of peace and the supreme person in the dynasty of King Yadu. O Lord, our father known as Kuvera, the demigod, is Your servant. Similarly, the great sage Nārada is also Your servitor, and by their grace only we have been able to see You personally. We therefore pray that we may always be engaged in Your transcendental loving service by speaking only about Your glories and hearing about Your transcendental activities. May our hands and other limbs be engaged in Your service and our minds always be concentrated at Your lotus feet and our heads always bowed down before the all-pervading universal form of Your Lordship."

When the demigods Nalakūvara and Maṇigrīva finished their prayers, the child, Lord Kṛṣṇa, the master and proprietor of Gokula, bound to the wooden grinding mortar by the ropes of Yaśodā, began to smile and said, "It was already known to Me that My great devotee-sage Nārada had shown his causeless mercy by saving you from the abominable condition of pride due to possessing extraordinary beauty and opulence in the family of the demigods. He has saved you from gliding down into the lowest condition of hellish life. All these facts are already known to Me. You are very fortunate because you were not only cursed by him, but you had the great opportunity to see him. If someone is able, by chance, to see a great saintly person like Nārada face to face, who is always serene and merciful to everyone, then immediately that conditioned soul becomes liberated. This is exactly like being situated in the full light of the sun: there cannot be any visionary impediment. Therefore, O Nalakūvara and Maṇigrīva, your lives have now become successful because you have developed ecstatic love for Me. This is your last birth within material existence. Now you can go back to your father's residence in the heavenly planet, and by remaining in the attitude of devotional service, you will be liberated in this very life."

After this, the demigods circumambulated the Lord many times and bowed down before Him again and again, and thus they left. The Lord remained bound up with ropes to the grinding mortar.

*Thus ends the Bhaktivedanta purport of the Tenth Chapter of* Kṛṣṇa, *"Deliverance of Nalakūvara and Maṇigrīva."*

# 11 / Killing the Demons Vatsāsura and Bakāsura

When the twin *arjuna* trees fell to the ground, making a sound like the falling of thunderbolts, all the inhabitants of Gokula, including Nanda Mahārāja, immediately came to the spot. They were very much astonished to see how the two great trees had suddenly fallen. Because they could find no reason for their falling down, they were puzzled. When they saw child Kṛṣṇa bound up to the wooden mortar by the ropes of Yaśodā, they began to think that it must have been caused by some demon. Otherwise, how was it possible? At the same time, they were very much perturbed because such uncommon incidences were always happening to the child Kṛṣṇa. While the elderly cowherd men were thus contemplating, the small children who were playing there informed the men that the trees fell due to Kṛṣṇa's pulling the wooden mortar with the ropes to which He was bound. "Kṛṣṇa came in between the two trees," they explained, "and the wooden mortar was topsy-turvied and stuck in between the trees. Kṛṣṇa began to pull the rope, and the trees fell down. When the trees fell down, two very dazzling men came out of the trees, and they began to talk to Kṛṣṇa."

Most of the cowherd men did not believe the statement of the children. They could not believe that such things were at all possible. Some of them, however, believed them and told Nanda Mahārāja, "Your child is different from all other children. He just might have done it." Nanda Mahārāja began to smile, hearing about the extraordinary abilities of his son. He came forward and untied the knot just to free his wonderful child. After being freed by Nanda Mahārāja, Kṛṣṇa was taken onto the laps of the elderly *gopīs.* They took Him away to the courtyard of the house and began to clap, praising His wonderful activities. Kṛṣṇa began to clap along with them, just like an ordinary child. The Supreme Lord Kṛṣṇa, being completely controlled by the *gopīs,* began to sing and dance, just like a puppet in their hands.

Sometimes mother Yaśodā used to ask Kṛṣṇa to bring her a wooden plank for sitting. Although the wooden plank was too heavy to be carried by a child, still somehow or other Kṛṣṇa would bring it to His mother. Sometimes while worshiping Nārāyaṇa, His father would ask Him to bring his wooden slippers, and Kṛṣṇa, with great difficulty, would put the slippers on His head and bring them to His father. When He was asked to lift some heavy article and was unable to lift it, He would simply move His arms. In this way, daily, at every moment, He was the reservoir of all pleasure to His parents. The Lord was exhibiting such childish activities before the inhabitants of Vṛndāvana because He wanted to show the great philosophers and sages searching after the Absolute Truth how the Supreme Absolute Truth Personality of Godhead is controlled by and subject to the desires of His pure devotees.

One day, a fruit vendor came before the house of Nanda Mahārāja. Upon hearing the vendor call, "If anyone wants fruits please come and take them from me!" child Kṛṣṇa immediately took some grains in His palm and went to get fruits in exchange. In those days exchange was by barter; therefore Kṛṣṇa might have seen His parents exchange fruits and other things by bartering grains, and so He imitated. But His palms were very small, and He was not very careful to hold them tight, so He was dropping the grains. The vendor who came to sell fruits saw this and was very much captivated by the beauty of the Lord, so he immediately accepted whatever few grains were left in His palm and filled His hands with fruits. In this meantime, the vendor saw that his whole basket of fruit had become filled with jewels. The Lord is the bestower of all benediction. If someone gives something to the Lord, he is not the loser; he is the gainer by a million times.

One day Lord Kṛṣṇa, the liberator of the twin *arjuna* trees, was playing with Balarāma and the other children on the bank of the Yamunā, and because it was already late in the morning, Rohiṇī, the mother of Balarāma, went to call them back home. But Balarāma and Kṛṣṇa were so engrossed in playing with Their friends that They did not wish to come back; They just engaged Themselves in playing more and more. When Rohiṇī was unable to take Them back home, she went home and sent mother Yaśodā to call Them again. Mother Yaśodā was so affectionate toward her son that as soon as she came out to call Him back home, her breast filled up with milk. She loudly cried, "My dear child, please come back home. Your time for lunch is already past." She then said, "My dear Kṛṣṇa, O my dear lotus-eyed child, please come and suck my breast. You have played enough. You must be very hungry, my dear little child.

You must be tired from playing for so long." She also addressed Balarāma thus: "My dear, the glory of Your family, please come back with Your younger brother Kṛṣṇa immediately. You have been engaged in playing since morning, and You must be very tired. Please come back and take Your lunch at home. Your father Nandarāja is waiting for You. He has to eat, so You must come back so that he can eat."

As soon as Kṛṣṇa and Balarāma heard that Nanda Mahārāja was waiting for Them and could not take his food in Their absence, They started to return. Their other playmates complained, "Kṛṣṇa is leaving us just at the point when our playing is at the summit. Next time we shall not allow Him to leave."

His playmates then threatened not to allow Him to play with them again. Kṛṣṇa became afraid, and instead of going back home, He went back again to play with the boys. At that time, mother Yaśodā scolded the children and told Kṛṣṇa, "My dear Kṛṣṇa, do You think that You are a street boy? You have no home? Please come back to Your home! I see that Your body has become very dirty from playing since early morning. Now come home and take Your bath. Besides, today is Your birthday ceremony; therefore You should come back home and give cows in charity to the *brāhmaṇas.* Don't You see how Your playmates are decorated with ornaments by their mothers? You should also be cleansed and decorated with nice dress and ornaments. Please, therefore, come back, take Your bath, dress Yourself nicely, and then again You may go on playing."

In this way mother Yaśodā called back Lord Kṛṣṇa and Balarāma who are worshipable by great demigods like Lord Brahmā and Lord Śiva. She was thinking of Them as her children.

When mother Yaśodā's children, Kṛṣṇa and Balarāma, came home, she bathed Them very nicely and dressed Them with ornaments. She then called for the *brāhmaṇas,* and through her children she gave many cows in charity for the occasion of Kṛṣṇa's birthday. In this way she performed the birthday ceremony of Kṛṣṇa at home.

After this incident, all the elderly members of the cowherd men assembled together, and Nanda Mahārāja presided. They began to consult amongst themselves how to stop great disturbances in the Mahāvana on account of the demons. In this meeting, Upananda, brother of Nanda Mahārāja, was present. He was considered to be learned and experienced, and he was a well-wisher of Kṛṣṇa and Balarāma. He was a leader, and he began to address the meeting as follows: "My dear friends! Now we should leave here for another place because we are continually finding that great demons are coming here to disturb the peaceful situation, and they are especially attempting to kill the small children. Just consider Pūtanā and Kṛṣṇa. It was simply by the grace of Lord Hari that Kṛṣṇa was saved from the hands of such a great demon. Next the whirlwind demon took Kṛṣṇa away in the sky, but by the grace of Lord Hari He was saved, and the demon fell down on a stone slab and died. Very recently, this child was playing between two trees, and the trees fell down violently, and yet there was no injury to the child. So Lord Hari saved Him again. Just imagine the calamity if this child or any other child playing with Him were crushed by the falling trees! Considering all these incidences, we must conclude that this place is no longer safe. Let us leave. We have all been saved from different calamities by the grace of Lord Hari. Now we should be cautious and leave this place and reside somewhere where we can live peacefully. I think that we should all go to the forest known as Vṛndāvana, where just now there are newly grown plants and herbs. It is very suitable for pasturing ground for our cows, and we and our families, the *gopīs* with their children, can very peacefully live there. Near Vṛndāvana there is Govardhana Hill, which is very beautiful, and there is newly grown grass and fodder for the animals, so there will be no difficulty in living there. I therefore suggest that we start immediately for that beautiful place, as there is no need to waste any more time. Let us prepare all our carts immediately, and, if you like, let us go, keeping all the cows in front."

On hearing the statement of Upananda, all the cowherd men immediately agreed. "Let us immediately go there." Everyone then loaded all their household furniture and utensils on the carts and prepared to go to Vṛndāvana. All the old men of the village, the children and women were arranged on seats, and the cowherd men equipped themselves with bows and arrows to follow the carts. All the cows and bulls along with their calves were placed in the front, and the men surrounded the flocks with their bows and arrows and began to blow on their horns and bugles. In this way, with tumultuous sound, they started for Vṛndāvana.

And who can describe the damsels of Vraja? They were all seated on the carts and were very beautifully dressed with ornaments and costly saris. They began to chant the pastimes of child Kṛṣṇa as usual. Mother Yaśodā and mother Rohiṇī were seated on a separate cart, and Kṛṣṇa and Balarāma were seated on their laps. While mother Rohiṇī and Yaśodā were riding on the cart, they talked to Kṛṣṇa and Balarāma, and feeling the pleasure of such talks, they looked very, very beautiful.

In this way, after reaching Vṛndāvana, where everyone lives eternally, very peacefully and happily, they encircled Vṛndāvana and kept the carts all together. After seeing the beautiful appearance of Govardhana on the bank of the River Yamunā, they began to construct their places of residence. While those of the same age were walking together and children were talking with their parents, the inhabitants of Vṛndāvana felt very happy.

At this time Kṛṣṇa and Balarāma were given charge of the calves. The first responsibility of the cowherd boys was to take care of the little calves. The boys are trained in this from the very beginning of their childhood. So along with other little cowherd boys, Kṛṣṇa and Balarāma went into the pasturing ground and took charge of the calves and played with Their playmates. While taking charge of the calves, sometimes the two brothers played on Their flutes. And sometimes They played with *āmalakī* fruits and *bael* fruits, just like small children play with balls. Sometimes They danced and made tinkling sounds with Their ankle bells. Sometimes They made Themselves into bulls and cows by covering Themselves with blankets. Thus Kṛṣṇa and Balarāma played. The two brothers also used to imitate the sounds of bulls and cows and play at bullfighting. Sometimes They used to imitate the sounds of various animals and birds. In this way, They enjoyed Their childhood pastimes apparently like ordinary, mundane children.

Once, when Kṛṣṇa and Balarāma were playing on the bank of the Yamunā, a demon of the name Vatsāsura assumed the shape of a calf and came there intending to kill the brothers. By taking the shape of a calf, the demon could mingle with other calves. Kṛṣṇa, however, specifically noticed this, and He immediately told Balarāma about the entrance of the demon. Both brothers then followed him and sneaked up upon him. Kṛṣṇa caught hold of the demon-calf by the two hind legs and tail, whipped him around very forcibly and threw him up into a tree. The demon lost his life and fell down from the top of the tree to the ground. When the demon lay dead on the ground, all the playmates of Kṛṣṇa congratulated Him, "Well done, well done," and the demigods in the sky began to shower flowers with great satisfaction. In this way, the maintainers of the complete creation, Kṛṣṇa and Balarāma, used to take care of the calves in the morning every day, and thus They enjoyed Their childhood pastimes as cowherd boys in Vṛndāvana.

All the cowherd boys would daily go to the bank of the River Yamunā to water their calves. Usually, when the calves drank water from the Yamunā, the boys also drank. One day, after drinking, when they were sitting on the bank of the river, they saw a huge animal which looked something like a duck and was as big as a hill. Its top was as strong as a thunderbolt. When they saw that unusual animal, they became afraid of it. The name of this beast was Bakāsura, and he was a friend of Kaṁsa's. He appeared on the scene suddenly and immediately attacked Kṛṣṇa with his pointed, sharp beaks and quickly swallowed Him up. When Kṛṣṇa was thus swallowed, all the boys, headed by Balarāma, became almost breathless, as if they had died. But when the Bakāsura demon was swallowing up Kṛṣṇa, he felt a burning fiery sensation in his throat. This was due to the glowing effulgence of Kṛṣṇa. The demon quickly threw Kṛṣṇa up and tried to kill Him by pinching Him in his beaks. Bakāsura did not know that although Kṛṣṇa was playing the part of a child of Nanda Mahārāja, He was still the original father of Lord Brahmā, the creator of the universe. The child of mother Yaśodā, who is the reservoir of pleasure for the demigods and who is the maintainer of saintly persons, caught hold of the beaks of the great gigantic duck and, before His cowherd boy friends, bifurcated his mouth, just as a child very easily splits a blade of grass. From the sky, the denizens of the heavenly planets showered flowers like the *cāmeli,* the most fragrant of all flowers, as a token of their congratulations. Accompanying the showers of flowers was a vibration of bugles, drums and conchshells.

When the boys saw the showering of flowers and heard the celestial sounds, they became struck with wonder. When they saw Kṛṣṇa, they all, including Balarāma, were so pleased that it seemed as if they had regained their very source of life. As soon as they saw Kṛṣṇa coming towards them, they one after another embraced the son of Nanda and held Him to their chests. After this, they assembled all the calves under their charge and began to return home.

When they arrived home, they began to speak of the wonderful activities of the son of Nanda. When the *gopīs* and cowherd men all heard the story from the boys, they felt great happiness because naturally they loved Kṛṣṇa, and hearing about His glories and victorious activities, they became still more affectionate toward Him. Thinking that the child Kṛṣṇa was saved from the mouth of death, they began to see His face with great love and affection. They were full of anxieties, but they could not turn their faces from the vision of Kṛṣṇa. The *gopīs* and the men began to converse amongst themselves about how the child Kṛṣṇa was attacked in so many ways and so many times by so many demons, and yet the demons were killed and Kṛṣṇa was uninjured. They continued to converse amongst themselves about how so many great demons in such fierce bodies attacked Kṛṣṇa to kill Him, but by the grace of Hari, they could not cause even a slight injury. Rather, they died like small flies in a fire. Thus they remembered the words of Gargamuni who foretold, by dint of his vast knowledge of the *Vedas* and astrology, that this boy would be attacked by many demons. Now they actually saw that this was coming true, word for word.

All the elderly cowherd men, including Nanda Mahārāja, used to talk of the wonderful activities of Lord Kṛṣṇa and Balarāma, and they were always so much absorbed in those talks that they forgot the threefold miseries of this material existence. This is the effect of Kṛṣṇa consciousness. What was enjoyed 5,000 years ago by Nanda Mahārāja can still be enjoyed by persons who are in Kṛṣṇa consciousness simply by talking about the transcendental pastimes of Kṛṣṇa and His associates.

Thus both Balarāma and Kṛṣṇa enjoyed Their childhood pastimes, imitating the monkeys of Lord Rāmacandra who constructed the bridge over the ocean and Hanumān, who jumped over the water to Ceylon. And They used to imitate such pastimes among Their friends and so happily passed Their childhood life.

*Thus ends the Bhaktivedanta purport of the Eleventh Chapter of* Kṛṣṇa, *"Killing the Demons Vatsāsura and Bakāsura."*

# 12 / The Killing of the Aghāsura Demon

Once the Lord desired to go early in the morning with all His cowherd boy friends to the forest, where they were to assemble together and take lunch. As soon as He got up from bed, He blew a buffalo horn and called all His friends together. Keeping the calves before them, they started for the forest. In this way, Lord Kṛṣṇa assembled thousands of His boy friends. They were each equipped with a stick, flute and horn as well as lunch bag, and each of them was taking care of thousands of calves. All the boys appeared very jolly and happy in that excursion. Each and every one of them was attentive for his personal calves. The boys were fully decorated with various kinds of golden ornaments, and out of sporting propensities they began to pick up flowers, leaves, twigs, peacock feathers and red clay from different places in the forest, and they began to dress themselves in different ways. While passing through the forest, one boy stole another boy's lunch package and passed it to a third. And when the boy whose lunch package was stolen came to know of it, he tried to take it back. But one threw it to another boy. This sportive playing went on amongst the boys as childhood pastimes.

When Lord Kṛṣṇa went ahead to a distant place in order to see some specific scenery, the boys behind Him tried to run to catch up and be the first to touch Him. So there was a great competition. One would say, "I will go there and touch Kṛṣṇa," and another would say, "Oh you cannot go. I'll touch Kṛṣṇa first." Some of them played on their flutes or vibrated bugles made of buffalo horn. Some of them gladly followed the peacocks and imitated the onomatopoetic sounds of the cuckoo. While the birds were flying in the sky, the boys ran after the birds' shadows along the ground and tried to follow their exact courses. Some of them went to the monkeys and silently sat down by them, and some of them imitated the dancing of the peacocks. Some of them caught the tails of the monkeys and played with them, and when the monkeys jumped in a tree, the boys also followed. When a monkey showed its face and teeth, a boy imitated and showed his teeth to the monkey. Some of the boys played with the frogs on the bank of the Yamunā, and when, out of fear, the frogs jumped in the water, the boys immediately dove in after them, and they would come out of the water when they saw their own shadows and stand imitating, making caricatures and laughing. They would also go to an empty well and make loud sounds, and when the echo came back, they would call it ill names and laugh.

As stated personally by the Supreme Personality of Godhead in the *Bhagavad-gītā,* He is realized proportionately by transcendentalists as Brahman, Paramātmā and the Supreme Personality of Godhead. Here, in confirmation of the same statement, Lord Kṛṣṇa, who awards the impersonalist Brahman realization by His bodily effulgence, also gives pleasure to the devotees as the Supreme Personality of Godhead. Those who are under the spell of external energy, *māyā,* take Him only as a beautiful child. Yet He gave full transcendental pleasure to the cowherd boys who played with Him. Only after accumulating heaps of pious activities, those boys were promoted to personally associate with the Supreme Personality of Godhead. Who can estimate the transcendental fortune of the residents of Vṛndāvana? They were personally visualizing the Supreme Personality of Godhead face to face, He whom many *yogīs* cannot find even after undergoing severe austerities, although He is sitting within the heart. This is also confirmed in the *Brahma-saṁhitā.* One may search for Kṛṣṇa the Supreme Personality of Godhead through the pages of the *Vedas* and *Upaniṣads,* but if one is fortunate enough to associate with a devotee, he can see the Supreme Personality of Godhead face to face. After accumulating pious activities in many, many previous lives, the cowherd boys were seeing Kṛṣṇa face to face and playing with Him as friends. They could not understand that Kṛṣṇa is the Supreme Personality of Godhead, but they were playing as intimate friends with intense love for Him.

When Lord Kṛṣṇa was enjoying His childhood pastimes with His boy friends, one Aghāsura demon became very impatient. He was unable to see Kṛṣṇa playing, so he appeared before the boys intending to kill them all. This Aghāsura was so dangerous that even the denizens of heaven were afraid of him. Although the denizens of heaven drank nectar daily to prolong their lives, they were afraid of this Aghāsura and were wondering, "When will the demon be killed?" The denizens used to drink nectar to become immortal, but actually they were not confident of their immortality. On the other hand, the boys who were playing with Kṛṣṇa had no fear of the demons. They were free of fear. Any material arrangement for protecting oneself from death is always unsure, but if one is in Kṛṣṇa consciousness, then immortality is confidently assured.

The demon Aghāsura appeared before Kṛṣṇa and His friends. Aghāsura happened to be the younger brother of Pūtanā and Bakāsura, and he thought, "Kṛṣṇa has killed my brother and sister. Now I shall kill Him along with all His friends and calves." Aghāsura was instigated by Kaṁsa, so he had come with determination. Aghāsura also began to think that when he would offer grains and water in memory of his brother and kill Kṛṣṇa and all the cowherd boys, then automatically all the inhabitants of Vṛndāvana would die. Generally, for the householders, the children are the life and breath force. When all the children die, then naturally the parents also die on account of strong affection for them.

Aghāsura, thus deciding to kill all the inhabitants of Vṛndāvana, expanded himself by the yogic *siddhi* called *mahimā*. The demons are generally expert in achieving almost all kinds of mystic powers. In the *yoga* system, by the perfection called *mahima-siddhi*, one can expand himself as he desires. The demon Aghāsura expanded himself up to eight miles and assumed the shape of a very fat serpent. Having attained this wonderful body, he stretched his mouth open just like a mountain cave. Desiring to swallow all the boys at once, including Kṛṣṇa and Balarāma, he sat on the path.

The demon in the shape of a big fat serpent expanded his lips from land to sky; his lower lip was touching the ground and his upper lip was touching the clouds. His jaws appeared like a big mountain cave, without limitation, and his teeth appeared just like mountain summits. His tongue appeared to be a broad traffic way, and he was breathing just like a hurricane. The fire of his eyes was blazing. At first the boys thought that the demon was a statue, but after examining it, they saw that it was more like a big serpent lying down in the road and widening his mouth. The boys began to talk among themselves: "This figure appears to be a great animal, and he is sitting in such a posture just to swallow us all. Just see—is it not a big snake that has widened his mouth to eat all of us?"

One of them said, "Yes, what you say is true. This animal's upper lip appears to be just like the sunshine, and its lower lip is just like the reflection of red sunshine on the ground. Dear friends, just look to the right and left hand side of the mouth of the animal. Its mouth appears to be like a big mountain cave, and its height cannot be estimated. The chin is also raised just like a mountain summit. That long highway appears to be its tongue, and inside the mouth it is as dark as in a mountain cave. The hot wind that is blowing like a hurricane is his breathing, and the fishy bad smell coming out from his mouth is the smell of his intestines."

Then they further consulted among themselves: "If we all at one time entered into the mouth of this great serpent, how could it possibly swallow all of us? And even if it were to swallow all of us at once, it could not swallow Kṛṣṇa. Kṛṣṇa will immediately kill him, as He did Bakāsura." Talking in this way, all the boys looked at the beautiful lotus-like face of Kṛṣṇa, and they began to clap and smile. And so they marched forward and entered the mouth of the gigantic serpent.

Meanwhile, Kṛṣṇa, who is the Supersoul within everyone's heart, could understand that the big statuesque figure was a demon. While He was planning how to stop the destruction of His intimate friends, all the boys along with their cows and calves entered the mouth of the serpent. But Kṛṣṇa did not enter. The demon was awaiting Kṛṣṇa's entrance, and he was thinking, "Everyone has entered except Kṛṣṇa, who has killed my brothers and sisters."

Kṛṣṇa is the assurance of safety to everyone. But when He saw that His friends were already out of His hands and were lying within the belly of a great serpent, He became, momentarily, aggrieved. He was also struck with wonder how the external energy works so wonderfully. He then began to consider how the demon should be killed and how he could save the boys and calves. Although there was no factual concern on Kṛṣṇa's part, He was thinking like that. Finally, after some deliberation, He also entered the mouth of the demon. When Kṛṣṇa entered, all the demigods, who had gathered to see the fun and who were hiding within the clouds, began to express their feelings with the words, "Alas! alas!" At the same time, all the friends of Aghāsura, especially Kaṁsa, who were all accustomed to eating flesh and blood, began to express their jubilation, understanding that Kṛṣṇa had also entered the mouth of the demon.

While the demon was trying to smash Kṛṣṇa and His companions, Kṛṣṇa heard the demigods crying, "Alas, alas," and He immediately began to expand Himself within the throat of the demon. Although he had a gigantic body, the demon choked by the expanding of Kṛṣṇa. His big eyes moved violently, and he quickly suffocated. His life-air could not come out from any source, and ultimately it burst out of a hole in the upper part of his skull. Thus his life-air passed off. After the demon dropped dead, Kṛṣṇa, with His transcendental glance alone, brought all the boys and calves back to consciousness and came with them out of the mouth of the demon. While Kṛṣṇa was within the mouth of Aghāsura, the demon's spirit soul came out like a dazzling light, illuminating all directions, and waited in the sky. As soon as Kṛṣṇa with His calves and friends came out of the mouth of the demon, that glittering effulgent light immediately merged into the body of Kṛṣṇa within the vision of all the demigods.

The demigods became overwhelmed with joy and began to shower flowers on the Supreme Personality of Godhead, Kṛṣṇa, and thus they worshiped Him. The denizens of heaven began to dance in jubilation, and the denizens in Gandharvaloka began to offer various kinds of prayers. Drummers began to beat drums in jubilation, the *brāhmaṇas* began to recite Vedic hymns, and all the devotees of the Lord began to chant the words, "*Jaya! Jaya!* All glories to the Supreme Personality of Godhead!"

When Lord Brahmā heard those auspicious vibrations which sounded throughout the higher planetary system, he immediately came down to see what had happened. He saw that the demon was killed, and he was struck with wonder at the uncommon glorious pastimes of the Personality of Godhead. The gigantic mouth of the demon remained in an open position for many days and gradually dried up; it remained a spot of pleasure pastimes for all the cowherd boys.

The killing of Aghāsura took place when Kṛṣṇa and all His boy friends were under five years old. Children under five years old are called *kaumāra.* After five years up to the tenth year they are called *paugaṇḍa,* and after the tenth year up to the fifteenth year they are called *kaiśora.* After the fifteenth year, boys are called youths. So for one year there was no discussion of the incident of the Aghāsura demon in the village of Vraja. But when they attained their sixth year, they informed their parents of the incident with great wonder. The reason for this will be clear in the next chapter.

For Śrī Kṛṣṇa, the Supreme Personality of Godhead, who is far greater than such demigods as Lord Brahmā, it is not at all difficult to award one the opportunity of merging with His eternal body. This He awarded to Aghāsura. Aghāsura was certainly the most sinful living entity, and it is not possible for the sinful to merge into the existence of the Absolute Truth. But in this particular case, because Kṛṣṇa entered into Aghāsura's body, the demon became fully cleansed of all sinful reaction. Persons constantly thinking of the eternal form of the Lord in the shape of the Deity or in the shape of a mental form are awarded the transcendental goal of entering into the kingdom of God and associating with the Supreme Personality of Godhead. So we can just imagine the elevated position of someone like Aghāsura into whose body the Supreme Personality of Godhead, Kṛṣṇa, personally entered. Great sages, meditators and devotees constantly keep the form of the Lord within the heart, or they see the Deity form of the Lord in the temples; in that way, they become liberated from all material contamination and at the end of the body enter into the kingdom of God. This perfection is possible simply by keeping the form of the Lord within the mind. But in the case of Aghāsura, the Supreme Personality of Godhead personally entered. Aghāsura's position was therefore greater than the ordinary devotee's or the greatest *yogī's.*

Mahārāja Parīkṣit, who was engaged in hearing the transcendental pastimes of Lord Kṛṣṇa (who saved the life of Mahārāja Parīkṣit while he was in the womb of his mother), became more and more interested to hear about Him. And thus he questioned the sage Śukadeva Gosvāmī, who was reciting *Śrīmad-Bhāgavatam* before the King.

King Parīkṣit was a bit astonished to understand that the killing of the Aghāsura demon was not discussed for one year, until after the boys attained the *paugaṇḍa* age. Mahārāja Parīkṣit was very inquisitive to learn this, for he was sure that such an incident was due to the working of Kṛṣṇa's different energies.

Generally, the *kṣatriyas* or the administrative class are always busy with their political affairs, and they have very little chance to hear about the transcendental pastimes of Lord Kṛṣṇa. But while Parīkṣit Mahārāja was hearing these transcendental pastimes, he considered himself to be very fortunate because he was hearing from Śukadeva Gosvāmī, the greatest authority on the *Śrīmad-Bhāgavatam.* Thus being requested by Mahārāja Parīkṣit, Śukadeva Gosvāmī continued to speak about the transcendental pastimes of Lord Kṛṣṇa in the matter of His form, quality, fame and paraphernalia.

*Thus ends the Bhaktivedanta purport of the Twelfth Chapter of* Kṛṣṇa, *"The Killing of the Aghāsura Demon."*

# 13 / The Stealing of the Boys and Calves by Brahmā

Śukadeva Gosvāmī was very much encouraged when Mahārāja Parīkṣit asked him why the cowherd boys did not discuss the death of Aghāsura until after one year had passed. He explained thus: "My dear King, you are making the subject matter of the transcendental pastimes of Kṛṣṇa fresher by your inquisitiveness."

It is said that it is the nature of a devotee to constantly apply his mind, energy, words, ears, etc., in hearing and chanting about Kṛṣṇa. This is called Kṛṣṇa consciousness, and for one who is rapt in hearing and chanting Kṛṣṇa, the subject matter never becomes hackneyed or old. That is the significance of transcendental subject matter in contrast to material subject matter. Material subject matter becomes stale, and one cannot hear a certain subject for a long time; he wants change. But as far as transcendental subject matter is concerned, it is called *nityanavanavāyamāna.* This means that one can go on chanting and hearing about the Lord and never feel tired but will remain fresh and eager to hear more and more.

It is the duty of the spiritual master to disclose all confidential subject matter to the inquisitive and sincere disciple. Thus Śukadeva Gosvāmī began to explain why the killing of Aghāsura was not discussed until one year had passed. Śukadeva Gosvāmī told the King, "Now hear of this secret with attention. After saving His friends from the mouth of Aghāsura and after killing the demon, Lord Kṛṣṇa brought His friends to the bank of Yamunā and addressed them as follows: 'My dear friends, just see how this spot is very nice for taking lunch and playing on the soft sandy Yamunā bank. You can see how the lotus flowers in the water are beautifully blown and how they distribute their flavor all around. The chirping of the birds along with cooing of the peacocks, surrounded by the whispering of the leaves in the trees, combine and present sound-vibrations that echo one another. And this just enriches the beautiful scenery created by the trees here. Let us have our lunch in this spot because it is already late and we are feeling hungry. Let the calves remain near us, and let them drink water from the Yamunā. While we engage in our lunch-taking, the calves may engage in eating the soft grasses that are in this spot.'"

On hearing this proposal from Kṛṣṇa, all the boys became very glad and said, "Certainly, let us all sit down here to take our lunch." They then let loose the calves to eat the soft grass. Sitting down on the ground and keeping Kṛṣṇa in the center, they began to open their different boxes brought from home. Lord Śrī Kṛṣṇa was seated in the center of the circle, and all the boys kept their faces toward Him. They ate and constantly enjoyed seeing the Lord face to face. Kṛṣṇa appeared to be the whorl of a lotus flower, and the boys surrounding Him appeared to be its different petals. The boys collected flowers, leaves of flowers and the barks of trees and placed them under their different boxes, and thus they began to eat their lunch, keeping company with Kṛṣṇa. While taking lunch, each boy began to manifest different kinds of relations with Kṛṣṇa, and they enjoyed each other's company with joking words. While thus enjoying lunch with His friends, Lord Kṛṣṇa's flute was pushed within the belt of His cloth, and His bugle and cane were pushed in on the left-hand side of His cloth. He was holding a lump of foodstuff prepared with yogurt, butter, rice and pieces of fruit salad in His left palm, which could be seen through His petal-like finger joints. The Supreme Personality of Godhead, who accepts the results of all great sacrifices, was laughing and joking, enjoying lunch with His friends in Vṛndāvana. And thus the scene was being observed by the demigods from heaven. As for the boys, they were simply enjoying transcendental bliss in the company of the Supreme Personality of Godhead.

At that time, the calves that were pasturing nearby entered into the deep forest, allured by new grasses, and gradually went out of sight. When the boys saw that the calves were not nearby, they became afraid for their safety, and they immediately cried out, "Kṛṣṇa!" Kṛṣṇa is the killer of fear personified. Everyone is afraid of fear personified, but fear personified is afraid of Kṛṣṇa. By crying out the word "Kṛṣṇa," the boys at once transcended the fearful situation. Out of His great affection, Kṛṣṇa did not want His friends to give up their pleasing lunch engagement and go searching for the calves. He therefore said, "My dear friends, you need not interrupt your lunch. Go on enjoying. I am going personally where the calves are." Thus Lord Kṛṣṇa immediately started to search out the calves in the caves and bushes. He searched in the mountain holes and in the forests, but nowhere could He find them.

At the time when Aghāsura was killed and the demigods were looking on the incident with great surprise, Brahmā, who was born out of the lotus flower growing out of the navel of Viṣṇu, also came to see. He was surprised how a little boy like Kṛṣṇa could act so wonderfully. Although he was informed that the little cowherd boy was the Supreme Personality of Godhead, he wanted to see more glorified pastimes of the Lord, and thus he stole all the calves and cowherd boys and took them to a different place. Lord Kṛṣṇa, therefore, in spite of searching for the calves, could not find them, and He even lost His boy friends on the bank of the Yamunā where they had been taking their lunch. In the form of a cowherd boy, Lord Kṛṣṇa was very little in comparison to Brahmā, but because He is the Supreme Personality of Godhead, He could immediately understand that all the calves and boys had been stolen by Brahmā. Kṛṣṇa thought, "Brahmā has taken away all the boys and calves. How can I alone return to Vṛndāvana? The mothers will be aggrieved!"

Therefore in order to satisfy the mothers of His friends as well as to convince Brahmā of the supremacy of the Personality of Godhead, He immediately expanded Himself as the cowherd boys and calves. In the *Vedas* it is said that the Supreme Personality of Godhead expands Himself in so many living entities by His energy. Therefore it was not very difficult for Him to expand Himself again into so many boys and calves. He expanded Himself to become exactly like the boys, who were of all different features, facial and bodily construction, and who were different in their clothing and ornaments and in their behavior and personal activities. In other words, everyone has different tastes; being individual soul, each person has entirely different activities and behavior. Yet Kṛṣṇa exactly expanded Himself into all the different positions of the individual boys. He also became the calves, who were also of different sizes, colors, activities, etc. This was possible because everything is an expansion of Kṛṣṇa's energy. In the *Viṣṇu Purāṇa* it is said, *parasya brahmaṇaḥ śakti.* Whatever we actually see in the cosmic manifestation—be it matter or the activities of the living entities—is simply an expansion of the energies of the Lord, as heat and light are the different expansions of fire.

Thus expanding Himself as the boys and calves in their individual capacities, and surrounded by such expansions of Himself, Kṛṣṇa entered the village of Vṛndāvana. The residents had no knowledge of what had happened. After entering the village, Vṛndāvana, all the calves entered their respective cowsheds, and the boys also went to their respective mothers and homes.

The mothers of the boys heard the vibration of their flutes before their entrance, and to receive them, they came out of their homes and embraced them. And out of maternal affection, milk was flowing from their breasts, and they allowed the boys to drink it. However, their offering was not exactly to their boys but to the Supreme Personality of Godhead who had expanded Himself into such boys. This was another chance for all the mothers of Vṛndāvana to feed the Supreme Personality of Godhead with their own milk. Therefore Lord Kṛṣṇa gave not only Yaśodā the chance of feeding Him, but this time He gave the chance to all the elderly *gopīs*.

All the boys began to deal with their mothers as usual, and the mothers also, on the approach of evening, began to bathe their respective children, decorate them with *tilaka* and ornaments and give them necessary food after the day's labor. The cows also, who were away in the pasturing ground, returned in the evening and began to call their respective calves. The calves immediately came to their mothers, and the mothers began to lick the bodies of the calves. These relations between the cows and the *gopīs* with their calves and boys remained unchanged, although actually the original calves and boys were not there. Actually the cows' affection for their calves and the elderly *gopīs'* affection for the boys causelessly increased. Their affection increased naturally, even though the calves and boys were not their offspring. Although the cows and elderly *gopīs* of Vṛndāvana had greater affection for Kṛṣṇa than for their own offspring, after this incident, their affection for their offspring increased exactly as it did for Kṛṣṇa. For one year continually, Kṛṣṇa Himself expanded as the calves and cowherd boys and was present in the pasturing ground.

As it is stated in the *Bhagavad-gītā*, Kṛṣṇa's expansion is situated in everyone's heart as the Supersoul. Similarly, instead of expanding Himself as the Supersoul, He expanded Himself as a portion of calves and cowherd boys for one continuous year.

One day, when Kṛṣṇa, along with Balarāma, was maintaining the calves in the forest, They saw some cows grazing on the top of Govardhana Hill. The cows could see down into the valley where the calves were being taken care of by the boys. Suddenly, on sighting their calves, the cows began to run towards them. They leaped downhill with joined front and rear legs. The cows were so melted with affection for their calves that they did not care about the rough path from the top of Govardhana Hill down to the pasturing ground. They began to approach the calves with their milk bags full of milk, and they raised their tails upwards. When they were coming down the hill, their milk bags were pouring milk on the ground out of intense maternal affection for the calves, although they were not their own calves. These cows had their own calves, and the calves that were grazing beneath Govardhana Hill were larger; they were not expected to drink milk directly from the milk bag but were satisfied with the grass. Yet all the cows came immediately and began to lick their bodies, and the calves also began to suck milk from the milk bags. There appeared to be a great bondage of affection between the cows and calves.

When the cows were running down from the top of Govardhana Hill, the men who were taking care of them tried to stop them. Elderly cows are taken care of by the men, and the calves are taken care of by the boys; and as far as possible, the calves are kept separate from the cows, so that the calves do not drink all the available milk. Therefore the men who were taking care of the cows on the top of Govardhana Hill tried to stop them, but they failed. Baffled by their failure, they were feeling ashamed and angry. They were very unhappy, but when they came down and saw their children taking care of the calves, they all of a sudden became very affectionate toward the children. It was very astonishing. Although the men came down disappointed, baffled and angry, as soon as they saw their own children, their hearts melted with great affection. At once their anger, dissatisfaction and unhappiness disappeared. They began to show paternal love for the children, and with great affection they lifted them in their arms and embraced them. They began to smell their children's heads and enjoy their company with great happiness. After embracing their children, the men again took the cows back to the top of Govardhana Hill. Along the way they began to think of their children, and affectionate tears fell from their eyes.

When Balarāma saw this extraordinary exchange of affection between the cows and their calves and between the fathers and their children—when neither the calves nor the children needed so much care—He began to wonder why this extraordinary thing happened. He was astonished to see all the residents of Vṛndāvana so affectionate for their own children, exactly as they had been for Kṛṣṇa. Similarly, the cows had grown affectionate for their calves—as much as for Kṛṣṇa. Balarāma therefore concluded that the extraordinary show of affection was something mystical, either performed by the demigods or by some powerful man. Otherwise, how could this wonderful change take place? He concluded that this mystical change must have been caused by Kṛṣṇa, whom Balarāma considered His worshipable Personality of Godhead. He thought, "It was arranged by Kṛṣṇa, and even I could not check its mystic power." Thus Balarāma understood that all those boys and calves were only expansions of Kṛṣṇa.

Balarāma inquired from Kṛṣṇa about the actual situation. He said, "My dear Kṛṣṇa, in the beginning I thought that all these cows, calves and cowherd boys were either great sages and saintly persons or demigods, but at the present it appears that they are actually Your expansions. They are all You; You Yourself are playing as the calves and cows and boys. What is the mystery of this situation? Where have those other calves and cows and boys gone? And why are You expanding Yourself as the cows, calves, and boys? Will You kindly tell Me what is the cause?" At the request of Balarāma, Kṛṣṇa briefly explained the whole situation: how the calves and boys were stolen by Brahmā and how He was concealing the incident by expanding Himself so people would not know that the original cows, calves, and boys were missing.

While Kṛṣṇa and Balarāma were talking, Brahmā returned after a moment's interval (according to the duration of his life). We have information of Lord Brahmā's duration of life from the *Bhagavad-gītā:* 1,000 times the duration of the four ages, or 4,300,000 x 1,000, comprise Brahmā's twelve hours. Similarly, one moment of Brahmā is equal to one year of our solar calculation. After one moment of Brahmā's calculation, Brahmā came back to see the fun caused by his stealing the boys and calves. But he was also afraid that he was playing with fire. Kṛṣṇa was his master, and he had played mischief for fun by taking away His calves and boys. He was really anxious, so he did not stay away very long; he came back after a moment (of his calculation). He saw that all the boys, calves and cows were playing with Kṛṣṇa in the same way as when he had come upon them, although he was confident that he had taken them and made them lie down asleep under the spell of his mystic power. Brahmā began to think, "All the boys, calves and cows were taken away by me, and I know they are still sleeping. How is it that a similar batch of cows, boys and calves are playing with Kṛṣṇa? Is it that they are not influenced by my mystic power? Have they been playing continually for one year with Kṛṣṇa?" Brahmā tried to understand who they were and how they were uninfluenced by his mystic power, but he could not ascertain it. In other words, he himself came under the spell of his own mystic power. The influence of his mystic power appeared like snow in darkness or the glow worm in daytime. During the night's darkness, the glow worm can show some glittering power, and the snow piled up on the top of a hill or on the ground can shine during the daytime. But at night the snow has no silver glitter; nor does the glow worm have any illuminating power during the daytime. Similarly, when the small mystic power exhibited by Brahmā was before the mystic power of Kṛṣṇa, it was just like snow or the glow worm. When a man of small mystic power wants to show potency in the presence of greater mystic power, he diminishes his own influence; he does not increase it. Even a great personality like Brahmā, when he wanted to show his mystic power before Kṛṣṇa, became ludicrous. Brahmā was thus confused about his own mystic power.

In order to convince Brahmā that all those cows, calves and boys were not the original ones, the cows, calves, and boys who were playing with Kṛṣṇa transformed into Viṣṇu forms. Actually, the original ones were sleeping under the spell of Brahmā's mystic power, but the present ones, seen by Brahmā, were all immediate expansions of Kṛṣṇa, or Viṣṇu. Viṣṇu is the expansion of Kṛṣṇa, so the Viṣṇu forms appeared before Brahmā. All the Viṣṇu forms were of bluish color and dressed in yellow garments; all of Them had four hands decorated with club, disc, lotus flower and conchshell. On Their heads were glittering golden jeweled helmets; They were bedecked with pearls and earrings, and garlanded with beautiful flowers. On Their chests was the mark of *śrīvatsa;* Their arms were decorated with armlets and other jewelry. Their necks were smooth just like the conchshell, Their legs were decorated with bells, Their waists decorated with golden bells, and Their fingers decorated with jeweled rings. Brahmā also saw that upon the whole body of Lord Viṣṇu, fresh *tulasī* buds were thrown, beginning from His lotus feet up to the top of the head. Another significant feature of the Viṣṇu forms was that all of Them were looking transcendentally beautiful. Their smiling resembled the moonshine, and Their glancing resembled the early rising of the sun. Just by Their glancing They appeared as the creators and maintainers of the modes of ignorance and passion. Viṣṇu represents the mode of goodness, Brahmā represents the mode of passion, and Lord Śiva represents the mode of ignorance. Therefore as maintainer of everything in the cosmic manifestation, Viṣṇu is also creator and maintainer of Brahmā and Lord Śiva.

After this manifestation of Lord Viṣṇu, Brahmā saw that many other Brahmās and Śivas and demigods and even insignificant living entities down to the ants and very small straws—movable and immovable living entities—were dancing, surrounding Lord Viṣṇu. Their dancing was accompanied by various kinds of music, and all of Them were worshiping Lord Viṣṇu. Brahmā realized that all those Viṣṇu forms were complete, beginning from the *aṇimā* perfection of becoming small like an atom, up to becoming infinite like the cosmic manifestation. All the mystic powers of Brahmā, Śiva, all the demigods and the twenty-four elements of cosmic manifestation were fully represented in the person of Viṣṇu. By the influence of Lord Viṣṇu, all subordinate mystic powers were engaged in

His worship. He was being worshiped by time, space, cosmic manifestation, reformation, desire, activity and the three qualities of material nature. Lord Viṣṇu, Brahmā also realized, is the reservoir of all truth, knowledge and bliss. He is the combination of three transcendental features, namely eternity, knowledge, and bliss, and He is the object of worship by the followers of the *Upaniṣads*. Brahmā realized that all the different forms of cows, boys and calves transformed into Viṣṇu forms were not transformed by a mysticism of the type that a *yogī* or a demigod can display by specific powers invested in him. The cows, calves and boys transformed into Viṣṇu *mūrtis* or Viṣṇu forms were not displays of Viṣṇu *māyā* or Viṣṇu energy, but were Viṣṇu Himself. The respective qualifications of Viṣṇu and Viṣṇu *māyā* are just like fire and heat. In the heat there is the qualification of fire, namely warmth; and yet heat is not fire. The manifestation of the Viṣṇu forms of the boys, cows and calves was not like the heat, but rather the fire—they were all actually Viṣṇu. Factually, the qualification of Viṣṇu is full truth, full knowledge and full bliss. Another example can be given with material objects, which are reflected in many, many forms. For example, the sun is reflected in many water pots, but the reflections of the sun in many pots are not actually the sun. There is no actual heat and light from the sun in the pot, although it appears as the sun. But the forms which Kṛṣṇa assumed were each and every one full Viṣṇu. *Satyam* means truth, *jñānam,* full knowledge, and *ānanda,* full bliss.

Transcendental forms of the Supreme Personality of Godhead in His person are so great that the impersonal followers of the *Upaniṣads* cannot reach the platform of knowledge to understand them. Particularly, the transcendental forms of the Lord are beyond the reach of the impersonalists who can only understand, through the studies of *Upaniṣads,* that the Absolute Truth is not matter and that the Absolute Truth is not materially restricted by limited potency. Lord Brahmā understood Kṛṣṇa and His expansion into Viṣṇu forms and could understand that, due to the expansion of energy of the Supreme Lord, everything movable and immovable within the cosmic manifestation is existing.

When Brahmā was thus standing baffled in his limited power and conscious of his limited activities within the eleven senses, he could at least realize that he was also a creation of the material energy, just like a puppet. As a puppet has no independent power to dance but dances according to the direction of the puppet master, so the demigods and living entities are all subordinate to the Supreme Personality of Godhead. As it is stated in the *Caitanya-caritāmṛta,* the only master is Kṛṣṇa, and all others are servants. The whole world is under the waves of the material spell, and beings are floating like straws in water. So their struggle for existence is continuing. But as soon as one becomes conscious that he is the eternal servant of the Supreme Personality of Godhead, this *māyā* or illusory struggle for existence is immediately stopped.

Lord Brahmā, who has full control over the goddess of learning and who is considered to be the best authority in Vedic knowledge, was thus perplexed, being unable to understand the extraordinary power manifested in the Supreme Personality of Godhead. In the mundane world, even a personality like Brahmā is unable to understand the potential mystic power of the Supreme Lord. Not only did Brahmā fail to understand, but he was perplexed even to see the display which was being manifested by Kṛṣṇa before him.

Kṛṣṇa took compassion upon Brahmā's inability to see even how He was displaying the force of Viṣṇu in transferring Himself into cows and cowherd boys, and thus, while fully manifesting the Viṣṇu expansion, He suddenly pulled His curtain of *yogamāyā* over the scene. In the *Bhagavad-gītā* it is said that the Supreme Personality of Godhead is not visible due to the curtain spread by *yogamāyā*. That which covers the reality is *mahā-māyā*, or the external energy, which does not allow a conditioned soul to understand the Supreme Personality of Godhead beyond the cosmic manifestation. But the energy which partially manifests the Supreme Personality of Godhead and partially does not allow one to see, is called *yogamāyā*. Brahmā is not an ordinary conditioned soul. He is far, far superior to all the demigods, and yet he could not comprehend the display of the Supreme Personality of Godhead; therefore Kṛṣṇa willingly stopped manifesting any further potency. The conditioned soul not only becomes bewildered, but he is completely unable to understand. The curtain of *yogamāyā* was drawn so that Brahmā would not become more and more perplexed.

When Brahmā was relieved from his perplexity, he appeared to be awakened from an almost dead state, and he began to open his eyes with great difficulty. Thus he could see the eternal cosmic manifestation with common eyes. He saw all around him the super-excellent view of Vṛndā-vana—full with trees—which is the source of life for all living entities. He could appreciate the transcendental land of Vṛndāvana where all the living entities are transcendental to ordinary nature. In the forest of Vṛndāvana, even ferocious animals like tigers and others live peacefully along with the deer and human being. He could understand that, because of the presence of the Supreme Personality of Godhead in Vṛndāvana, that place is transcendental to all other places and that there is no lust and greed there. Brahmā thus found Śrī Kṛṣṇa, the Supreme Personality of Godhead, playing the part of a small cowherd boy; he saw that little child with a lump of food in His left hand, searching out His friends, cows and calves, just as He was actually doing one year before, after their disappearance.

Immediately Brahmā descended from his great swan carrier and fell down before the Lord just like a golden stick. The word used among the Vaiṣṇavas for offering respect is *daṇḍavat.* This word means falling down like a stick; one should offer respect to the superior Vaiṣṇava by falling down straight, with his body just like a stick. So Brahmā fell down before the Lord just like a stick to offer respect; and because the complexion of Brahmā is golden, he appeared to be like a golden stick lying down before Lord Kṛṣṇa. All the four helmets on the heads of Brahmā touched the lotus feet of Kṛṣṇa. Brahmā, being very joyful, began to shed tears, and he washed the lotus feet of Kṛṣṇa with his tears. Repeatedly he fell and rose as he recalled the wonderful activities of the Lord. After repeating obeisances for a long time, Brahmā stood up and smeared his hands over his eyes. Seeing the Lord before him, he, trembling, began to offer prayers with great respect, humility and attention.

*Thus ends the Bhaktivedanta purport of the Thirteenth Chapter of* Kṛṣṇa, *"The Stealing of the Boys and Calves by Brahmā."*

# 14 / Prayers Offered by Lord Brahmā to Lord Kṛṣṇa

Brahmā said, "My dear Lord, You are the only worshipful Supreme Lord, Personality of Godhead; therefore I am offering my humble obeisances and prayers just to please You. Your bodily features are of the color of clouds filled with water. You are glittering with a silver electric aura emanating from Your yellow garments.

"Let me offer my respectful repeated obeisances unto the son of Mahārāja Nanda who is standing before me with conchshell, earrings and peacock feather on His head. His face is beautiful; He is wearing a helmet, garlanded by forest flowers, and He stands with a morsel of food in His hand. He is decorated with cane and bugle, and He carries a buffalo horn and flute. He stands before me with small lotus feet.

"My dear Lord, people may say that I am the master of all Vedic knowledge, and I am supposed to be the creator of this universe, but it has been proved now that I cannot understand Your personality, even though You are present before me just like a child. You are playing with Your boy friends, calves and cows, which might imply that You do not even have sufficient education. You are appearing just like a village boy, carrying Your food in Your hand and searching for Your calves. And yet there is so much difference between Your body and mine that I cannot estimate the potency of Your body. As I have already stated in the *Brahma-saṁhitā,* Your body is not material."

In the *Brahma-saṁhitā* it is stated that the body of the Lord is all spiritual; there is no difference between the Lord's body and His self. Each limb of His body can perform the actions of all the others. The Lord can see with His hands, He can hear with His eyes, He can accept offerings with His legs and He can create with His mouth.

Brahmā continued: "Your appearance as a cowherd child is for the benefit of the devotees, and although I have committed offenses at Your lotus feet by stealing away Your cows, boys and calves, I can understand that You have mercy upon me. That is Your transcendental quality; You are very affectionate toward Your devotees. In spite of Your affection for me, I cannot estimate the potency of Your bodily activities. It is to be understood that when I, Lord Brahmā, the supreme personality of this universe, cannot estimate the child-like body of the Supreme Personality of Godhead, then what to speak of others? And if I cannot estimate the spiritual potency of Your child-like body, then what can I understand about Your transcendental pastimes? Therefore, as it is said in the *Bhagavad-gītā,* anyone who can understand a little of the transcendental pastimes, appearance and disappearance of the Lord becomes immediately eligible to enter into the kingdom of God after quitting the material body. This statement is also confirmed in the *Vedas,* and it is stated simply: by understanding the Supreme Personality of Godhead, one can overcome the chain of repeated birth and death. I therefore recommend that people should not try to understand You by their speculative knowledge.

"The best process of understanding You is to submissively give up the speculative process and try to hear about You, either from Yourself as You have given statements in the *Bhagavad-gītā* and many similar Vedic literatures, or from a realized devotee who has taken shelter at Your lotus feet. One has to hear from a devotee without speculation. One does not even need to change his worldly position; he simply has to hear Your message. Although You are not understandable by the material senses simply by hearing about You, one can gradually conquer the nescience of misunderstanding. By Your own grace only, You become revealed to a devotee. You are unconquerable by any other means. Speculative knowledge without any trace of devotional service is simply a useless waste of time in the search for You. Devotional service is so important that even a little attempt can raise one to the highest perfectional platform. One should not, therefore, neglect this auspicious process of devotional service and take to the speculative method. By the speculative method one may gain partial knowledge of Your cosmic manifestation, but it is not possible to understand You, the origin of everything. The attempt of persons who are interested only in speculative knowledge is simply wasted labor, like the labor of a person who attempts to gain something by beating the empty husk of a rice paddy. A little quantity of paddy can be husked by the grinding wheel, and one can gain some grains of rice, but if the skin of the paddy is already beaten by the grinding wheel, there is no further gain in beating the husk. It is simply useless labor.

"My dear Lord, there are many instances in the history of human society where a person, after failing to achieve the transcendental platform, engaged himself in devotional service with his body, mind and words and thus attained the highest perfectional state of entering into Your abode. The processes of understanding You by speculation or mystic meditation are all useless without devotional service. One should therefore engage himself in Your devotional service even in his worldly activities, and one should always keep himself near You by the process of hearing and chanting Your transcendental glories. Simply by being attached to hearing and chanting Your glories, one can attain the highest perfectional stage and enter into Your kingdom. If a person, therefore, always keeps in touch with You by hearing and chanting Your glories and offers the results of his work for Your satisfaction only, he very easily and happily attains entrance into Your supreme abode. You are realizable by persons who have cleansed their hearts of all contamination. This cleansing of the heart is made possible by chanting and hearing the glories of Your Lordship."

The Lord is all-pervading. As it is stated by Lord Kṛṣṇa in the *Bhagavad-gītā*, "Everything is sustained by Me, but at the same time I am not in everything." Since the Lord is all-pervading, there is nothing existing without His knowledge. The all-pervasive nature of the Supreme Personality of Godhead can never be within the limited knowledge of a living entity; therefore, a person who has attained steadiness of the mind by fixing the mind on the lotus feet of the Lord is able to understand the Supreme Lord to some extent. It is the business of the mind to wander over varied subject matter for sense gratification. Therefore only a person who engages the senses always in the service of the Lord can control the mind and be fixed at the lotus feet of the Lord. This concentration of the mind upon the lotus feet of the Lord is called *samādhi.* Until one reaches the stage of *samādhi,* or trance, he cannot understand the nature of the Supreme Personality of Godhead. There may be some philosophers or scientists who can study the cosmic nature from atom to atom; they may be so advanced that they can count the atomic composition of the cosmic atmosphere or all the planets and stars in the sky, or even the shining molecular parts of the sun or other stars and luminaries in the sky. But it is not possible to count the qualities of the Supreme Personality of Godhead.

As described in the beginning of *Vedānta-sūtra,* the Supreme Person is the origin of all qualities. He is generally called *nirguṇa. Nirguṇa* means without qualities. *Guṇa* means quality, and *nir* means without. But impersonalists interpret this word *nirguṇa* as "having no quality." Because they are unable to estimate the qualities of the Lord in transcendental realization, they conclude that the Supreme Lord has no qualities. But that is actually not the position. The real position is that He is the original source of all qualities. All qualities are emanating constantly from Him. How, therefore, can a limited person count the qualities of the Lord? One may estimate the qualities of the Lord for one moment, but the next moment the qualities are increased; so it is not possible to make an estimation of the transcendental qualities of the Lord. He is therefore called *nirguṇa*. His qualities cannot be estimated.

One should not uselessly labor in mental speculation to estimate the Lord's qualities. There is no need of adopting the speculative method or exercising the body to attain mystic *yoga* perfection. One should simply understand that the distress and happiness of this body are predestined; there is no need to try to avoid the distress of this bodily existence or to attempt to achieve happiness by different types of exercises. The best course is to surrender unto the Supreme Personality of Godhead with body, mind and words and always be engaged in His service. This transcendental labor is fruitful, but other attempts to understand the Absolute Truth are never successful. Therefore an intelligent man does not try to understand the Supreme Person, Absolute Truth, by speculative or mystic power. Rather, he engages in devotional service and depends on the Supreme Personality of Godhead. He knows that whatever may happen to the body is due to his past fruitive activities. If one lives such a simple life in devotional service, then automatically he can inherit the transcendental abode of the Lord. Actually, every living entity is part and parcel of the Supreme Lord and a son of the Godhead. Each has the natural right to inherit and share the transcendental pleasures of the Lord, but due to the contact of matter, conditioned living entities have been practically disinherited. If one adopts the simple method of engaging himself in devotional service, automatically he becomes eligible to become freed from the material contamination and elevated to the transcendental position of associating with the Supreme Lord.

Lord Brahmā presented himself to Lord Kṛṣṇa as the most presumptuous living creature because he wanted to examine the wonder of His personal power. He stole the boys and calves of the Lord in order to see how the Lord would recover them. After his maneuver, Lord Brahmā admitted that his attempt was most presumptuous, for he was attempting to test his energy before the person of original energy. Coming to his senses, Lord Brahmā saw that although he was a very powerful living creature in the estimation of all other living creatures within this material world, in comparison to the power and energy of the Supreme Personality of

Godhead, his power was nothing. The scientists of the material world have discovered wonders such as atomic weapons, and when tested in a city or insignificant place on this planet, such powerful weapons create so-called havoc, but if the atomic weapons are tested on the sun, what is their significance? They are insignificant there. Similarly, Brahmā's stealing the calves and boys from Śrī Kṛṣṇa may be a wonderful display of mystic power, but when Śrī Kṛṣṇa exhibited His expansive power in so many calves and boys and maintained them without effort, Brahmā could understand that his own power was insignificant.

Brahmā addressed Lord Kṛṣṇa as *Acyuta* because the Lord is never forgetful of a little service rendered by His devotee. He is so kind and affectionate towards His devotees that a little service by them is accepted by Him as a great deal. Brahmā has certainly rendered much service to the Lord. As the supreme personality in charge of this particular universe, he is, without a doubt, a faithful servant of Kṛṣṇa; therefore he could appease Kṛṣṇa. He asked that the Lord understand him as a subordinate servant whose little mistake and impudence might be excused. He admitted that he was puffed up by his powerful position as Lord Brahmā. Because he is the qualitative incarnation of the mode of passion within this material world, this was natural for him, and therefore he committed the mistake. But after all, Lord Kṛṣṇa would kindly take compassion upon His subordinate and excuse him for his gross mistake.

Lord Brahmā realized his actual position. He is certainly the supreme teacher of this universe, in charge of the production of material nature consisting of complete material elements, false ego, sky, air, fire, water and earth. Such a universe may be gigantic, but it can be measured, just as we measure our body as seven cubits. Generally everyone's personal bodily measurement is calculated to be seven cubits of his hand. This particular universe may appear as a very gigantic body, but it is nothing but the measurement of seven cubits for Lord Brahmā. Aside from this universe, there are unlimited other universes which are outside the jurisdiction of this particular Lord Brahmā. Just as innumerable atomic infinitesimal fragments pass through the holes of a screened window, so millions and trillions of universes in their seedling form are coming out from the bodily pores of Mahā-Viṣṇu, and that Mahā-Viṣṇu is but a part of the plenary expansion of Kṛṣṇa. Under these circumstances, although Lord Brahmā is the supreme creature within this universe, what is his importance in the presence of Lord Kṛṣṇa?

Lord Brahmā therefore compared himself to a little child within the womb of his mother. If the child within the womb plays with his hands and legs, and while playing touches the body of the mother, is the mother offended with the child? Of course she isn't. Similarly, Lord Brahmā may be a very great personality, and yet not only Brahmā but everything that be is existing within the womb of the Supreme Personality of Godhead. The Lord's energy is all-pervading; there is no place in the creation where it is not acting. Everything is existing within the energy of the Lord, so the Brahmā of this universe or the Brahmās of the many other millions and trillions of universes are existing within the energy of the Lord; therefore the Lord is considered to be the mother, and everything existing within the womb of the mother is considered to be the child. And the good mother is never offended with the child, even if he touches the body of the mother by kicking his legs.

Lord Brahmā then admitted that his birth was from the lotus flower which blossomed from the navel of Nārāyaṇa after the dissolution of the three worlds, or three planetary systems, known as *Bhurloka, Bhuvarloka* and *Svarloka.* The universe is divided into three divisions, namely Svarga, Martya and Pātāla. These three planetary systems are merged into water at the time of dissolution. At that time Nārāyaṇa, the plenary portion of Kṛṣṇa, lies down on the water and gradually a lotus stem grows from His navel, and from that lotus flower, Brahmā is born. It is naturally concluded that the mother of Brahmā is Nārāyaṇa. Because the Lord is the resting place of all the living entities after the dissolution of the universe, He is called Nārāyaṇa. The word *nāra* means the aggregate total of all living entities, and *ayana* means the resting place. The form of Garbhodakaśāyī Viṣṇu is called Nārāyaṇa because He rests Himself on that water. In addition, He is the resting place of all living creatures. Besides that, Nārāyaṇa is also present in everyone's heart, as it is confirmed in the *Bhagavad-gītā.* In that sense, also, He is Nārāyaṇa, as *ayana* means the source of knowledge as well as the resting place. It is also confirmed in the *Bhagavad-gītā* that remembrance of the living entity is due to the presence of the Supersoul within the heart. After changing the body, a living creature forgets everything of his past life, but because Nārāyaṇa the Supersoul is present within his heart, he is reminded by Him to act according to his past desire. Lord Brahmā wanted to prove that Kṛṣṇa is the original Nārāyaṇa, that He is the source of Nārāyaṇa, and that Nārāyaṇa is not an exhibition of the external energy, *māyā,* but is an expansion of spiritual energy. The activities of the external energy or *māyā* are exhibited after the creation of this cosmic world, and the original spiritual energy of Nārāyaṇa was acting before the creation. So the expansions of Nārāyaṇa, from Kṛṣṇa to Garbhodakaśāyī Viṣṇu, from

Garbhodakaśāyī Viṣṇu to Kṣīrodakaśāyī Viṣṇu, and from Kṣīrodakaśāyī Viṣṇu to everyone's heart, are manifestations of His spiritual energy. They are not conducted by the material energy; therefore they are not temporary. Anything conducted by the material energy is temporary, but everything executed by the spiritual energy is eternal.

Lord Brahmā reconfirmed his statement establishing Kṛṣṇa as the original Nārāyaṇa. He said that the gigantic universal body is still resting on the water known as Garbhodaka. He spoke as follows: "This gigantic body of the universe is another manifestation of Your energy. On account of His resting on the water, this universal form is also Nārāyaṇa, and we are all within the womb of this Nārāyaṇa form. I see Your different Nārāyaṇa forms everywhere. I can see You on the water, I can feel You within my heart, and I can also see You before me now. You are the original Nārāyaṇa.

"My dear Lord, in this incarnation You have proved that You are the supreme controller of *māyā*. You remain within the cosmic manifestation, and yet the whole creation is within You. This fact has already been proved by You when You exhibited the whole universal creation within Your mouth before Your mother Yaśodā. By Your inconceivable potency of *yogamāyā*, You can make such things effective without external help.

"My dear Lord Kṛṣṇa, the whole cosmic manifestation that we are visualizing at present is all within Your body. Yet I am seeing You outside, and You are also seeing me outside. How can such things happen without being influenced by Your inconceivable energy?"

Lord Brahmā stressed herein that without accepting the inconceivable energy of the Supreme Personality of Godhead, one cannot explain things as they are. He continued: "My dear Lord, leaving aside all other things and just considering today's happenings–what I have seen–are they not all due to Your inconceivable energies? First of all I saw You alone; thereafter You expanded Yourself as Your friends, the calves and all the existence of Vṛndāvana; then I saw You and all the boys as four-handed Viṣṇus, and They were being worshiped by all elements and all demigods, including myself. Again They all became cowherd boys, and You remained alone as You were before. Does this not mean that You are the Supreme Lord Nārāyaṇa, the origin of everything, and from You everything emanates, and again everything enters unto You, and You remain the same as before?"

"Persons who are unaware of Your inconceivable energy cannot understand that You alone expand Yourself as the creator Brahmā, maintainer Viṣṇu, and annihilator Śiva. Persons who are not in awareness of things as they are contemplate that I, Brahmā, am the creator, Viṣṇu is the maintainer, and Lord Śiva is the annihilator. Actually, You are alone everything —creator, maintainer, and annihilator. Similarly, You expand Yourself in different incarnations; among the demigods You incarnate as Vāmanadeva, among the great sages You incarnate as Paraśurāma, among the human beings You appear as Yourself, as Lord Kṛṣṇa, or Lord Rāma, among the animals You appear as the boar incarnation, and among the aquatics You appear as the incarnation of fish. And yet You have no appearance; You are always eternal. Your appearance and disappearance are made possible by Your inconceivable energy just to give protection to the faithful devotees and to annihilate the demons. O my Lord, O all-pervading Supreme Personality of Godhead, O Supersoul, controller of all mystic powers, no one can appreciate Your transcendental pastimes as they are exhibited within these three worlds. No one can estimate how You have expanded Your *yogamāyā* and Your incarnation and how You act by Your transcendental energy. My dear Lord, this whole cosmic manifestation is just like a flashing dream, and its temporary existence simply disturbs the mind. As a result, we are full of anxiety in this existence; to live within this material world means simply to suffer and to be full of all miseries. And yet this temporary existence of the material world appears to be pleasing and dear on account of its having evolved from Your body, which is eternal and full of bliss and knowledge.

"My conclusion is, therefore, that You are the Supreme Soul, Absolute Truth, and the supreme original person; and although You have expanded Yourself in so many Viṣṇu forms, or in living entities and energies, by Your inconceivable transcendental potencies, You are the supreme one without a second, You are the supreme Supersoul. The innumerable living entities are simply like sparks of the original fire. Your Lordship, the conception of the Supersoul as impersonal is wrongly accepted because I see that You are the original person. A person with a poor fund of knowledge may think that, because You are the son of Mahārāja Nanda, You are not the original person, that You are born just like a human being. They are mistaken. You are the actual original person; that is my conclusion. In spite of Your being the son of Nanda, You are the original person, and there is no doubt about it. You are the Absolute Truth, and You are not of this material darkness. You are the source of the original *brahmajyoti* as well as the material luminaries. Your transcendental effulgence is identical with *brahmajyoti.* As it is described in the *Brahma-saṁhitā,* the *brahmajyoti* is nothing but Your personal bodily effulgence. There are many Viṣṇu incarnations and incarnations of Your different qualities, but all those incarnations are not on the same level. You are the original lamp. Other incarnations may possess the same candle power as the original lamp, but the original lamp is the beginning of all light. And because You are not one of the creations of this material world, even after the annihilation of this world, Your existence as You are will continue.

"Because You are the original person, You are therefore described in the *Gopāla-tāpanī* (the Vedic *Upaniṣad*), as well as in the *Brahma-saṁhitā*, as *govindam ādi-puruṣam.* Govinda is the original person, the cause of all causes. In the *Bhagavad-gītā* also it is stated that You are the source of the Brahman effulgence. No one should conclude that Your body is like an ordinary material body. Your body is *akṣara,* indestructible. The material body is always full of threefold miseries, but Your body is *sac-cid-ānanda-vigraha:* full of being, bliss, knowledge and eternality. You are also *nirañjana* because Your pastimes, as the little son of mother Yaśodā or the Lord of the *gopīs,* are never contaminated by the material qualities. And although You exhibited Yourself in so many cowherd boys, calves and cows, Your transcendental potency is not reduced. You are always complete. As it is described in the Vedic literature, even if the complete is taken away from the complete–Supreme Absolute Truth–it yet remains the complete, Supreme Absolute Truth. And although many expansions from the complete are visible, the complete is one without a second. Since all Your pastimes are spiritual, there is no possibility of their being contaminated by the material modes of nature. When You place Yourself subordinate to Your father and mother, Nanda and Yaśodā, You are not reduced in Your potency; this is an expression of Your loving attitude for Your devotees. There is no other competitor of second identity than Yourself. A person with a poor fund of knowledge concludes that Your pastimes and appearance are simply material designations. You are transcendental to both nescience and knowledge, as it is confirmed in the *Gopāla-tāpanī.* You are the original *amṛta* (nectar of immortality), indestructible. As it is confirmed in the *Vedas, amṛtaṁ śāśvataṁ brahme.* Brahman is the eternal, the supreme origin of everything, who has no birth or death.

"In the *Upaniṣads* it is stated that the Supreme Brahman is as effulgent as the sun and is the origin of everything, and anyone who can understand that original person becomes liberated from the material conditional life. Anyone who can simply be attached to You by devotional service can know Your actual position, Your birth, appearance, disappearance and activities. As confirmed in the *Bhagavad-gītā,* simply by understanding Your constitutional position, appearance and disappearance, one can be immediately elevated to the spiritual kingdom after quitting this present body. Therefore to cross over the ocean of material nescience, an intelligent person takes shelter of Your lotus feet and is easily transferred to the spiritual world. There are many so-called meditators who do not know that You are the Supreme Soul. As stated in the *Bhagavad-gītā,* You are the Supreme Soul present in everyone's heart. Therefore there is no necessity of one's meditating on something beyond You. One who is always absorbed in meditation on Your original form of Kṛṣṇa easily crosses over the ocean of material nescience. But persons who do not know that You are the Supreme Soul remain within this material world in spite of their so-called meditation. If, by the association of Your devotees, a person comes to the knowledge that Lord Kṛṣṇa is the original Supersoul, then it is possible for him to cross over the ocean of material ignorance. For instance, a person becomes transcendental to the mistake of thinking a rope is a snake; as soon as one understands that the rope is not a snake, he is liberated from fear. For one who understands You, therefore, through Your personal teachings, as stated in the *Bhagavad-gītā,* or through Your pure devotees, as stated in the *Śrīmad-Bhāgavatam* and all Vedic literatures –that You are the ultimate goal of understanding–he need no more fear this material existence.

"So-called liberation and bondage have no meaning for a person who is already engaged in Your devotional service, just as a person who knows that the rope is not a snake is unafraid. A devotee knows that this material world belongs to You, and he therefore engages everything in Your transcendental loving service. Thus there is no bondage for him. For a person who is already situated in the sun planet, there is no question of the appearance or disappearance of the sun in the name of day or night. It is also said that You, Kṛṣṇa, are just like the sun, and *māyā* is like darkness. When the sun is present, there is no question of darkness; so, for those who are always in Your presence, there is no question of bondage or liberation. They are already liberated. On the other hand, persons who falsely think themselves to be liberated without taking shelter of Your lotus feet, fall down because their intelligence is not pure.

"If one therefore thinks that the Supersoul is something different from Your personality and thus searches out the Supersoul somewhere else, in the forest or in the caves of the Himālayas, his condition is very lamentable.

"Your teachings in the *Bhagavad-gītā* are that one should give up all other processes of self-realization and simply surrender unto You, for that is complete. Because You are supreme in everything, those who are searching after the Brahman effulgence are also searching after You. And those who are searching after Supersoul realization are also searching after You. You have stated in the *Bhagavad-gītā* that You Yourself, by Your partial representation as the Supersoul, have entered into this material cosmic manifestation. You are present in everyone's heart, and there is no need to search out the Supersoul anywhere else. If someone does so, he is simply in ignorance. One who is transcendental to such a position understands that You are unlimited; You are both within and without. Your presence is everywhere. Instead of searching for the Supersoul anywhere else, a devotee only concentrates his mind on You within. Actually one who is liberated from the material concept of life can search for You; others cannot. The simile of thinking the rope to be a snake is applicable only to those who are still in ignorance of You. Actually the existence of a snake besides the rope is only within the mind. The existence of *māyā*, similarly, is only within the mind. *Māyā* is nothing but ignorance of Your personality. When one forgets Your personality, that is the conditional state of *māyā*. Therefore one who is fixed upon You both internally and externally is not illusioned.

"One who has attained a little devotional service can understand Your glories. Even one striving for Brahman realization or Paramātmā realization cannot understand the different features of Your personality unless he treads the devotional path. One may be the spiritual master of many impersonalists, or he may go to the forest or to a cave or mountain and meditate as a hermit for many, many years, but he cannot understand Your glories without being favored by a slight degree of devotional service. Brahman realization or Paramātmā realization are also not possible even after one searches for many, many years unless one is touched by the wonderful effect of devotional service.

"My dear Lord, I pray that I may be so fortunate that, in this life or in another life, wherever I may take my birth, I may be counted as one of Your devotees. Wherever I may be, I pray that I may be engaged in Your devotional service. I do not even care what form of life I get in the future, because I can see that even in the form of cows and calves or cowherd boys, the devotees are so fortunate to be always engaged in Your transcendental loving service and association. Therefore I wish to be one of them instead of such an exalted person as I am now, for I am full of ignorance. The *gopīs* and cows of Vṛndāvana are so fortunate that they have been able to supply their breast milk to You. Persons who are engaged in performing great sacrifices and offering many valuable goats in the sacrifice cannot attain the perfection of understanding You, but simply by devotional service these innocent village women and cows are all able to satisfy You with their milk. You have drunk their milk to satisfaction, yet You are never satisfied by those engaged in performing sacrifices. I am simply surprised, therefore, with the fortunate position of Mahārāja Nanda, mother Yaśodā and the cowherd men and *gopīs,* because You, the Supreme Personality of Godhead, the Absolute Truth, are existing here as their most intimate lovable object. My dear Lord, no one can actually appreciate the good fortune of these residents of Vṛndāvana. We are all demigods, controlling deities of the various senses of the living entities, and we are proud of enjoying such privileges, but actually there is no comparison between our position and the position of these fortunate residents of Vṛndāvana because they are actually relishing Your presence and enjoying Your association by dint of their activities. We may be proud of being controllers of the senses, but here the residents of Vṛndāvana are so transcendental that they are not under our control. Actually they are enjoying the senses through service to You. I shall therefore consider myself fortunate to be given a chance to take birth in this land of Vṛndāvana in any of my future lives.

"My dear Lord, I am therefore not interested in either material opulences or liberation. I am most humbly praying at Your lotus feet for You to please give me any sort of birth within this Vṛndāvana forest so that I may be able to be favored by the dust of the feet of some of the devotees of Vṛndāvana. Even if I am given the chance to grow just as the humble grass in this land, that will be a glorious birth for me. But if I am not so fortunate to take birth within the forest of Vṛndāvana, I beg to be allowed to take birth outside the immediate area of Vṛndāvana so that when the devotees go out they will walk over me. Even that would be a great fortune for me. I am just aspiring for a birth in which I will be smeared by the dust of the devotees' feet.

"I can see that everyone here is simply full of Kṛṣṇa consciousness; they do not know anything but Mukunda. All the *Vedas* are indeed searching after the lotus feet of Kṛṣṇa."

It is confirmed in the *Bhagavad-gītā* that the purpose of Vedic knowledge is to find Kṛṣṇa. And it is said in the *Brahma-saṁhitā* that it is very difficult to find Kṛṣṇa, the Supreme Personality of Godhead, by systematic reading of the Vedic literature. But He is very easily available through the mercy of a pure devotee. The pure devotees of Vṛndāvana are fortunate because they can see Mukunda (Lord Kṛṣṇa) all the time. This word "*mukunda*" can be understood in two ways. *Muk* means liberation. Lord Kṛṣṇa can give liberation and therefore transcendental bliss. The word also refers to His smiling face, which is just like the *kunda* flower. *Mukha* also means face. The *kunda* flower is very beautiful, and it appears to be smiling. Thus the comparison is made.

The difference between the pure devotees of Vṛndāvana and other devotees is that the residents of Vṛndāvana have no other desire but to be associated with Kṛṣṇa. Kṛṣṇa, being very kind to His devotees, fulfills their desire; because they always want Kṛṣṇa's association, the Lord is always prepared to give it to them. The devotees of Vṛndāvana are also spontaneous lovers. They do not follow the regulative principles. They are not required to strictly follow regulative principles because they are already naturally developed in transcendental love for Kṛṣṇa. Regulative principles are required for persons who have not achieved the position of transcendental love. Brahmā is also a devotee of the Lord, but he is subject to follow the regulative principles. He prays to Kṛṣṇa to give him the chance to take birth in Vṛndāvana so that he might be elevated to the platform of spontaneous love.

Lord Brahmā continued: "My Lord, sometimes I am puzzled as to how Your Lordship will be able to repay, in gratitude, the devotional service of these residents of Vṛndāvana. Although I know that You are the supreme source of all benediction, I am puzzled to know how You will be able to repay all the service that You are receiving from these residents of Vṛndāvana. I think of how You are so kind, so magnanimous, that even Pūtanā, who came to cheat You by dressing herself as a very affectionate mother, was awarded liberation and the actual post of a mother. And other demons belonging to the same family, such as Aghāsura and Bakāsura, were also favored with liberation. Under the circumstances, I am puzzled. These residents of Vṛndāvana have given You everything—their bodies, their minds, their love, their homes. Everything is being utilized for Your purpose. So how will You be able to repay their debt? You have already given Yourself to Pūtanā! I surmise that You shall ever remain a debtor to the residents of Vṛndāvana, being unable to repay their loving service. My Lord, I can understand that the superexcellent service of the residents of Vṛndāvana is due to their spontaneously engaging all natural instincts in Your service. It is said that attachment for material objects and home is due to illusion, which makes a living entity conditioned in the material world. But this is only the case for persons who are not in Kṛṣṇa consciousness. In the case of the residents of Vṛndāvana, such obstructions, as attachment to hearth and home, are nonexistent. Because their attachment has been converted unto You, and their home has been converted into a temple because You are always there, and because they have forgotten everything for Your sake, there is no impediment. For a Kṛṣṇa conscious person, there is no such thing as impediments in hearth and home. Nor is there illusion.

"I can also understand that Your appearance as a small cowherd boy, a child of the cowherd men, is not at all a material activity. You are so much obliged by their affection that You are here to enthuse them with more loving service by Your transcendental presence. In Vṛndāvana there is no distinction between material and spiritual because everything is dedicated to Your loving service. My dear Lord, Your Vṛndāvana pastimes are simply to enthuse Your devotees. If someone takes Your Vṛndāvana pastimes to be material, he will be misled.

"My dear Lord Kṛṣṇa, those who deride You, claiming that You have a material body like an ordinary man, are described in the *Bhagavad-gītā* as demonic and less intelligent. You are always transcendental. The non-devotees are cheated because they consider You to be a material creation. Actually, You have assumed this body, which resembles that of an ordinary cowherd boy, simply to increase the devotion and transcendental bliss of Your devotees.

"My dear Lord, I have nothing to say about people who advertise that they have already realized God or that by their realization they have themselves become God. But as far as I am concerned, I admit frankly that for me it is not possible to realize You by my body, mind or speech. What can I say about You, or how can I realize You by my senses? I cannot even think of You perfectly with my mind, which is the master of the senses. Your qualities, Your activities and Your body cannot be conceived by any person within this material world. Only by Your mercy can one understand, to some extent, what You are. My dear Lord, You are the Supreme Lord of all creation, although I sometimes falsely think that I am the master of this universe. I may be master of this universe, but there are innumerable universes, and there are innumerable Brahmās also who preside over these universes. But actually You are the master of them all. As the Supersoul in everyone's heart, You know everything. Please, therefore accept me as Your surrendered servant. I hope that You will excuse me for disturbing You in Your pastimes with Your friends and calves. Now if You will kindly allow me, I will immediately leave so You can enjoy Your friends and calves without my presence.

"My dear Lord Kṛṣṇa, Your very name suggests that You are all-attractive. The attraction of the sun and the moon are all due to You. By the attraction of the sun, You are beautifying the very existence of the Yadu dynasty. With the attraction of the moon, You are enhancing the potency of the land, the demigods, the *brāhmaṇas,* the cows and the oceans. Because of Your supreme attraction, demons like Kaṁsa and others are annihilated. Therefore it is my deliberate conclusion that You are the only worshipable Deity within the creation. Accept my humble obeisances until the annihilation of this material world. As long as there is sunshine within this material world, kindly accept my humble obeisances."

In this way, Brahmā, the master of this universe, after offering humble and respectful obeisances unto the Supreme Personality of Godhead and circumambulating Him three times, was ready to return to his abode known as Brahmaloka. By His gesture, the Supreme Personality of Godhead gave him permission to return. As soon as Brahmā left, Lord Śrī Kṛṣṇa immediately appeared as He had on the very day the cows and cowherd boys had vanished.

Kṛṣṇa had left His friends on the bank of the Yamunā while they were engaged in lunch, and although He returned exactly one year later, the cowherd boys thought that He had returned within a second. That is the way of Kṛṣṇa's different energies and activities. It is stated in the *Bhagavad-gītā* that Kṛṣṇa Himself is residing in everyone's heart, and He causes both remembrance and forgetfulness. All living entities are controlled by the supreme energy of the Lord, and sometimes they remember and sometimes they forget their constitutional position. His friends, being controlled in such a way, could not understand that for one whole year they were absent from the Yamunā bank and were under the spell of Brahmā's illusion. When Kṛṣṇa appeared before the boys, they thought, "Kṛṣṇa has returned within a minute." They began to laugh, thinking that Kṛṣṇa was not willing to leave their lunchtime company. They were very jubilant and invited Him, "Dear friend Kṛṣṇa, You have come back so quickly! All right, we have not as yet begun our lunch, not even taken one morsel of food. So please come and join us and let us eat together." Kṛṣṇa smiled and accepted their invitation, and He began to enjoy the lunchtime company of His friends. While eating, Kṛṣṇa was thinking, "These boys believe that I have come back within a second, but they do not know that for the last year I have been involved with the mystic activities of Lord Brahmā."

After finishing their lunch, Kṛṣṇa and His friends and calves began to return to their Vrajabhūmi homes. While passing, they enjoyed seeing the dead carcass of Aghāsura in the shape of a gigantic serpent. When Kṛṣṇa returned home to Vrajabhūmi, He was seen by all the inhabitants of Vṛndāvana. He was wearing a peacock feather in His helmet, which was also decorated with forest flowers. Kṛṣṇa was also garlanded with flowers and painted with different colored minerals collected from the caves of Govardhana Hill. Govardhana Hill is always famous for supplying natural red dyes, and Kṛṣṇa and His friends painted their bodies with them. Each of them had a bugle made of buffalo horn and a stick and a flute, and each called his respective calves by their particular names. They were so proud of Kṛṣṇa's wonderful activities that, while entering the village, they all sang His glories. All the *gopīs* in Vṛndāvana saw beautiful Kṛṣṇa entering the village. The boys composed nice songs describing how they were saved from being swallowed by the great serpent and how the serpent was killed. Some described Kṛṣṇa as the son of Yaśodā, and others as the son of Nanda Mahārāja. "He is so wonderful that He saved us from the clutches of the great serpent and killed him," they said. But little did they know that one year had passed since the killing of Aghāsura.

In this regard, Mahārāja Parīkṣit asked Śukadeva Gosvāmī how the inhabitants of Vṛndāvana suddenly developed so much love for Kṛṣṇa, although Kṛṣṇa was not a member of any of their families. Mahārāja Parīkṣit enquired, "During the absence of the original cowherd boys, when Kṛṣṇa expanded Himself, why is it that the boys' parents became more loving toward Him than toward their own sons? Also, why did the cows become so loving toward the calves, more than toward their own calves?"

Śukadeva Gosvāmī told Mahārāja Parīkṣit that every living entity is actually most attached to his own self. Outward paraphernalia such as home, family, friends, country, society, wealth, opulence, reputation, etc., are all only secondary in pleasing the living entity. They please only because they bring pleasure to the self. For this reason, one is self-centered and is attached to his body and self more than he is to relatives like wife, children, and friends. If there is some immediate danger to one's own person, he first of all takes care of himself, then others. That is natural. That means, more than anything else, he loves his own self. The next important object of affection, after his own self, is his material body. A person who has no information of the spirit soul is very much attached to his material body, so much so that even in old age he wants to preserve the body in so many artificial ways, thinking that his old and broken body can be saved. Everyone is working hard day and night just to give pleasure to his own self, under either the bodily or spiritual concept of life. We are attached to material possessions because they give pleasure to the senses or to the body. The attachment to the body is there only because the "I," the spirit soul, is within the body. Similarly, when one is further advanced, he knows that the spirit soul is pleasing because it is part and parcel of Kṛṣṇa. Ultimately, it is Kṛṣṇa who is pleasing and all-attractive. He is the Supersoul of everything. And in order to give us this information, Kṛṣṇa descends and tells us that the all-attractive center is He Himself. Without being an expansion of Kṛṣṇa, nothing can be attractive.

Whatever is attractive within the cosmic manifestation is due to Kṛṣṇa. Kṛṣṇa is therefore the reservoir of all pleasure. The active principle of everything is Kṛṣṇa, and highly elevated transcendentalists see everything in connection with Him. In the *Caitanya-caritāmṛta* it is stated that a *mahābhāgavata,* or highly advanced devotee, sees Kṛṣṇa as the active principle in all movable and immovable living entities. Therefore he sees everything within this cosmic manifestation in relation to Kṛṣṇa. For the fortunate person who has taken shelter of Kṛṣṇa as everything, liberation is already there. He is no longer in the material world. This is also confirmed in the *Bhagavad-gītā.* Whoever is engaged in the devotional service of Kṛṣṇa is already on the *brahma-bhūta* or spiritual platform. The very name Kṛṣṇa suggests piety and liberation. Anyone who takes shelter of the lotus feet of Kṛṣṇa enters the boat for crossing over the ocean of nescience. For him, this vast expansion of the material manifestation becomes as insignificant as a hoofprint. Kṛṣṇa is the center of all great souls, and He is the shelter of the material worlds.

For one who is on the platform of Kṛṣṇa consciousness, Vaikuṇṭha, or the spiritual world, is not far away. He does not live within the material world where there is danger at every step. In this way, Kṛṣṇa consciousness was fully explained by Śukadeva Gosvāmī to Mahārāja Parīkṣit. Śukadeva Gosvāmī even recited to the king the statements and prayers of Lord Brahmā. These descriptions of Lord Kṛṣṇa's pastimes with His cowherd boys, His eating with them on the bank of the Yamunā and Lord Brahmā's prayers unto Him, are all transcendental subject matters. Anyone who hears, recites or chants them surely gets all his spiritual desires fulfilled. Thus Kṛṣṇa's childhood appearance, His sporting with Balarāma in Vṛndāvana, was described.

*Thus ends the Bhaktivedanta purport of the Fourteenth Chapter of* Kṛṣṇa, *"Prayers Offered by Lord Brahmā to Lord Kṛṣṇa."*

# 15 / Killing of Dhenukāsura

In this way, Śrī Kṛṣṇa, along with His elder brother Balarāma, passed the childhood age known as *kaumāra* and stepped into the age of *paugaṇḍa,* from the sixth year up to the tenth. At that time, all the cowherd men conferred and agreed to give those boys who had passed their fifth year charge of the cows in the pasturing ground. Given charge of the cows, Kṛṣṇa and Balarāma traversed Vṛndāvana, purifying the land with Their footprints.

Accompanied by the cowherd boys and Balarāma, Kṛṣṇa brought forward the cows and played on His flute through the forest of Vṛndāvana, which was full of flowers, vegetables, and pasturing grass. The Vṛndāvana forest was as sanctified as the clear mind of a devotee and was full of bees, flowers and fruits. There were chirping birds and clear water lakes with waters that could relieve one of all fatigues. Sweet flavored breezes blew always, refreshing the mind and body. Kṛṣṇa, with His friends and Balarāma, entered the forest and, seeing the favorable situation, enjoyed the atmosphere to the fullest extent. Kṛṣṇa saw all the trees, overloaded with fruits and fresh twigs, coming down to touch the ground as if welcoming Him by touching His lotus feet. He was very pleased by the behavior of the trees, fruits and flowers, and He began to smile realizing their desires.

Kṛṣṇa then spoke to His elder brother Balarāma as follows: "My dear brother, You are superior to all of us, and Your lotus feet are worshiped by the demigods. Just see how these trees, full with fruits, have bent down to worship Your lotus feet. It appears that they are trying to get out of the darkness of being obliged to accept the form of trees. Actually, the trees born in the land of Vṛndāvana are not ordinary living entities. Having held the impersonal point of view in their past lives, they are now put into this stationary condition of life, but now they have the opportunity of seeing You in Vṛndāvana, and they are praying for further advancement in spiritual life through Your personal association. Generally the trees are living entities in the modes of darkness. The impersonalist philosophers are in that darkness, but they eradicate it by taking full advantage of Your presence. I think the drones that are buzzing all around You must have been Your devotees in their past lives. They cannot leave Your company because no one can be a better, more affectionate master than You. You are the supreme and original Personality of Godhead, and the drones are just trying to spread Your glories by chanting every moment. I think some of them must be great sages, devotees of Your Lordship, and they are disguising themselves in the form of drones because they are unable to give up Your company even for a moment. My dear brother, You are the supreme worshipable Godhead. Just see how the peacocks in great ecstasy are dancing before You. The deer, whose behavior is just like the *gopīs,* are welcoming You with the same affection. And the cuckoos who are residing in this forest are receiving You with great joy because they consider that Your appearance is so auspicious in their home. Even though they are trees and animals, these residents of Vṛndāvana are glorifying You. They are prepared to welcome You to their best capacity, as is the practice of great souls in receiving another great soul at home. As for the land, it is so pious and fortunate that the footprints of Your lotus feet are marking its body.

"It is quite natural for these Vṛndāvana inhabitants to thus receive a great personality like You. The herbs, creepers and plants are also so fortunate to touch Your lotus feet. And by Your touching the twigs with Your hands, these small plants are also made glorious. As for the hills and the rivers, they too are now glorious because You are glancing at them. Above all, the damsels of Vraja, the *gopīs,* attracted by Your beauty, are the most glorious, because You embrace them with Your strong arms."

In this way, both Lord Kṛṣṇa and Balarāma began to enjoy the residents of Vṛndāvana to their full satisfaction, along with the calves and cows on the bank of the Yamunā. In some places both Kṛṣṇa and Balarāma were accompanied by Their friends. The boys were singing, imitating the humming sound of the drones and accompanying Kṛṣṇa and Balarāma, who were garlanded with forest flowers. While walking, the boys sometimes imitated the quacking sound of the swans in the lakes, or when they saw the peacocks dancing, they imitated them before Kṛṣṇa. Kṛṣṇa also moved His neck, imitating the dancing and making His friends laugh.

The cows taken care of by Kṛṣṇa had different names, and Kṛṣṇa would call them with love. After hearing Kṛṣṇa calling, the cows would immediately respond by mooing, and the boys would enjoy this exchange to their hearts' content. They would all imitate the sound vibrations made by the different kinds of birds, especially the *cakoras,* peacocks, cuckoo and *bhāradvājas.* Sometimes, when they would see the weaker animals fleeing out of fear of the sounds of tigers and lions, the boys, along with Kṛṣṇa and Balarāma, would imitate the animals and run away with them. When they felt some fatigue, they would sit down, and Balarāma would put His head on the lap of one of the boys just to take rest, and Kṛṣṇa would immediately come and begin massaging the legs of Balarāma. And sometimes He would take a palm fan and fan the body of Balarāma, causing a pleasing breeze to relieve Him of His fatigue. Other boys would sometimes dance or sing while Balarāma took rest, and sometimes they would wrestle amongst themselves or jump. When the boys were thus engaged, Kṛṣṇa would immediately join them, and catching their hands, He would enjoy their company and laugh and praise their activities. When Kṛṣṇa would feel tired and fatigued, He would sometimes take shelter of the root of a big tree, or the lap of a cowherd boy, and lie down. When He would lie down with a boy or a root as His pillow, some of the boys would come and massage His legs, and some would fan His body with a fan made from leaves. Some of the more talented boys would sing in very sweet voices to please Him. Thus very soon His fatigue would go away. The Supreme Personality of Godhead, Kṛṣṇa, whose legs are tended by the goddess of fortune, shared Himself with the cowherd boys as one of them, expanding His internal potency to appear exactly like a village boy. But despite His appearing just like a village boy, there were occasions when He proved Himself to be the Supreme Personality of Godhead. Sometimes men pose themselves as the Supreme Personality of Godhead and cheat innocent people, but they can only cheat; they cannot exhibit the potency of God.

While Kṛṣṇa was thus engaged in exhibiting His internal potency along with the supermost fortunate friends, there occurred another chance for Him to exhibit the superhuman powers of Godhead. His most intimate friends Śrīdāmā, Subala and Stokakṛṣṇa began to address Kṛṣṇa and Balarāma with great love and affection thus: "Dear Balarāma, You are very powerful; Your arms are very strong. Dear Kṛṣṇa, You are very expert in killing all kinds of disturbing demons. Will You kindly note that just near this place there is a big forest of the name Tālavana. This forest is full of palm trees, and all the trees are filled with fruits. Some are falling down, and some of them are very ripe even in the trees. It is a very nice place, but because of a great demon, Dhenukāsura, it is very difficult to go there. No one can reach the trees to collect the fruits. Dear Kṛṣṇa and Balarāma, this demon is present there in the form of an ass, and he is surrounded by similar demon friends who assume the same shape. All of them are very strong, so it is very difficult to approach this place. Dear brothers, You are the only persons who can kill such demons. Other than You, no one can go there for fear of being killed. Not even animals go there, and no birds are sleeping there; they have all left. One can only appreciate the sweet aroma that is coming from that place. It appears that up until now, no one has tasted the sweet fruits there, either on the tree or on the ground. Dear Kṛṣṇa, to tell You frankly, we are very attracted by this sweet aroma. Dear Balarāma, let us all go there and enjoy these fruits. The aroma of the fruits is now spread everywhere. Don't You smell it from here?"

When Balarāma and Kṛṣṇa were thus petitioned by Their smiling, intimate friends, They were inclined to please them, and They began to proceed towards the forest, surrounded by all Their friends. Immediately upon entering the Tālavana, Balarāma began to yank the trees with His arms, exhibiting the strength of an elephant. Because of this jerking, all the ripe fruits fell down on the ground. Upon hearing the sound of the falling fruits, the demon Dhenukāsura, who was living there in the form of an ass, began to approach with great force, shaking the whole field so that all the trees began to move as if there were an earthquake. The demon appeared first before Balarāma and began to kick His chest with his hind legs. At first, Balarāma did not say anything, but the demon with great anger began to kick Him again more vehemently. This time Balarāma immediately caught hold of the legs of the ass with one hand and, wheeling him around, threw him into the treetops. While he was being wheeled around by Balarāma, the demon lost his life. Balarāma threw the demon into the biggest palm tree about, and the demon's body was so heavy that the palm tree fell upon other trees, and several fell down. It appeared as if a great hurricane had passed through the forest, and all the trees were falling down, one after another. This exhibition of extraordinary strength is not astonishing because Balarāma is the Personality of Godhead known as Ananta Śeṣanāga, who is holding all the planets on the hoods of His millions of heads. The whole cosmic manifestation is maintained by Him exactly as two threads hold the weaving of a cloth.

After the demon was thrown into the trees, all the friends and associates of Dhenukāsura immediately assembled and attacked Balarāma and Kṛṣṇa with great force. They were determined to retaliate and avenge the death of their friend. But Kṛṣṇa and Balarāma began to catch each of the asses by the hind legs and, exactly in the same way, wheel them around. Thus They killed all of them by throwing them into the palm trees. Because of the dead bodies of the asses, there was a panoramic scene. It appeared as if clouds of various colors were assembled in the trees. Hearing of this great incident, the demigods from the higher planets began to shower flowers on Kṛṣṇa and Balarāma and began to beat their drums and offer devotional prayers.

A few days after the killing of Dhenukāsura, people began to come into the Tālavana forest to collect the fruits, and animals began to return without fear to feed on the nice grasses grown there. Just by chanting or hearing these transcendental activities and pastimes of the brothers Kṛṣṇa and Balarāma, one can amass pious activities.

When Kṛṣṇa, Balarāma and Their friends entered the village of Vṛndāvana, They played Their flutes, and the boys praised Their uncommon activities in the forest. Their faces were decorated with *tilaka* and smeared with the dust raised by the cows, and Kṛṣṇa's head was decorated with a peacock feather. Both He and Balarāma played Their flutes, and the young *gopīs* were joyous to see Kṛṣṇa returning home. All the *gopīs* in Vṛndāvana remained very morose on account of Kṛṣṇa's absence. All day they were thinking of Kṛṣṇa in the forest or of Him herding cows in the pasture. When they saw Kṛṣṇa returning, all their anxieties were immediately relieved, and they began to look at His face the way drones hover over the honey of the lotus flower. When Kṛṣṇa entered the village, the young *gopīs* smiled and laughed. Kṛṣṇa, while playing the flute, enjoyed the beautiful smiling faces of the *gopīs*.

Then Kṛṣṇa and Balarāma were immediately received by Their affectionate mothers, Yaśodā and Rohiṇī, and, according to the time's demands, they began to fulfill the desires of their affectionate sons. Simultaneously, the mothers rendered service and bestowed benediction upon their transcendental sons. They very nicely took care of their children by bathing and dressing Them. Kṛṣṇa was dressed in bluish garments, and Balarāma was dressed in yellowish garments, and They were given all sorts of ornaments and flower garlands. Being relieved of the fatigue of Their day's work in the pasturing ground, They looked refreshed and very beautiful.

They were given palatable dishes by Their mothers, and They pleasantly ate everything. After eating, They were seated nicely on clean bedding, and the mothers began to sing various songs of Their activities. As soon as They sat down on the bedding, They very quickly fell fast asleep. In this way, Kṛṣṇa and Balarāma used to enjoy Vṛndāvana life as cowherd boys.

Sometimes Kṛṣṇa used to go with His boy friends and with Balarāma, and sometimes He used to go alone with His friends to the bank of the Yamunā and tend the cows. Gradually, the summer season arrived, and one day, while in the field, the boys and cows became very thirsty and began to drink the water of the Yamunā. The river, however, was made poisonous by the venom of the great serpent known as Kāliya.

Because the water was so poisonous, the boys and cows became visibly affected immediately after drinking. They suddenly fell down on the ground, apparently dead. Then Kṛṣṇa, who is the life of all lives, simply cast His merciful glance over them, and all the boys and cows regained consciousness and began to look at one another with great astonishment. They could understand that by drinking the water of Yamunā they had died and that the merciful glance of Kṛṣṇa restored their life. Thus they appreciated the mystic power of Kṛṣṇa, who is known as Yogeśvara, the master of all mystic *yogīs*.

*Thus ends the Bhaktivedanta purport of the Fifteenth Chapter of* Kṛṣṇa, *"Killing of Dhenukāsura."*

# 16 / Subduing Kāliya

When He understood that the water of the Yamunā was being polluted by the black serpent Kāliya, Lord Kṛṣṇa took action against him and made him leave the Yamunā and go elsewhere, and thus the water became purified.

When this story was being narrated by Śukadeva Gosvāmī, Mahārāja Parīkṣit became eager to hear more about Kṛṣṇa's childhood pastimes. He inquired from Śukadeva Gosvāmī how Kṛṣṇa chastised Kāliya, who was living in the water for many years. Actually, Mahārāja Parīkṣit was becoming more and more enthusiastic to hear the transcendental pastimes of Kṛṣṇa, and his inquiry was made with great interest.

Śukadeva Gosvāmī narrated the story as follows. Within the River Yamunā there was a great lake, and in that lake the black serpent Kāliya used to live. Because of his poison, the whole area was so contaminated that it emanated a poisonous vapor twenty-four hours a day. If a bird happened to even pass over the spot, he would immediately fall down in the water and die.

Due to the poisonous effect of the Yamunā's vapors, the trees and grass near the bank of the Yamunā had all dried up. Lord Kṛṣṇa saw the effect of the great serpent's poison: the whole river that ran before Vṛndāvana was now deadly.

Kṛṣṇa, who advented Himself just to kill all undesirable elements in the world, immediately climbed up in a big *kadamba* tree on the bank of the Yamunā. The *kadamba* is a round yellow flower, generally seen only in the Vṛndāvana area. After climbing to the top of the tree, He tightened His belt cloth, and, flapping His arms just like a wrestler, jumped in the midst of the poisonous lake. The *kadamba* tree from which Kṛṣṇa had jumped was the only tree there which was not dead. Some commentators say that due to touching the lotus feet of Kṛṣṇa, the tree became immediately alive. In some other *Purāṇas* it is stated that Garuḍa, the eternal carrier of Viṣṇu, knew that Kṛṣṇa would take this action in the future, so he put some nectar on this tree to preserve it. When Lord Kṛṣṇa jumped into the water, the river overflooded its banks, as if something very large had fallen into it. This exhibition of Kṛṣṇa's strength is not at all uncommon because He is the reservoir of all strength.

When Kṛṣṇa was swimming about, just like a great strong elephant, He made a tumultuous sound which the great black serpent Kāliya could hear. The tumult was intolerable for him, and he could understand that this was an attempt to attack his home. Therefore he immediately came before Kṛṣṇa. Kāliya saw that Kṛṣṇa was indeed worth seeing because His body was so beautiful and delicate; its color resembled that of a cloud, and His legs resembled a lotus flower. He was decorated with Śrīvatsa, jewels and yellow garments. He was smiling with a beautiful face and was playing in the River Yamunā with great strength. But in spite of Kṛṣṇa's beautiful features, Kāliya felt great anger within his heart, and thus he grabbed Kṛṣṇa with his mighty coils. Seeing the incredible way in which Kṛṣṇa was enveloped in the coils of the serpent, the affectionate cowherd boys and inhabitants of Vṛndāvana immediately became stunned out of fear. They had dedicated everything to Kṛṣṇa, their lives, property, affection, activities —everything was for Kṛṣṇa—and when they saw Him in that condition, they became overwhelmed with fear and fell down on the ground. All the cows, bulls and small calves became overwhelmed with grief, and they began to look at Him with great anxiety. Out of fear they could only cry in agony and stand erect on the bank, unable to help their beloved Kṛṣṇa.

While this scene was taking place on the bank of the Yamunā, there were ill omens manifest. The earth trembled, meteors fell from the sky, and the bodies of men shivered. All these are indications of great immediate danger. Observing the inauspicious signs, the cowherd men, including Mahārāja Nanda, became very anxious out of fear. At the same time they were informed that Kṛṣṇa had gone to the pasturing ground without His elder brother, Balarāma. As soon as Nanda and Yaśodā and the cowherd men heard this news, they became even more anxious. Out of their great affection for Kṛṣṇa, unaware of the extent of Kṛṣṇa's potencies, they became overwhelmed with grief and anxiety because they had nothing dearer than Kṛṣṇa and because they dedicated their everything—life, property, affection, mind and activities—to Kṛṣṇa. Because of their great attachment for Kṛṣṇa, they thought, "Today Kṛṣṇa is surely going to be vanquished!"

All the inhabitants of Vṛndāvana came out of the village to see Kṛṣṇa.

The assembly consisted of children, young and old men, women, animals and all living entities; they knew that Kṛṣṇa was their only means of sustenance. While this was happening, Balarāma, who is the master of all knowledge, stood there simply smiling. He knew how powerful His younger brother Kṛṣṇa was and that there was no cause for anxiety when Kṛṣṇa was fighting with an ordinary serpent of the material world. He did not, therefore, personally take any part in their concern. On the other hand, all the inhabitants of Vṛndāvana, being disturbed, began to search out Kṛṣṇa by following the impression of His footprints on the ground, and thus they moved towards the bank of the Yamunā. Finally, by following the footprints marked with flag, bow and conchshell, the inhabitants of Vṛndāvana arrived at the river bank and saw that all the cows and boys were weeping to behold Kṛṣṇa enwrapped in the coils of the black serpent. Then they became still more overwhelmed with grief. While Balarāma was smiling to see their lamentation, all the inhabitants of Vrajabhūmi merged into the ocean of grief because they thought that Kṛṣṇa was finished. Although the residents of Vṛndāvana did not know much about Kṛṣṇa, their love for Him was beyond comparison. As soon as they saw that Kṛṣṇa was in the River Yamunā enveloped by the serpent Kāliya and that all the boys and cows were lamenting, they simply began to think of Kṛṣṇa's friendship, His smiling face, His sweet words and His dealings with them. Thinking of all these and believing that their Kṛṣṇa was now within the clutches of Kāliya, they at once felt that the three worlds had become vacant. Lord Caitanya also said that He was seeing the three worlds as vacant for want of Kṛṣṇa. This is the highest stage of Kṛṣṇa consciousness. Almost all of the inhabitants of Vṛndāvana had the highest ecstasy, love for Kṛṣṇa.

When mother Yaśodā arrived, she wanted to enter the River Yamunā, and being checked, she fainted. Other friends who were equally aggrieved were shedding tears like torrents of rain or waves of the river, but in order to bring mother Yaśodā to consciousness, they began to speak loudly about the transcendental pastimes of Kṛṣṇa. Mother Yaśodā remained still, as if dead, because her consciousness was concentrated on the face of Kṛṣṇa. Nanda and all others who dedicated everything, including their lives, to Kṛṣṇa were ready to enter the waters of the Yamunā, but Lord Balarāma checked them because He was in perfect knowledge that there was no danger.

For two hours Kṛṣṇa remained like an ordinary child gripped in the coils of Kāliya, but when He saw that all the inhabitants of Gokula—including His mother and father, the *gopīs*, the boys and the cows—were just on the point of death and that they had no shelter for salvation from imminent death, Kṛṣṇa immediately freed Himself. He began to expand His body, and when the serpent tried to hold Him, he felt a great strain. On account of the strain, his coils slackened, and he had no other alternative but to let loose the Personality of Godhead, Kṛṣṇa, from his grasp. Kāliya then became very angry, and his great hoods expanded. He exhaled poisonous fumes from his nostrils, his eyes blazed like fire, and flames issued from his mouth. The great serpent remained still for some time, looking at Kṛṣṇa. Licking his lips with bifurcated tongues, the serpent looked at Kṛṣṇa with double hoods, and his eyesight was full of poison. Kṛṣṇa immediately pounced upon him, just as Garuḍa swoops upon a snake. Thus attacked, Kāliya looked for an opportunity to bite Him, but Kṛṣṇa moved around him. As Kṛṣṇa and Kāliya moved in a circle, the serpent gradually became fatigued, and his strength seemed to diminish considerably. Kṛṣṇa immediately pressed down the serpent's hoods and jumped up on them. The Lord's lotus feet became tinged with red from the rays of the jewels on the snake's hoods. Then He who is the original artist of all fine arts, such as dancing, began to dance upon the hoods of the serpent, although they were moving to and fro. Upon seeing this, denizens from the upper planets began to shower flowers, beat drums, play different types of flutes and sing various prayers and songs. In this way, all the denizens of heaven, such as the Gandharvas, Siddhas and demigods, became very pleased.

While Kṛṣṇa was dancing on his hoods, Kāliya tried to push Him down with some of his other hoods. Kāliya had about a hundred hoods, but Kṛṣṇa took control of them. He began to dash Kāliya with His lotus feet, and this was more than the serpent could bear. Gradually, Kāliya was reduced to struggling for his very life. He vomited all kinds of refuse and exhaled fire. While throwing up poisonous material from within, Kāliya became reduced in his sinful situation. Out of great anger, he began to struggle for existence and tried to raise one of his hoods to kill the Lord. The Lord immediately captured that hood and subdued it by kicking it and dancing on it. It actually appeared as if the Supreme Personality of Godhead Viṣṇu was being worshiped; the poisons emanating from the mouth of the serpent appeared to be like flower offerings. Kāliya then began to vomit blood instead of poison; he was completely fatigued. His whole body appeared to be broken by the kicks of the Lord. Within his mind, however, he finally began to understand that Kṛṣṇa was the Supreme Personality of Godhead, and he began to surrender unto Him. He realized that Kṛṣṇa was the Supreme Lord, the master of everything.

The wives of the serpent, known as the Nāgapatnīs, saw that their husband was being subdued by the kicking of the Lord, within whose womb the whole universe remains. Kāliya's wives prepared to worship the Lord, although, in their haste, their dress, hair and ornaments became disarrayed. They also surrendered unto the Supreme Lord and began to pray. They appeared before Him, put forward their offspring and anxiously offered respectful obeisances, falling down on the bank of the Yamunā. The Nāgapatnīs knew that Kṛṣṇa is the shelter of all surrendered souls, and they desired to release their husband from the impending danger by pleasing the Lord with their prayers.

The Nāgapatnīs began to offer their prayers as follows: "O dear Lord, You are equal to everyone. For You there is no distinction between Your sons, friends or enemies. Therefore the punishment which You have so kindly offered to Kāliya is exactly befitting. O Lord, You have descended especially for the purpose of annihilating all kinds of disturbing elements within the world, and because You are the Absolute Truth, there is no difference between Your mercy and punishment. We think, therefore, that this apparent punishment to Kāliya is actually some benediction. We consider that Your punishment is Your great mercy upon us because when You punish someone it is to be understood that the reactions of his sinful activities are eradicated. It is already clear that this creature appearing in the body of a serpent must have been overburdened with all kinds of sin; otherwise, how could he have the body of a serpent? Your dancing on his hoods reduces all the sinful results of actions caused by his having this body of a serpent. It is, therefore, very auspicious that You have become angry and have punished him in this way. We are very astonished to see how You have become so pleased with this serpent who evidently performed various religious activities in his past lives. Everyone must have been pleased by his undergoing all kinds of penances and austerities, and he must have executed universal welfare activities for all living creatures."

The Nāgapatnīs confirm that one cannot come in contact with Kṛṣṇa without having executed pious activities in devotional service in his previous lives. As Lord Caitanya advised in His *Śikṣāṣṭaka,* one has to execute devotional service by humbly chanting the Hare Kṛṣṇa *mantra,* thinking oneself lower than the straw in the street and not expecting honor for himself but offering all kinds of honor to others. The Nāgapatnīs were astonished that, although Kāliya had the body of a serpent as the result of grievous sinful activities, at the same time he was in contact with the Lord to the extent that the Lord's lotus feet were touching his hoods. Certainly this was not the ordinary result of pious activities. These two contradictory facts astonished them. Thus they continued to pray: "O dear Lord, we are simply astonished to see that he is so fortunate as to have the the dust of Your lotus feet on his head. This is a fortune sought after by great saintly persons. Even the goddess of fortune underwent severe austerities just to have the blessing of the dust of Your lotus feet, so how is it that Kāliya is so easily getting this dust on his head? We have heard from authoritative sources that those who are blessed with the dust of Your lotus feet do not care even for the highest post within the universe, namely the post of Lord Brahmā, or the kingship of heavenly planets, or the sovereignty of this planet. Nor do such persons desire to rule the planets above this earth, such as Siddhaloka; nor do they aspire for the mystic powers achieved by the *yoga* process. Nor do the pure devotees aspire for liberation by becoming one with You. My Lord, although he is born in a species of life which is fostered by the most abominable modes of material nature, accompanied with the quality of anger, this King of the serpents has achieved something very, very rare. Living entities who are wandering within this universe and getting different species of life can very easily achieve the greatest benediction only by Your mercy."

It is also confirmed in the *Caitanya-caritāmṛta* that the living entities are wandering within the universe in various species of life, but by the mercy of Kṛṣṇa and the spiritual master, they can get the seed of devotional service, and thus their path of liberation can be cleared.

"We therefore offer our respectful obeisances unto You," the Nāgapatnīs continued, "our dear Lord, because You are the Supreme Person, You are living as the Supersoul within every living entity; although You are transcendental to the cosmic manifestation, everything is resting in You. You are the personified indefatigable eternal time. The entire time force is existing in You, and You are therefore the seer and the embodiment of total time in the shape of past, present and future, month, day, hour, moment—everything. In other words, O Lord, You can see perfectly all the activities happening in every moment, in every hour, in every day, every year, past, present and future. You are Yourself the universal form, and yet You are different from this universe. You are simultaneously one and different from the universe. We therefore offer our respectful obeisances unto You. You are Yourself the whole universe, and yet You are the creator of the whole universe. You are the superintendent and maintainer of this whole universe, and You are its original cause. Although You are present within this universe by Your three qualitative incarnations, Brahmā, Viṣṇu, and Maheśvara, You are transcendental to the material creation. Although You are the cause of the appearance of all kinds of living entities—their senses, their lives, their minds, their intelligence—You are to be realized by Your internal energy. Let us therefore offer our respectful obeisances unto You, who are unlimited, finer than the finest, the center of all creation and knower of everything. Different varieties of philosophical speculators try to reach You. You are the ultimate goal of all philosophical efforts, and You are actually described by all philosophies and by different kinds of doctrines. Let us offer our respectful obeisances unto You, because You are the origin of all scripture and the source of knowledge. You are the root of all evidences, and You are the Supreme Person who can bestow upon us the supreme knowledge. You are the cause of all kinds of desires, and You are the cause of all kinds of satisfaction. You are the *Vedas* personified. Therefore we offer You our respectful obeisances.

"Our dear Lord, You are the Supreme Personality of Godhead, Kṛṣṇa, and You are also the supreme enjoyer now appeared as the son of Vasudeva, who is a manifestation of the pure state of goodness. You are the predominating Deity of mind and intelligence, Pradyumna and Aniruddha, and You are the Lord of all Vaiṣṇavas. By Your expansion as *caturvyūha*—namely Vāsudeva, Saṅkarṣaṇa, Aniruddha and Pradyumna—You are the cause of the development of mind and intelligence. By Your activities only, the living entities become covered by forgetfulness or discover their real identity. This is also confirmed in the *Bhagavad-gītā* (Fifteenth Chapter): the Lord is sitting as the Supersoul in everyone's heart, and due to His presence the living entity either forgets himself or revives his original identity. We can partially understand that You are within our hearts as the witness of all our activities, but it is very difficult to appreciate Your presence, although every one of us can do so to some extent. You are the supreme controller of both the material and spiritual energies; therefore You are the supreme leader, although You are different from this cosmic manifestation. You are the witness and creator and the very ingredient of this cosmic manifestation. We therefore offer our respectful obeisances unto You. Our dear Lord, in the matter of creating this cosmic manifestation, personally You have nothing to exert; by expending Your different kinds of energy—namely the mode of goodness, the mode of passion and the mode of ignorance—You can create, maintain and annihilate this cosmic manifestation. As the controller of the entire time force, You can simply glance over the material energy, create this universe and energize the different forces of material nature which are acting differently in different creatures. No one can estimate, therefore, how Your activities are going on within this world. Our dear Lord, although You have expanded into the three principal Deities of this universe—namely Lord Brahmā, Lord Viṣṇu and Lord Śiva—for creation, maintenance and destruction, Your appearance as Lord Viṣṇu is actually for the benediction of living creatures. Therefore, for those who are actually peaceful and who are aspiring after the supreme peace, worship of Your peaceful appearance as Lord Viṣṇu is recommended. O Lord, we are submitting our prayers unto You. You can appreciate that this poor serpent is going to give up his life. You know that for us women our lives and everything are our husband's; therefore, we are praying unto You that You kindly excuse Kāliya, our husband, because if this serpent dies, then we shall be in great difficulty. Looking upon us only, please excuse this great offender. Our dear Lord, every living creature is Your offspring, and You maintain everyone. This serpent is also Your offspring, and You can excuse him although he has offended You, undoubtedly without knowing Your potency. We are praying that he may be excused for this time. Our dear Lord, we are offering our loving service unto You because we are all eternal servitors of Your Lordship. You can order us and ask us to do whatever You please. Every living being can be relieved from all kinds of despair if he agrees to abide by Your orders."

After the Nāgapatnīs submitted their prayers, Lord Kṛṣṇa released Kāliya from his punishment. Kāliya was already unconscious from being struck by the Lord. Upon regaining consciousness and being released from the punishment, Kāliya got back his life force and the working power of his senses. With folded hands, he humbly began to pray to the Supreme Lord Kṛṣṇa: "My dear Lord, I have been born in such a species that by nature I am angry and envious, being in the darkest region of the mode of ignorance. Your Lordship knows well that it is very difficult to give up one's natural instincts, although by such instincts the living creature transmigrates from one body to another." It is also confirmed in the *Bhagavad-gītā* that it is very difficult to get out of the clutches of material nature, but if anyone surrenders unto the Supreme Personality of Godhead, Kṛṣṇa, the modes of material nature can no longer act on him. "My dear Lord," Kāliya continued, "You are therefore the original creator of all kinds of modes of material nature by which the universe is created. You are the cause of the different kinds of mentality possessed by living creatures by which they have obtained different varieties of bodies. My dear Lord, I am born as a serpent; therefore, by natural instinct, I am very angry. How is it then possible to give up my acquired nature without Your mercy? It is very difficult to get out of the clutches of Your *māyā*. By Your *māyā* we remain enslaved. My dear Lord, kindly excuse me for my inevitable material tendencies. Now You can punish me or save me as You desire."

After hearing this, the Supreme Personality of Godhead, who was acting as a small human child, ordered the serpent thus: "You must immediately leave this place and go to the ocean. Leave without delay. You can take with you all your offspring, wives and everything that you possess. Don't pollute the waters of the Yamunā. Let it be drunk by My cows and cowherd boys without hindrance." The Lord then declared that the order given to the Kāliya snake be recited and heard by everyone so that no one need fear Kāliya any longer.

Anyone who hears the narration of the Kāliya serpent and his punishment will need fear no more the envious activities of snakes. The Lord also declared: "If one takes a bath in the Kāliya lake where My cowherd boy friends and I have bathed, or if one, fasting for a day, offers oblations to the forefathers from the water of this lake, he will be relieved from all kinds of sinful reaction." The Lord also assured Kāliya: "You came here out of fear of Garuḍa, who wanted to eat you in the beautiful land by the ocean. Now, after seeing the marks where I have touched your head with My lotus feet, Garuḍa will not disturb you."

The Lord was pleased with Kāliya and his wives. Immediately after hearing His order, the wives began to worship Him with great offerings of nice garments, flowers, garlands, jewels, ornaments, sandal pulp, lotus flowers, and nice eatable fruits. In this way they pleased the master of Garuḍa, of whom they were very much afraid. Then, obeying the orders of Lord Kṛṣṇa, all of them left the lake within the Yamunā.

*Thus ends the Bhaktivedanta purport of the Sixteenth Chapter of* Kṛṣṇa, *"Subduing Kāliya."*

# 17 / Extinguishing the Forest Fire

King Parīkṣit, after hearing of the chastisement of Kāliya, inquired from Śukadeva Gosvāmī as to why Kāliya left his beautiful land and why Garuḍa was so antagonistic to him. Śukadeva Gosvāmī informed the King that the island known as Nāgālaya was inhabited by serpents and that Kāliya was one of the chief serpents there. Being accustomed to eating snakes, Garuḍa used to come to this island and kill many serpents at his will. Some of them he actually ate, but some were unnecessarily killed. The reptile society became so disturbed that their leader, Vāsuki, appealed to Lord Brahmā for protection. Lord Brahmā made an arrangement by which Garuḍa would not create a disturbance: on each half-moon day, the reptile community would offer a serpent to Garuḍa. The serpent was to be kept underneath a tree as a sacrificial offering to Garuḍa. Garuḍa was satisfied with this offering, and therefore he did not disturb any other serpents.

But gradually, Kāliya took advantage of this situation. He was unnecessarily puffed up by the volume of his accumulated poison, as well as by his material power, and he thought, "Why should Garuḍa be offered this sacrifice?" He then ceased offering any sacrifice; instead, he himself ate the offering intended for Garuḍa. When Garuḍa, the great devotee-carrier of Viṣṇu, understood that Kāliya was eating the offered sacrifices, he became very angry and quickly rushed to the island to kill the offensive serpent. Kāliya tried to fight Garuḍa and faced him with his many hoods and poisonous sharp teeth. Kāliya attempted to bite him, and Garuḍa, the son of Tārkṣya, in great anger and with the great force deserving the carrier of Lord Viṣṇu, struck the body of Kāliya with his effulgent golden wings. Kāliya, who is also known as Kadrūsuta, son of Kadrū, immediately fled to the lake known as Kāliyadaha, underneath the Yamunā River, which Garuḍa could not approach.

Kāliya took shelter within the water of the Yamunā for the following reason. Just as Garuḍa went to the island of the Kāliya snake, so he also used to go to the Yamunā to catch fish to eat. There was, however, a great *yogī* known as Saubhari Muni, who used to meditate within the water there and who was sympathetic with the fish. He asked Garuḍa not to come there and disturb the fish. Although Garuḍa was not under anyone's order, being the carrier of Lord Viṣṇu, he did not disobey the order of the great *yogī*. Instead of staying and eating many fish, he carried off one big fish, who was their leader. Saubhari Muni was sorry that one of the leaders of the fish was taken away by Garuḍa, and thinking of their protection, he cursed Garuḍa in the following words: "Henceforward from this day, if Garuḍa comes here to catch fish, then—I say this with all my strength—he will be immediately killed."

This curse was known only to Kāliya. Kāliya was, therefore, confident that Garuḍa would not be able to come there, and so he thought it wise to take shelter of the lake within the Yamunā. But Kāliya's taking shelter of Saubhari Muni was not successful; he was driven away from the Yamunā by Kṛṣṇa, the master of Garuḍa. It may be noted that Garuḍa is directly related to the Supreme Personality of Godhead and is so powerful that he is never subjected to anyone's order or curse. Actually the cursing of Garuḍa—who is stated in the *Śrīmad-Bhāgavatam* to be of the stature of the Supreme Personality of Godhead, Bhagavān—was an offense on the part of Saubhari Muni. Although Garuḍa did not try to retaliate, the Muni was not saved from his offensive act against a great Vaiṣṇava personality. Due to this offence, Saubhari fell down from his yogic position and afterwards became a householder, a sense enjoyer in the material world. The falldown of Saubhari Muni, who was supposed to be absorbed in spiritual bliss by meditation, is an instruction to the offender of Vaiṣṇavas.

When Kṛṣṇa finally came out of Kāliya's lake, He was seen by all His friends and relatives on the bank of Yamunā. He appeared before them nicely decorated, smeared all over with *candana* pulp, bedecked with valuable jewels and stones, and almost completely covered with gold. The inhabitants of Vṛndāvana, cowherd boys and men, mother Yaśodā, Mahārāja Nanda and all the cows and calves, saw Kṛṣṇa coming from the Yamunā, and it was as though they had recovered their very life. When a person regains his life, naturally he becomes absorbed in pleasure and joyfulness. They each in turn pressed Kṛṣṇa to their chests, and thus they felt a great relief. Mother Yaśodā, Rohiṇī, Mahārāja Nanda and the cowherd men became so happy that they embraced Kṛṣṇa and thought they had achieved their ultimate goal of life.

Balarāma also embraced Kṛṣṇa, but He was laughing because He had known what would happen to Kṛṣṇa when everyone else was so overwhelmed with anxiety. All the trees on the bank of the Yamunā, all the cows, bulls and calves were full of pleasure because of Kṛṣṇa's appearance there. The *brāhmaṇa* inhabitants of Vṛndāvana, along with their wives, immediately came to congratulate Kṛṣṇa and His family members. *Brāhmaṇas* are considered to be the spiritual masters of society. They offered their blessings to Kṛṣṇa and the family on account of Kṛṣṇa's release. They also asked Mahārāja Nanda to give them some charity on that occasion. Being so pleased by Kṛṣṇa's return, Mahārāja Nanda began to give many cows and much gold in charity to the *brāhmaṇas.* While Nanda Mahārāja was thus engaged, mother Yaśodā simply embraced Kṛṣṇa and made Him sit on her lap while she shed tears continually.

Since it was almost night, and all the inhabitants of Vṛndāvana, including the cows and calves, were very tired, they decided to take their rest on the river bank. In the middle of the night, while they were taking rest, there was suddenly a great forest fire, and it quickly appeared that the fire would soon devour all the inhabitants of Vṛndāvana. As soon as they felt the warmth of the fire, they immediately took shelter of Kṛṣṇa, the Supreme Personality of Godhead, although He was playing just like their child. They began to say, "Our dear Kṛṣṇa! O Supreme Personality of Godhead! Our dear Balarāma, the reservoir of all strength! Please try to save us from this all-devouring and devastating fire. We have no other shelter than You. This devastating fire will swallow us all!" Thus they prayed to Kṛṣṇa, saying that they could not take any shelter other than His lotus feet. Lord Kṛṣṇa, being compassionate upon His own townspeople, immediately swallowed up the whole forest fire and saved them. This was not impossible for Kṛṣṇa because He is unlimited. He has unlimited power to do anything He desires.

*Thus ends the Bhaktivedanta purport of the Seventeenth Chapter of* Kṛṣṇa, *"Extinguishing the Forest Fire."*

# 18 / Killing the Demon Pralambāsura

After extinguishing the devastating fire, Kṛṣṇa, surrounded by His relatives, friends, cows, calves and bulls and glorified by their singing, again entered Vṛndāvana, which is always full of cows. While Kṛṣṇa and Balarāma were enjoying life in Vṛndāvana, in the midst of the cowherd boys and girls, the season gradually changed to summer. The summer season in India is not very much welcomed because of the excessive heat, but in Vṛndāvana everyone was pleased because summer there appeared just like spring. This was possible only because Lord Kṛṣṇa and Balarāma, who are the controllers even of Lord Brahmā and Lord Śiva, were residing there. In Vṛndāvana there are many falls which are always pouring water, and the sound is so sweet that it covers the sound of the crickets. And because water flows all over, the forest always looks very green and beautiful.

The inhabitants of Vṛndāvana were never disturbed by the scorching heat of the sun or the high summer temperatures. The lakes of Vṛndāvana are surrounded by green grasses, and various kinds of lotus flowers bloom there, such as the *kalhāra-kañjotpala,* and the air blowing in Vṛndāvana carries the aromatic pollen of those lotus flowers. When the particles of water from the waves of the Yamunā, the lakes and the waterfalls, touched the bodies of the inhabitants of Vṛndāvana, they automatically felt a cooling effect. Therefore they were practically undisturbed by the summer season.

Vṛndāvana is such a nice place. Flowers are always blooming, and there are even various kinds of decorated deer. Birds are chirping, peacocks are crowing and dancing, and bees are humming. The cuckoos there sing nicely in five kinds of tunes.

Kṛṣṇa, the reservoir of pleasure, blowing His flute, accompanied by His elder brother Balarāma and other cowherd boys and cows, entered the beautiful forest of Vṛndāvana to enjoy the atmosphere. They walked into the midst of newly grown leaves of trees whose flowers resembled peacock feathers. They were garlanded by those flowers and decorated with saffron chalk. Sometimes they were dancing and singing and sometimes wrestling with one another. While Kṛṣṇa danced, some of the cowherd boys sang, and others played on flutes; some bugled on buffalo horns or clapped their hands, praising Kṛṣṇa, "Dear brother, You are dancing very nicely." Actually, all these boys were demigods descended from higher planets to assist Kṛṣṇa in His pastimes. The demigods garbed in the dress of the cowherd boys were encouraging Kṛṣṇa in His dancing, just as one artist encourages another with praise. Up to that time, neither Balarāma nor Kṛṣṇa had undergone the haircutting ceremony; therefore Their hair was clustered like crows' feathers. They were always playing hide-and-seek with Their boy friends or jumping or fighting with one another. Sometimes, while His friends were chanting and dancing, Kṛṣṇa would praise them, "My dear friends, you are dancing and singing very nicely." The boys played at catching ball with bell shaped fruits and round *āmalakī.* They played blindman's buff, challenging and touching one another. Sometimes they imitated the forest deer and various kinds of birds. They joked with one another by imitating croaking frogs, and they enjoyed swinging underneath the trees. Sometimes they would play like a king and his subjects amongst themselves. In this way, Balarāma and Kṛṣṇa, along with all Their friends, played all kinds of sports and enjoyed the soothing atmosphere of Vṛndāvana, full of rivers, lakes, rivulets, fine trees and excellent fruits and flowers.

Once while they were engaged in their transcendental pastimes, a great demon of the name Pralambāsura entered their company, desiring to kidnap both Balarāma and Kṛṣṇa. Although Kṛṣṇa was playing the part of a cowherd boy, as the Supreme Personality of Godhead He could understand everything—past, present and future. So when Pralambāsura entered their company, Kṛṣṇa began to think how to kill the demon, but externally He received him as a friend. "O My dear friend," He said. "It is very good that you have come to take part in our pastimes." Kṛṣṇa then called all His friends and ordered them: "Now we shall play in pairs. We shall challenge one another in pairs." With this proposal, all the boys assembled together. Some of them took the side of Kṛṣṇa, and some of them took the side of Balarāma, and they arranged to play in duel. The defeated members in duel fighting had to carry the victorious members on their backs. They began playing, and at the same time tended the cows as they proceeded through the Bhāṇḍīravana forest. The party of Balarāma, accompanied by Śrīdāmā and Vṛṣabha, came out victorious, and Kṛṣṇa's party had to carry them on their backs through the Bhāṇḍīravana forest. The Supreme Personality of Godhead, Kṛṣṇa, being defeated, had to carry Śrīdāmā on His back, and Bhadrasena carried Vṛṣabha. Imitating their play, Pralambāsura, who appeared there as a cowherd boy, carried Balarāma on his back. Pralambāsura was the greatest of the demons, and he had calculated that Kṛṣṇa was the most powerful of the cowherd boys.

In order to avoid the company of Kṛṣṇa, Pralambāsura carried Balarāma far away. The demon was undoubtedly very strong and powerful, but he was carrying Balarāma, who is compared with a mountain; therefore he began to feel the burden, and thus he assumed his real form. When he appeared in his real feature, he was decorated with a golden helmet and earrings and looked just like a cloud with lightning carrying the moon. Balarāma observed the demon's body expanding up to the limits of the clouds, his eyes dazzling like blazing fire and his mouth flashing with sharpened teeth. At first, Balarāma was surprised by the demon's appearance, and He began to wonder, "How is it that all of a sudden this carrier has changed in every way?" But with a clear mind He could quickly understand that He was being carried away from His friends by a demon who intended to kill Him. Immediately He struck the head of the demon with His strong fist, just as the king of the heavenly planets strikes a mountain with his thunderbolt. Being stricken by the fist of Balarāma, the demon fell down dead, just like a snake with a smashed head, and blood poured from his mouth. When the demon fell, he made a tremendous sound, and it sounded as if a great hill were falling upon being struck by the thunderbolt of King Indra. All the boys then rushed to the spot. Being astonished by the ghastly scene, they began to praise Balarāma with the words, "Well done, well done." All of them then began to embrace Balarāma with great affection, thinking that He had returned from death, and they offered their blessings and congratulations. All the demigods in the heavenly planets became very satisfied and showered flowers on the transcendental body of Balarāma, and they also offered their blessings and congratulations for His having killed the great demon Pralambāsura.

*Thus ends the Bhaktivedanta purport of the Eighteenth Chapter of* Kṛṣṇa, *"Killing the Demon Pralambāsura."*

# 19 / Devouring the Forest Fire

While Kṛṣṇa and Balarāma and Their friends were engaged in the pastimes described above, the cows, being unobserved, began to wander off on their own, entering farther and farther into the deepest part of the forest, allured by fresh grasses. The goats, cows and buffalo travelled from one forest to another and entered the forest known as Iṣikāṭavi. This forest was full of green grass, and therefore they were allured; but when they entered, they saw that there was a forest fire, and they began to cry. On the other side, Balarāma and Kṛṣṇa, along with Their friends, could not find their animals, and they became very aggrieved. They began to trace the cows by following their footprints, as well as the path of eaten grass. All of the boys were fearing that their very means of livelihood, the cows, were now lost. Soon, however, they heard the crying of their cows. Kṛṣṇa began to call the cows by their respective names, with great noise. Upon hearing Kṛṣṇa calling, the cows immediately replied with joy. But by this time the forest fire surrounded all of them, and the situation appeared to be very fearful. The flames increased as the wind blew very quickly, and it appeared that everything movable and immovable would be devoured. All the cows and the boys became very frightened, and they looked towards Balarāma the way a dying man looks at the picture of the Supreme Personality of Godhead. They said, "Dear Kṛṣṇa and Balarāma, we are now burning from the heat of this blazing fire. Let us take shelter of Your lotus feet. We know You can protect us from this great danger. Our dear friend Kṛṣṇa, we are Your intimate friends. It is not right that we should suffer in this way. We are all completely dependent on You, and You are the knower of all religious life. We do not know anyone except You."

The Personality of Godhead heard the appealing voices of His friends, and casting a pleasing glance over them, He began to answer. By speaking through His eyes, He impressed His friends that there was no cause for fear. Then Kṛṣṇa, the supreme mystic, the powerful Personality of Godhead, immediately swallowed up all the flames of the fire. The cows and boys were thus saved from imminent danger. Out of fear, the boys were almost unconscious, but when they regained their consciousness and opened their eyes, they saw that they were again in the forest with Kṛṣṇa, Balarāma and the cows. They were astonished to see that they were completely free from the attack of the blazing fire and that the cows were saved. They secretly thought that Kṛṣṇa must not be an ordinary boy, but some demigod.

In the evening, Kṛṣṇa and Balarāma, along with the boys and cows, returned to Vṛndāvana, playing Their flutes. As they approached the village, all the *gopīs* became very joyous. Throughout the day the *gopīs* used to think of Kṛṣṇa while He was in the forest, and in His absence they were considering one moment to be like twelve years.

*Thus ends the Bhaktivedanta purport of the Nineteenth Chapter of* Kṛṣṇa, *"Devouring the Forest Fire."*

# 20 / Description of Autumn

The killing of Pralambāsura and the devouring of the devastating forest fire by Kṛṣṇa and Balarāma became household topics in Vṛndāvana. The cowherd men described these wonderful activities to their wives and to everyone else, and all were struck with wonder. They concluded that Kṛṣṇa and Balarāma were demigods who had kindly come to Vṛndāvana to become their children. In this way, the rainy season ensued. In India, after the scorching heat of the summer, the rainy season is very welcome. The clouds accumulating in the sky, covering the sun and the moon, become very pleasing to the people, and they expect rainfall at every moment. After summer, the advent of the rainy season is considered to be a life-giving source for everyone. The thunder and occasional lightning are also pleasurable to the people.

The symptoms of the rainy season may be compared to the symptoms of the living entities who are covered by the three modes of material nature. The unlimited sky is like the Supreme Brahman, and the tiny living entities are like the covered sky, or Brahman covered by the three modes of material nature. Originally, everyone is part and parcel of Brahman. The Supreme Brahman, or the unlimited sky, can never be covered by a cloud, but a portion of it can be covered. As stated in the *Bhagavad-gītā,* the living entities are part and parcel of the Supreme Personality of Godhead. But they are only an insignificant portion of the Supreme Lord. This portion is covered by the modes of material nature, and therefore the living entities are residing within this material world. The *brahmajyoti*–spiritual effulgence–is just like the sunshine; as the sunshine is full of molecular shining particles, so the *brahmajyoti* is full of minute portions of the Supreme Personality of Godhead. Out of that unlimited expansion of minute portions of the Supreme Lord, some are covered by the influence of material nature, whereas others are free.

Clouds are accumulated water drawn from the land by the sunshine. Continually for eight months the sun evaporates all kinds of water from the surface of the globe, and this water is accumulated in the shape of clouds, which are distributed as water when there is need. Similarly, a government exacts various taxes from the citizens which the citizens are able to pay by their different material activities: agriculture, trade and industry; thus the government can also exact taxes in the form of income tax and sales tax. This is compared to the sun drawing water from the earth. When there is again need of water on the surface of the globe, the same sunshine converts the water into clouds and distributes it all over the globe. Similarly, the taxes collected by the government must be distributed to the people again, as educational work, public work, sanitary work, etc. This is very essential for a good government. The government should not simply exact tax for useless squandering; the tax collection should be utilized for the public welfare of the state.

During the rainy season, there are strong winds blustering all over the country and carrying clouds from one place to another to distribute water. When water is urgently needed after the summer season, the clouds are just like a rich man who, in times of need, distributes his money even by exhausting his whole treasury. So the clouds exhaust themselves by distributing water all over the surface of the globe.

When Mahārāja Daśaratha, the father of Lord Rāmacandra, used to fight with his enemies, it was said that he approached them just like a farmer uprooting unnecessary plants and trees. And when there was need of giving charity, he used to distribute money exactly as the cloud distributes rain. The distribution of rain by clouds is so sumptuous that it is compared to the distribution of wealth by a great, munificent person. The clouds' downpour is so sufficient that the rains even fall on rocks and hills and on the oceans and seas where there is no need for water. It is like a charitable person who opens his treasury for distribution and who does not discriminate whether the charity is needed or not. He gives in charity openhandedly.

Before the rainfall, the whole surface of the globe becomes almost depleted of all kinds of energies and appears very lean. After the rainfall, the whole surface of the earth becomes green with vegetation and appears to be very healthy and strong. Here, a comparison is made with the person undergoing austerities for fulfillment of a material desire. The flourishing condition of the earth after a rainy season is compared with the fulfillment of material desires. Sometimes, when a country is subjected by an undesirable government, persons and parties undergo severe penances and austerities to get control of the government, and when they attain control, they flourish by giving themselves generous salaries. This also is like the flourishing of the earth in the rainy season. Actually, one should undergo severe austerities and penances only to achieve spiritual happiness. In the *Śrīmad-Bhāgavatam* it is recommended that *tapasa* or penance should be accepted for realizing the Supreme Lord. By accepting austerity in devotional service, one regains his spiritual life, and as soon as one regains his spiritual life, he enjoys unlimited spiritual bliss. But if someone undertakes austerities and penances for some material gain, it is stated in the *Bhagavad-gītā* that the results are temporary and that they are desired by persons of less intelligence.

During the rainy season, in the evening, there are many glowworms visible about the tops of trees, hither and thither, and they glitter just like lights. But the luminaries of the sky, the stars and the moons, are not visible. Similarly, in the age of Kali, persons who are atheists or miscreants become very prominently visible, whereas persons who are actually following the Vedic principles for spiritual emancipation are practically obscured. This age, Kaliyuga, is compared to the cloudy season of the living entities. In this age, real knowledge is covered by the influence of material advancement of civilization. The cheap mental speculators, atheists and manufacturers of so-called religious principles become prominent like the glowworms, whereas persons strictly following the Vedic principles or scriptural injunctions become covered by the clouds of this age. People should learn to take advantage of the actual luminaries of the sky, the sun, moon, and stars, instead of the glowworm's light. Actually, the glowworm cannot give any light in the darkness of night. As clouds sometimes clear, even in the rainy season, and sometimes the moon, stars and sun become visible, so even in this Kaliyuga there are sometimes advantages. The Vedic movement of Lord Caitanya's—the distribution of chanting the Hare Kṛṣṇa *mantra*—is heard in this way. People seriously anxious to find real life should take advantage of this movement instead of looking toward the light of mental speculators and atheists.

After the first rainfall, when there is a thundering sound in the clouds, all the frogs begin to croak, like students suddenly engaged in reading their studies. Students are generally supposed to rise early in the morning. They do not usually arise of their own accord, however, but only when there is a bell sounded in the temple or in the cultural institution. By the order of the spiritual master they immediately rise, and after finishing their morning duties, they sit down to study the *Vedas* or chant Vedic *mantras*. Everyone is sleeping in the darkness of Kaliyuga, but when there is a great *ācārya*, by his calling only, everyone takes to the study of the *Vedas* to acquire actual knowledge. During the rainy season, many small ponds, lakes and rivulets become filled with water; otherwise the rest of the year they remain dry. Similarly, materialistic persons are dry, but sometimes, when they are in a so-called opulent position, with a home or children or a little bank balance, they appear to be flourishing, but immediately afterwards they become dry again, like the small rivulets and ponds. The poet Vidyāpati said that in the society of friends, family, children, wife, etc., there is certainly some pleasure, but that pleasure is compared to a drop of water in the desert. Everyone is hankering after happiness, just as in the desert everyone is hankering after water. If, in the desert, there is a drop of water, the water is there of course, but the benefit from that drop of water is very insignificant. In our materialistic way of life, we are hankering after an ocean of happiness, but in the form of society, friends and mundane love, we are getting no more than a drop of water. Our satisfaction is never achieved, as the small rivulets, lakes and ponds are never filled with water in the dry season.

Due to rainfall, the grass, trees and vegetation look very green. Some times the grass is covered by a certain kind of red insect, and when the green and red combine with umbrella-like mushrooms, the entire scene changes, just like a person who has suddenly become rich. The farmer then becomes very happy to see his field full of grains, but the capitalists—who are always unaware of the activities of a supernatural power—become unhappy because they are afraid of a competitive price. In some places certain capitalists in government restrict the farmer from producing too much grains, not knowing the actual fact that all food grains are supplied by the Supreme Personality of Godhead. According to the Vedic injunction, *eko bahūnāṁ yo vidadhāti kāmān,* the Supreme Personality of Godhead maintains this creation; therefore, He arranges for a supply of whatever is required for all living entities. When there is population increase, it is the business of the Supreme Lord to feed them. But persons who are atheistṣ or miscreants do not like abundant production of food grains, especially if their business might be hampered.

During the rainy season, all living entities, in the land, sky and water, become very refreshed, exactly like one who engages in the transcendental loving service of the Lord. We have practical experience of this with our students in the International Society for Krishna Consciousness. Before becoming students, they were dirty looking, although they had naturally beautiful personal features; but due to having no information of Kṛṣṇa consciousness they appeared very dirty and wretched. Since they have taken to Kṛṣṇa consciousness, their health has improved, and by following the rules and regulations, their bodily luster has increased. When they are dressed with saffron colored cloth, with *tilaka* on their foreheads and beads in their hands and on their necks, they look exactly as if they come directly from Vaikuṇṭha.

In the rainy season, when the rivers swell and rush to the oceans and seas, they appear to agitate the ocean. Similarly, if a person who is engaged in the *yoga*-mystic process is not very advanced in spiritual life, he can become agitated by the sex impulse. High mountains, however, although splashed by torrents of rain, do not change; so a person who is advanced in Kṛṣṇa consciousness, even if put into difficulties, is not embarrassed because a person who is spiritually advanced accepts any adverse condition of life as the mercy of the Lord, and thus he is completely eligible to enter into the spiritual kingdom.

In the rainy season some of the roads are not frequently used, and they become covered with long grasses. This is exactly like a *brāhmaṇa* who is not accustomed to studying and practicing the reformatory methods of Vedic injunctions—he becomes covered with the long grasses of *māyā*. In that condition, forgetful of his constitutional nature, he forgets his position of eternal servitorship to the Supreme Personality of Godhead. By being deviated by the seasonal overgrowth of long grasses created by *māyā*, a person identifies himself with mayic production and succumbs to illusion, forgetting his spiritual life.

During the rainy season, lightning appears in one group of clouds and then immediately in another group of clouds. This phenomena is compared to a lusty woman who does not fix her mind on one man. A cloud is compared to a qualified person because it pours rain and gives sustenance to many people; a man who is qualified similarly gives sustenance to many living creatures, such as family members or many workers in business. Unfortunately, his whole life can be disturbed by a wife who divorces him; when the husband is disturbed, the whole family is ruined, the children are dispersed or the business is closed, and everything is affected. It is therefore recommended that a woman desiring to advance in Kṛṣṇa consciousness peacefully live with a husband and that the couple not separate under any condition. The husband and wife should control sex indulgence and concentrate their minds on Kṛṣṇa consciousness so their life may be successful. After all, in the material world a man requires a woman, and a woman requires a man. When they are combined, they should live peacefully in Kṛṣṇa consciousness and should not be restless like the lightning, flashing from one group of clouds to another.

Sometimes, in addition to the roaring thunder of the clouds, there is an appearance of a rainbow, which stands as a bow without a string. Actually, a bow is in the curved position, being tied at its two ends by the bowstring; but in the rainbow there is no such string, and yet it rests in the sky so beautifully. Similarly, when the Supreme Personality of Godhead descends to this material world, He appears just like an ordinary human being, but He is not resting on any material condition. In the *Bhagavad-gītā,* the Lord says that He appears by His internal potency, which is free from the bondage of the external potency. What is bondage for the ordinary creature is freedom for the Personality of Godhead. In the rainy season, the moonlight is covered by clouds but is visible at intervals. It sometimes appears that the moon is moving with the movement of the clouds, but actually the moon is still; due to the clouds it also appears to move. Similarly, for one who has identified himself with the moving material world, his actual spiritual luster is covered by illusion, and with the movement of material activities, he thinks that he is moving through different spheres of life. This is due to false ego, which is the demarcation between spiritual and material existence, just as the moving cloud is the demarcation between moonlight and darkness. In the rainy season, when the clouds appear for the first time, after seeing their appearance, the peacocks begin to dance with joy. This can be compared to persons who are very harassed in the materialistic way of life. If they can find the association of a person engaged in the loving devotional service of the Lord, they become enlightened, just like the peacocks when they dance. We have practical experience of this, because many of our students were dry and morose previous to their coming to Kṛṣṇa consciousness, but having come into contact with devotees, they are now dancing like jubilant peacocks.

Plants and creepers grow by drinking water from the ground. Similarly, a person practicing austerities becomes dry; after the austere performances are completed and he gets the result, he begins to enjoy life in sense gratification, with family, society, love, home and other paraphernalia. Sometimes it is seen that cranes and ducks meander continually on the banks of the lakes and rivers, although the banks are filled with muddy garbage and thorny creepers. Similarly, persons who are householders without Kṛṣṇa consciousness are constantly tarrying in material life, in spite of all kinds of inconveniences. In family life, or any life, one cannot be perfectly happy without being Kṛṣṇa conscious. Śrīla Narottama dāsa Ṭhākur prays that he will have the association of a person—either a householder or a man in the renounced order of life—who is engaged in the transcendental loving service of the Lord and is always crying the holy name of Lord Caitanya.

For the materialistic person, worldly affairs become too aggressive, whereas to a person who is in Kṛṣṇa consciousness, everything appears to be happily situated.

The barriers around the agricultural field sometimes break due to heavy torrents of rain. Similarly, the unauthorized atheistic propaganda in the age of Kali breaks the boundary of the Vedic injunctions. Thus people gradually degenerate to godlessness. In the rainy season, the clouds, tossed by the wind, deliver water which is welcomed like nectar. When the Vedic followers, the *brāhmaṇas,* inspire rich men like kings and the wealthy mercantile community to give charity in the performance of great sacrifices, the distribution of such wealth is also nectarean. The four sections of human society, namely the *brāhmaṇas,* the *kṣatriyas,* the *vaiśyas* and the *śūdras,* are meant to live peacefully in a cooperative mood; this is possible when they are guided by the expert Vedic *brāhmaṇas* who perform sacrifices and distribute wealth equally.

Vṛndāvana forest improved from the rains and was replete with ripened dates, mangoes, blackberries and other fruits. Lord Kṛṣṇa, the Supreme Personality of Godhead, and His boy friends and Lord Balarāma, entered the forest to enjoy the new seasonal atmosphere. The cows, being fed by new grasses, became very healthy, and their milk bags were all very full. When Lord Kṛṣṇa called them by name, they immediately came to Him out of affection, and in their joyful condition the milk flowed from their bags. Lord Kṛṣṇa was very pleased when passing through the Vṛndāvana forest by the side of Govardhana Hill. On the bank of the Yamunā He saw all the trees decorated with bee hives pouring honey. There were many waterfalls on Govardhana Hill, and their flowing made a nice sound. Kṛṣṇa heard them as He looked into the caves of the hill. When the rainy season was not ended completely but was gradually turning to autumn, sometimes, especially when there was rainfall within the forest, Kṛṣṇa and His companions would sit under a tree or within the caves of Govardhana Hill and enjoy eating the ripened fruits and talking with great pleasure. When Kṛṣṇa and Balarāma were in the forest all day, mother Yaśodā used to send Them some rice mixed with yogurt, fruits and sweetmeat. Kṛṣṇa would take them and sit on a slab of stone on the bank of the Yamunā. While Kṛṣṇa and Balarāma and Their friends were eating, they watched the cows, calves and bulls. The cows appeared to be tired from standing with their heavy milk bags. By sitting and chewing grass, they became happy, and Kṛṣṇa was pleased to see them. He was proud to see the beauty of the forest, which was nothing but the manifestation of His own energy.

At such times Kṛṣṇa would praise nature's special activities during the rainy season. It is stated in the *Bhagavad-gītā* that the material energy, or nature, is not independent in its actions. Nature is acting under the superintendence of Kṛṣṇa. It is also stated in the *Brahma-saṁhitā* that material nature, known as Durgā, is acting as the shadow of Kṛṣṇa. Whatever order is sent from Kṛṣṇa, material nature obeys. Therefore the natural beauty created by the rainy season was acted out according to the indications of Kṛṣṇa. Soon all the water reservoirs became very clean and pleasing, and refreshing air was blowing everywhere because of the appearance of autumn. The sky was completely cleared of all clouds, and it recovered its natural blue color. The blooming lotus flower in the clear water in the forest appeared like a person who has fallen down from *yoga* practice but again has become beautiful by resuming his spiritual life.

Everything becomes naturally beautiful with the appearance of the autumn season. Similarly, when a materialistic person takes to Kṛṣṇa consciousness and spiritual life, he also becomes as clear as the sky and water in autumn. The autumn season takes away the rolling of dark clouds in the sky as well as the polluted water. Filthy conditions on the ground also become cleansed. Similarly, a person who takes to Kṛṣṇa consciousness immediately becomes cleansed of all dirty things within and without. Kṛṣṇa is therefore known as Hari. "*Hari*" means "he who takes away." Kṛṣṇa immediately takes away all unclean habits from anyone who takes to Kṛṣṇa consciousness. The clouds of autumn are white, for they do not carry any water. Similarly, a retired man, being freed from all responsibility of family affairs (namely, maintaining the home, wife and children) and taking completely to Kṛṣṇa consciousness, becomes freed from all anxieties and looks as white as clouds in autumn. Sometimes in autumn the falls come down from the top of the hill to supply clean water, and sometimes they stop. Similarly, sometimes great saintly persons distribute clear knowledge, and sometimes they are silent. The small ponds which were filled with water because of the rainy season, gradually dry up in autumn. As for the tiny aquatics living in the reservoirs, they cannot understand that their numbers are diminishing day by day, as the materially engrossed persons cannot understand that their duration of life is being reduced day by day. Such persons are engaged in maintaining cows, property, children, wife, society and friendship. Due to the reduced water and scorching heat from the sun in the autumn season, the small creatures living in small reservoirs of water are much disturbed; they are exactly like uncontrolled persons who are always unhappy from being unable to enjoy life or maintain their family members. The muddy earth gradually dries up, and newly grown fresh vegetables begin to wither. Similarly, for one who has taken to Kṛṣṇa consciousness, desire for family enjoyment gradually dries up.

Because of the appearance of the autumn season, the water of the ocean becomes calm and quiet, just as a person developed in self-realization is no longer disturbed by the three modes of material nature. In autumn, farmers save the water within the fields by building strong walls so that the water contained within the field cannot run out. There is hardly any hope for new rainfalls; therefore they want to save whatever is in the field. Similarly, a person who is actually advanced in self-realization protects his energy by controlling the senses. It is advised that after the age of fifty, one should retire from family life and should conserve the energy of the body for utilization in the advancement of Kṛṣṇa consciousness. Unless one is able to control the senses and engage them in the transcendental loving service of Mukunda, there is no possibility of salvation.

During the daytime in autumn, the sun is very scorching, but at night, due to the clear moonshine, people get relief from the day's fatigue. If a person takes shelter of Mukunda, or Kṛṣṇa, he can be saved from the fatigue of misidentifying the body with the self. Mukunda, or Kṛṣṇa, is also the source of solace to the damsels of Vṛndāvana. The damsels of Vrajabhūmi are always suffering because of separation from Kṛṣṇa. When they meet Kṛṣṇa during the moonlit autumn night, their fatigue of separation is also satiated. When the sky is clear of all clouds, the stars at night shine very beautifully; similarly, when a person is actually situated in Kṛṣṇa consciousness, he is cleared of all dirty things, and he becomes as beautiful as the stars in the autumn sky. Although the *Vedas* prescribe *karma* in the form of offering sacrifices, their ultimate purpose is stated in the *Bhagavad-gītā:* one has to accept Kṛṣṇa consciousness after thoroughly understanding the purpose of the *Vedas.* Therefore the clean heart exhibited by a devotee in Kṛṣṇa consciousness can be compared to the clean sky of the autumn season. During autumn, the moon looks very bright along with the stars in the clear sky. Lord Kṛṣṇa Himself appeared in the sky of the Yadu dynasty, and He was exactly like the moon surrounded by the stars, or the members of the Yadu dynasty. When there are ample blooming flowers in the gardens in the forest, the fresh, aromatic breeze gives a great relief to the person who has suffered during the summer and rainy seasons. Unfortunately, such breezes could not give any relief to the *gopīs* because of their hearts' dedication to Kṛṣṇa. People in general might have taken pleasure in that nice autumn breeze, but the *gopīs,* not being embraced by Kṛṣṇa, were not very satisfied.

On arrival of the autumn season, all the cows, deer, birds and females in general become pregnant, because in that season generally all the husbands become impelled by sex desire. This is exactly like the transcendentalists who, by the grace of the Supreme Lord, are bestowed with the benediction of their destinations in life. Śrīla Rūpa Gosvāmī has instructed in his *Upadeśāmṛta* that one should follow devotional service with great enthusiasm, patience and conviction and should follow the rules and regulations, keep oneself clean from material contamination and stay in the association of devotees. By following these principles, one is sure to achieve the desired result of devotional service. For he who patiently follows the regulative principles of devotional service, the time will come when he will achieve the result, as the wives who reap results by becoming pregnant.

During the autumn, the lotus flowers in the lakes grow in large numbers because of the absence of lilies; both the lilies and the lotus flowers grow by sunshine, but during the autumn season, the scorching sunshine helps only the lotus. This example is given in the case of a country where the king or the government is strong; the rise of unwanted elements like thieves and robbers cannot prosper. When the citizens become confident that they will not be attacked by robbers, they develop very satisfactorily. A strong government is compared to the scorching sunshine in the autumn season; the lilies are compared to unwanted persons like robbers, and the lotus flowers are compared to the satisfied citizens of the government. During autumn, the fields become filled with ripened grains. At that time, the people become happy over the harvest and observe various ceremonies, such as Navānna–the offering of new grains to the Supreme Personality of Godhead. The new grains are first offered to the Deities in various temples, and all are invited to take sweet rice made of these new grains. There are other religious ceremonies and methods of worship, particularly in Bengal, where the greatest of all such ceremonies is held, called *Durgā Pūjā*.

In Vṛndāvana the autumn season was very beautiful then because of the presence of the Supreme Personality of Godhead, Kṛṣṇa and Balarāma. The mercantile community, the royal order and great sages were free to move to achieve their desired benedictions. Similarly, the transcendentalists, when freed from the encagement of the material body, also achieved their desired goal. During the rainy season, the mercantile community cannot move from one place to another and so do not get their desired profit. Nor can the royal order go from one place to another to collect taxes from the people. As for saintly persons who must travel to preach transcendental knowledge, they also are restrained by the rainy season. But during the autumn, all of them leave their confines. In the case of the transcendentalist, be he a *jñānī*, a *yogī*, or a devotee, because of the material body he cannot actually enjoy spiritual achievement. But as soon as he gives up the body, or after death, the *jñānī* merges into the spiritual effulgence of the Supreme Lord; the *yogī* transfers himself to the various higher planets, and the devotee goes to the planet of the Supreme Lord, Goloka Vṛndāvana, or the Vaikuṇṭhas, and thus enjoys his eternal spiritual life.

*Thus ends the Bhaktivedanta purport of the Twentieth Chapter of* Kṛṣṇa, *"Description of Autumn."*

# 21 / The Gopīs Attracted by the Flute

Kṛṣṇa was very pleased with the atmosphere of the forest where flowers bloomed and bees and drones hummed very jubilantly. While the birds, trees and branches were all looking very happy, Kṛṣṇa, tending the cows, accompanied by Śrī Balarāma and the cowherd boys, began to vibrate His transcendental flute. After hearing the vibration of the flute of Kṛṣṇa, the *gopīs* in Vṛndāvana remembered Him and began to talk amongst themselves about how nicely Kṛṣṇa was playing His flute. When the *gopīs* were describing the sweet vibration of Kṛṣṇa's flute, they also remembered their pastimes with Him; thus their minds became disturbed, and they were unable to describe completely the beautiful vibrations. While discussing the transcendental vibration, they remembered also how Kṛṣṇa dressed, decorated with a peacock feather on His head, just like a dancing actor, and with blue flowers pushed over His ear. His garment glowed yellow-gold, and He was garlanded with a *vaijayantī* necklace. Dressed in such an attractive way, Kṛṣṇa filled up the holes of His flute with the nectar emanating from His lips. So they remembered Him, entering the forest of Vṛndāvana, which is always glorified by the footprints of Kṛṣṇa and His companions.

Kṛṣṇa was very expert in playing the flute, and the *gopīs* were captivated by the sound vibration, which was not only attractive to them, but to all living creatures who heard it. One of the *gopīs* told her friends, "The highest perfection of the eyes is to see Kṛṣṇa and Balarāma entering the forest and playing Their flutes and tending the cows with Their friends."

Persons who are constantly engaged in the transcendental meditation of seeing Kṛṣṇa, internally and externally, by thinking of Him playing the flute and entering the Vṛndāvana forest, have really attained the perfection of *samādhi. Samādhi* (trance) means absorption of all the activities of the senses on a particular object, and the *gopīs* indicate that the pastimes of

Kṛṣṇa are the perfection of all meditation and *samādhi.* It is also confirmed in the *Bhagavad-gītā* that anyone who is always absorbed in the thought of Kṛṣṇa is the topmost of all *yogīs.*

Another *gopī* expressed her opinion that Kṛṣṇa and Balarāma, while tending the cows, appeared just like actors going to play on a dramatic stage. Kṛṣṇa was dressed in glowing garments of yellow, Balarāma in blue, and They held new twigs of mango tree, peacock feathers, and bunches of flowers in Their hands. Dressed with garlands of lotus flowers, They were sometimes singing very sweetly among Their friends. One *gopī* told her friend, "How is it Kṛṣṇa and Balarāma are looking so beautiful?" Another *gopī* said, "My dear friend, we cannot even think of His bamboo flute—what sort of pious activities did it execute so that it is now enjoying the nectar of the lips of Kṛṣṇa?" Kṛṣṇa sometimes kisses the *gopīs;* therefore the transcendental nectar of His lips is available only to them, and His lips are considered their property. Therefore the *gopīs* asked: "How is it possible that the flute, which is nothing but a bamboo rod, is always engaged in enjoying the nectar from Kṛṣṇa's lips? Because the flute is engaged in the service of the Supreme Lord, the mother and the father of the flute must be happy."

The lakes and the rivers are considered to be the mothers of the trees because the trees live simply by drinking water. So the waters of the lakes and rivers of Vṛndāvana were full of happy lotus flowers because the waters were thinking, "How is it our son, the bamboo rod, is enjoying the nectar of Kṛṣṇa's lips?" The bamboo trees standing by the banks of the rivers and the lakes were also happy to see their descendant so engaged in the service of the Lord, just as persons who are advanced in knowledge take pleasure to see their descendants engage in the service of the Lord. The trees were overwhelmed with joy and were incessantly yielding honey, which flowed from the beehives hanging on the branches.

Sometimes the *gopīs* spoke thus to their friends about Kṛṣṇa: "Dear friends, our Vṛndāvana is proclaiming the glories of this entire earth because this planet is glorified by the lotus footprints of the son of Devakī. Besides that, when Govinda plays His flute, the peacocks immediately become mad. When all the animals and trees and plants, either on the top of Govardhana Hill or in the valley, see the dancing of the peacock, they all stand still and listen to the transcendental sound of the flute with great attention. We think that this boon is not possible or available on any other planet." Although the *gopīs* were village cowherd women and girls, they had knowledge of Kṛṣṇa. Similarly, one can learn the highest truths simply by hearing the *Vedas* from authoritative sources.

Another *gopī* said, "My dear friends, just see the deer! Although they are dumb animals, they have approached the son of Mahārāja Nanda, Kṛṣṇa. Not only are they attracted by the dress of Kṛṣṇa and Balarāma, but as soon as they hear the playing of the flute, the deer, along with their husbands, offer respectful obeisances unto the Lord by looking at Him with great affection." The *gopīs* were envious of the deer because the deer were able to offer their service to Kṛṣṇa along with their husbands. The *gopīs* thought themselves not so fortunate because whenever they wanted to go to Kṛṣṇa, their husbands were not very happy.

Another *gopī* said, "My dear friends, Kṛṣṇa is so nicely dressed that He appears to be the impetus to various kinds of ceremonies held by the womenfolk. Even the wives of the denizens of heaven become attracted after hearing the transcendental sound of His flute. Although they are travelling in the air in their airplanes, enjoying the company of their husbands, on hearing the sound of Kṛṣṇa's flute, they immediately become perturbed. Their hair is loosened and their tight dresses are slackened." This means that the transcendental sound of the flute of Kṛṣṇa extended to all corners of the universe. Also, it is significant that the *gopīs* knew about the different kinds of airplanes flying in the sky.

Another *gopī* said to her friends, "My dear friends, the cows are also charmed as soon as they hear the transcendental sound of the flute of Kṛṣṇa. It sounds to them like the pouring of nectar, and they immediately spread their long ears just to catch the liquid nectar of the flute. As for the calves, they are seen with the nipples of their mothers pressed in their mouths, but they cannot suck the milk. They remain struck with devotion, and tears glide down their eyes, illustrating vividly how they are embracing Kṛṣṇa heart to heart." These phenomena indicate that even the cows and calves in Vṛndāvana knew how to cry for Kṛṣṇa and embrace Him heart to heart. Actually, Kṛṣṇa conscious affection can be culminated in shedding tears from the eyes.

A younger *gopī* told her mother, "My dear mother, the birds, who are all looking at Kṛṣṇa playing on His flute, are sitting very attentively on the branches and twigs of different trees. From their features it appears that they have forgotten everything and are engaged only in hearing Kṛṣṇa's flute. This proves that they are not ordinary birds; they are great sages and devotees, and just to hear Kṛṣṇa's flute they have appeared in Vṛndāvana forest as birds." Great sages and scholars are interested in Vedic knowledge, but the essence of Vedic knowledge is stated in the *Bhagavad-gīta: vedaiś ca sarvair aham eva vedyaḥ*. Through the knowledge of the *Vedas*, Kṛṣṇa has to be understood. From the behavior of these birds, it appeared that they were great scholars in Vedic knowledge and that they took to Kṛṣṇa's transcendental vibration and rejected all branches of Vedic knowledge. Even the River Yamunā, being desirous to embrace the lotus feet of Kṛṣṇa after hearing the transcendental vibration of His flute, broke her fierce waves to flow very nicely with lotus flowers in her hands, just to present flowers to Mukunda with deep feeling.

The scorching heat of the autumn sunshine was sometimes intolerable, and therefore the clouds in the sky appeared in sympathy above Kṛṣṇa and Balarāma and Their boy friends while They engaged in blowing Their flutes. The clouds served as a soothing umbrella over Their heads just to make friendship with Kṛṣṇa. The wanton aborigine girls also became fully satisfied when they smeared their faces and breasts with the dust of Vṛndāvana, which was reddish from the touch of Kṛṣṇa's lotus feet. The aborigine girls had very full breasts, and they were also very lusty, but when their lovers felt their breasts, they were not very satisfied. When they came out into the midst of the forest, they saw that while Kṛṣṇa was walking, some of the leaves and creepers of Vṛndāvana turned reddish from the *kuṅkuma* powder which fell from His lotus feet. His lotus feet were held by the *gopīs* on their breasts, which were also smeared with *kuṅkuma* powder, but when Kṛṣṇa travelled in the Vṛndāvana forest with Balarāma and His boy friends, the reddish powder fell on the ground of the Vṛndāvana forest. So the lusty aborigine girls, while looking toward Kṛṣṇa playing His flute, saw the reddish *kuṅkuma* on the ground and immediately took it and smeared it over their faces and breasts. In this way they became fully satisfied, although they were not satisfied when their lovers touched their breasts. All material lusty desires can be immediately satisfied if one comes in contact with Kṛṣṇa consciousness.

Another *gopī* began to praise the unique position of Govardhana Hill in this way: "How fortunate is this Govardhana Hill, for it is enjoying the association of Lord Kṛṣṇa and Balarāma who are accustomed to walk on it. Thus Govardhana is always in touch with the lotus feet of the Lord. And because Govardhana Hill is so obliged to Lord Kṛṣṇa and Balarāma, it is supplying different kinds of fruits, roots and herbs, as well as very pleasing crystal water from its lakes, in presentation to the Lord." The best presentation offered by Govardhana Hill, however, was newly grown grass for the cows and calves. Govardhana Hill knew how to please the Lord by pleasing His most beloved associates, the cows and the cowherd boys.

Another *gopī* said that everything appeared wonderful when Kṛṣṇa and Balarāma travelled in the forest of Vṛndāvana playing Their flutes and making intimate friendship with all kinds of moving and nonmoving living creatures. When Kṛṣṇa and Balarāma played on Their transcendental flutes, the moving creatures became stunned and stopped their activities, and the nonmoving living creatures, like trees and plants, began to shiver with ecstasy.

Kṛṣṇa and Balarāma carried binding ropes on Their shoulders and in Their hands, just like ordinary cowherd boys. While milking the cows, the boys bound the hind legs with a small rope. This rope almost always hung from the shoulders of the boys, and it was not absent on the shoulders of Kṛṣṇa and Balarāma. In spite of Their being the Supreme Personality of Godhead, They played exactly like cowherd boys, and therefore everything became wonderful and attractive. While Kṛṣṇa was engaged in tending the cows in the forest of Vṛndāvana or on Govardhana Hill, the *gopīs* in the village were always absorbed in thinking of Him and discussing His different pastimes. This is the perfect example of Kṛṣṇa consciousness: to somehow or other remain always engrossed in thoughts of Kṛṣṇa. The vivid example is always present in the behavior of the *gopīs;* therefore Lord Caitanya declared that no one can worship the Supreme Lord by any method which is better than the method of the *gopīs.* The *gopīs* were not born in very high *brāhmaṇa* or *kṣatriya* families; they were born in the families of *vaiśyas,* and not in big mercantile communities but in the families of cowherd men. They were not very well educated, although they heard all sorts of knowledge from the *brāhmaṇas,* the authorities of Vedic knowledge. The *gopīs'* only purpose was to remain always absorbed in thoughts of Kṛṣṇa.

*Thus ends the Bhaktivedanta purport of the Twenty-first Chapter of* Kṛṣṇa, *"The Gopīs Attracted by the Flute."*

# 22 / Stealing the Garments of the Unmarried Gopī Girls

According to Vedic civilization, unmarried girls from ten to fourteen years of age are supposed to worship either Lord Śiva or the goddess Durgā in order to get a nice husband. But the unmarried girls of Vṛndāvana were already attracted by the beauty of Kṛṣṇa. They were, however, engaged in the worship of the goddess Durgā in the beginning of the *hemanta* season (just prior to the winter season). The first month of *hemanta* is called Agrahāyana (October-November), and at that time all the unmarried *gopīs* of Vṛndāvana began to worship goddess Durgā with a vow. They first ate *haviṣyānna,* a kind of foodstuff prepared by boiling together mung dahl and rice without any spices or turmeric. According to Vedic injunction, this kind of foodstuff is recommended to purify the body before one enacts a ritualistic ceremony. All the unmarried *gopīs* in Vṛndāvana used to daily worship goddess Kātyāyanī early in the morning after taking bath in the River Yamunā. Kātyāyanī is another name for goddess Durgā. The goddess is worshiped by preparing a doll made out of sand mixed with earth from the bank of the Yamunā. It is recommended in the Vedic scriptures that a deity may be made from different kinds of material elements; it can be painted, made of metal, made of jewels, made of wood, earth or stone or can be conceived within the heart of the worshiper. The Māyāvādī philosopher takes all these forms of the deity to be imaginary, but actually they are accepted in the Vedic literatures to be identical with either the Supreme Lord or a respective demigod.

The unmarried *gopīs* used to prepare the deity of goddess Durgā and worship it with *candana* pulp, garlands, incense lamps and all kinds of presentations—fruits, grains and twigs of plants. After worshiping, it is the custom to pray for some benediction. The unmarried girls used to pray with great devotion to goddess Kātyāyanī, addressing her as follows: "O supreme eternal energy of the Personality of Godhead, O supreme mystic power, O supreme controller of this material world, O goddess, please be kind to us and arrange for our marriage with the son of Nanda Mahārāja, Kṛṣṇa." The Vaiṣṇavas generally do not worship any demigods. Śrīla Narottama dāsa Ṭhākur has strictly forbidden all worship of the demigods for anyone who wants to advance in pure devotional service. Yet the *gopīs,* who are beyond compare in their affection for Kṛṣṇa, were seen to worship Durgā. The worshipers of demigods also sometimes mention that the *gopīs* also worshiped goddess Durgā, but we must understand the purpose of the *gopīs.* Generally, people worship goddess Durgā for some material benediction. Here, the *gopīs* prayed to the goddess to become wives of Lord Kṛṣṇa. The purport is that if Kṛṣṇa is the center of activity, a devotee can adopt any means to achieve that goal. The *gopīs* could adopt any means to satisfy or serve Kṛṣṇa. That was the superexcellent characteristic of the *gopīs.* They worshiped goddess Durgā completely for one month in order to have Kṛṣṇa as their husband. Every day they prayed for Kṛṣṇa, the son of Nanda Mahārāja, to become their husband.

Early in the morning, the *gopīs* used to go to the bank of the Yamunā to take bath. They would assemble together, capturing each other's hands, and loudly sing of the wonderful pastimes of Kṛṣṇa. It is an old system among Indian girls and women that when they take bath in the river they place their garments on the bank and dip into the water completely naked. The portion of the river where the girls and women take bath was strictly prohibited to any male member, and this is still the system. The Supreme Personality of Godhead, knowing the minds of the unmarried young *gopīs,* benedicted them with their desired objective. They had prayed for Kṛṣṇa to become their husband, and Kṛṣṇa wanted to fulfill their desires.

At the end of the month, Kṛṣṇa, along with His friends, appeared on the scene. Another name of Kṛṣṇa is Yogeśvara, or master of all mystic powers. By practicing meditation, the *yogī* can study the psychic movement of other men, and certainly Kṛṣṇa could understand the desire of the *gopīs.* Appearing on the scene, Kṛṣṇa immediately collected all the garments of the *gopīs,* climbed up in a nearby tree, and with smiling face began to speak to them.

"My dear girls," He said. "Please come here one after another and pray for your garments and then take them away. I'm not joking with you. I'm just telling the truth. I have no desire to play any joke with you, for you have observed the regulative principles for one month by worshiping goddess Kātyāyanī. Please do not come here all at once. Come alone; I want to see each of you in your complete beauty, for you all have thin waists. I have requested you to come alone. Now please comply."

When the girls in the water heard such joking words from Kṛṣṇa, they began to look at one another and smile. They were very joyous to hear such a request from Kṛṣṇa because they were already in love with Him. Out of shyness, they looked at one another, but they could not come out of the water because they were naked. Due to remaining in the water for a long time, they felt cold and were shivering, yet upon hearing the pleasing and joking words of Govinda, their minds were perturbed with great joy. They began to tell Kṛṣṇa, "Dear son of Nanda Mahārāja, please do not joke with us in that way. It is completely unjust to us. You are a very respectable boy because You are the son of Nanda Mahārāja, and You are very dear to us, but You should not play this joke on us because now we are all shivering from the cold water. Kindly deliver our garments immediately, otherwise we shall suffer." They then began to appeal to Kṛṣṇa with great submission. "Dear Śyāmasundara," they said, "we are all Your eternal servitors. Whatever You order us to do, we are obliged to perform without hesitation because we consider it our religious duty. But if You insist on putting this proposal to us, which is impossible to perform, then certainly we will have to go to Nanda Mahārāja and lodge a complaint against You. If Nanda Mahārāja does not take action, then we shall tell King Kaṁsa about Your misbehavior."

Upon hearing this appeal by the unmarried *gopīs,* Kṛṣṇa answered, "My dear girls, if you think that you are My eternal servitors and you are always ready to execute My order, then My request is that, with your smiling faces, you please come here alone, one after another, and take away your garments. If you do not come here, however, and if you lodge complaints to My father, I shall not care anyway, for I know My father is old and cannot take any action against Me."

When the *gopīs* saw that Kṛṣṇa was strong and determined, they had no alternative but to abide by His order. One after another they came out of the water, but because they were completely naked, they tried to cover their nakedness by placing their left hand over their pubic area. In that posture they were all shivering. Their simple presentation was so pure that Lord Kṛṣṇa immediately became pleased with them. All the unmarried *gopīs* who prayed to Kātyāyanī to have Kṛṣṇa as their husband were thus satisfied. A woman cannot be naked before any male except her husband. The unmarried *gopīs* desired Kṛṣṇa as their husband, and He fulfilled their desire in this way. Being pleased with them, He took their garments on His shoulder and began to speak as follows. "My dear girls, you have committed a great offense by going naked in the River Yamunā. Because of this, the predominating deity of the Yamunā, Varuṇadeva, has become displeased with you. Please, therefore, just touch your foreheads with folded palms and bow down before the demigod Varuṇa in order to be excused from this offensive act." The *gopīs* were all simple souls, and whatever Kṛṣṇa said they took to be true. In order to be freed from the wrath of Varuṇadeva, as well as to fulfill the desired end of their vows and ultimately to please their worshipable Lord, Kṛṣṇa, they immediately abided by His order. Thus they became the greatest lovers of Kṛṣṇa, and His most obedient servitors.

Nothing can compare to the Kṛṣṇa consciousness of the *gopīs.* Actually, the *gopīs* did not care for Varuṇa or any other demigod; they only wanted to satisfy Kṛṣṇa. Kṛṣṇa became very ingratiated and satisfied by the simple dealings of the *gopīs,* and He immediately delivered their respective garments, one after another. Although Kṛṣṇa cheated the young unmarried *gopīs* and made them stand naked before Him and enjoyed joking words with them, and although He treated them just like dolls and stole their garments, they were still pleased with Him and never lodged complaints against Him. This attitude of the *gopīs* is described by Lord Caitanya Mahāprabhu when He prays, "My dear Lord Kṛṣṇa, You may embrace me or trample me under Your feet, or You may make me brokenhearted by never being present before me. Whatever You like, You can do, because You have complete freedom to act. But in spite of all Your dealings, You are my Lord eternally, and I have no other worshipable object." This is the attitude of the *gopīs* toward Kṛṣṇa.

Lord Kṛṣṇa was pleased with them, and since they all desired to have Him as their husband, He told them, "My dear well-behaved girls, I know of your desire for Me and why you worship goddess Kātyāyanī, and I completely approve of your action. Anyone whose full consciousness is always absorbed in Me, even if in lust, is elevated. As a fried seed cannot fructify, so any desire in connection with My loving service cannot produce any fruitive result, as in ordinary *karma.*"

There is a statement in the *Brahma-saṁhitā: karmāṇi nirdahati kintu ca bhakti-bhājām.* Everyone is bound by his fruitive activities, but the devotees, because they work completely for the satisfaction of the Lord, suffer no reactions. Similarly, the *gopīs'* attitude toward Kṛṣṇa, although seemingly lusty, should not be considered to be like the lusty desires of ordinary women. The reason is explained by Kṛṣṇa Himself. Activities in devotional service to Kṛṣṇa are transcendental to any fruitive result.

"My dear *gopīs,*" Kṛṣṇa continued, "your desire to have Me as your husband will be fulfilled because with this desire you have worshiped goddess Kātyāyanī. I promise you that during the next autumn season you shall be able to meet with Me, and you shall enjoy Me as your husband."

Taking shelter of the shade of the trees, Kṛṣṇa became very happy. While walking He began to address the inhabitants of Vṛndāvana. "My dear Stokakṛṣṇa, My dear Varūthapa, My dear Bhadrasena, My dear Sudāmā, My dear Subala, My dear Arjuna, My dear Viśāla, My dear Ṛṣabha—just look at these most fortunate trees of Vṛndāvana. They have dedicated their lives to the welfare of others. Individually they are tolerating all kinds of natural disturbances, such as hurricanes, torrents of rain, scorching heat and piercing cold, but they are very careful to relieve our fatigues and give us shelter. My dear friends, I think they are glorified in this birth as trees. They are so careful to give shelter to others that they are like noble, highly elevated charitable men who never deny charity to one who approaches them. No one is denied shelter by these trees. They supply various kinds of facilities to human society, such as leaves, flowers, fruit, shade, roots, bark, flavor extracts and fuel. They are the perfect example of noble life. They are like a noble person who has sacrificed everything possible—his body, mind, activities, intelligence and words—in engaging in the welfare of all living entities."

Thus the Supreme Personality of Godhead walked on the bank of the Yamunā, touching the leaves of the trees and their fruits, flowers and twigs, and praising their glorious welfare activities. Different people may accept certain welfare activities to be beneficial for human society, according to their own views, but the welfare activity that can be rendered to people in general, for eternal benefit, is the spreading of the Kṛṣṇa consciousness movement. Everyone should be prepared to propagate this movement. As instructed by Lord Caitanya, one should be humbler than the grass on the ground and more tolerant than the tree. The tolerance of the trees is explained by Lord Kṛṣṇa Himself, and those who are engaged in the preaching of Kṛṣṇa consciousness should learn lessons from the teachings of Lord Kṛṣṇa and Lord Caitanya through Their direct disciplic succession.

While passing through the forest of Vṛndāvana on the bank of the Yamunā, Kṛṣṇa sat down at a beautiful spot and allowed the cows to drink the cold and transparent water of the Yamunā. Being fatigued, the cowherd boys, Kṛṣṇa and Balarāma also drank. After seeing the young *gopīs* taking bath in the Yamunā, Kṛṣṇa passed the rest of the morning with the boys.

*Thus ends the Bhaktivedanta purport of the Twenty-second Chapter of* Kṛṣṇa, *"Stealing the Garments of the Unmarried Gopī Girls."*

# 23 / Delivering the Wives of the Brāhmaṇas Who Performed Sacrifices

The morning passed, and the cowherd boys were very hungry because they had not eaten breakfast. They immediately approached Kṛṣṇa and Balarāma and said, "Dear Kṛṣṇa and Balarāma, You are both all-powerful; You can kill many, many demons, but today we are much afflicted with hunger, and this is disturbing us. Please arrange for something that will mitigate our hunger."

Requested in this way by Their friends, Lord Kṛṣṇa and Balarāma immediately showed compassion on certain wives of *brāhmaṇas* who were performing sacrifices. These wives were great devotees of the Lord, and Kṛṣṇa took this opportunity to bless them. He said, "My dear friends, please go to the house of the *brāhmaṇas* nearby. They are now engaged in performing Vedic sacrifices known as *āṅgirasa,* for they desire elevation to heavenly planets. All of you please go to them." Then Lord Kṛṣṇa warned His friends, "These *brāhmaṇas* are not Vaiṣṇavas. They cannot even chant Our names, Kṛṣṇa and Balarāma. They are very busy in chanting the Vedic hymns, although the purpose of Vedic knowledge is to find Me. But because they are not attracted by the names of Kṛṣṇa and Balarāma, you had better not ask them for anything in My name. Better ask for some charity in the name of Balarāma."

Charity is generally given to high class *brāhmaṇas,* but Kṛṣṇa and Balarāma did not appear in a *brāhmaṇa* family. Balarāma was known as the son of Vasudeva, a *kṣatriya,* and Kṛṣṇa was known in Vṛndāvana as the son of Nanda Mahārāja, who was a *vaiśya.* Neither belonged to the *brāhmaṇa* community. Therefore, Kṛṣṇa considered that the *brāhmaṇas* engaged in performing sacrifices might not be induced to give charity to a *kṣatriya* and *vaiśya.* "But at least if you utter the name of Balarāma, they may prefer to give in charity to a *kṣatriya,* rather than to Me, because I am only a *vaiśya.*"

Being thus ordered by the Supreme Personality of Godhead, all the boys went to the *brāhmaṇas* and began to ask for some charity. They approached them with folded hands and fell down on the ground to offer respect. "O earthly gods, kindly hear us who are ordered by Lord Kṛṣṇa and Balarāma. We hope you know Them both very well, and we wish you all good fortune. Kṛṣṇa and Balarāma are tending cows nearby, and we have accompanied Them. We have come to ask for some food from you. You are all *brāhmaṇas* and knowers of religious principles, and if you think that you should give us charity, then give us some food and we shall all eat along with Kṛṣṇa and Balarāma. You are the most respectable *brāhmaṇas* within the human society, and you are expected to know all the principles of religious procedure."

Although the boys were village boys and were not expected to be learned in all the Vedic principles of religious ritual, they hinted that because of their association with Kṛṣṇa and Balarāma, they knew all those principles. When the Supreme Personality of Godhead Kṛṣṇa and Balarāma asked for food, the boys would immediately deliver it without hesitation because it is stated in the *Bhagavad-gītā* that one should perform *yajña* (sacrifices) only for the satisfaction of Viṣṇu.

The boys continued, "Lord Viṣṇu as Kṛṣṇa and Balarāma is standing waiting, and you should immediately deliver whatever food you have in your stock." They also explained to the *brāhmaṇas* how foodstuffs are to be accepted. Generally, the Vaiṣṇavas, or pure devotees of the Lord, do not take part in ordinary sacrificial performances. But they know very well the ceremonials called *dīkṣā paśusamtha sautrāmnya.* One is permitted to take food after the procedure of *dīkṣā* and before the animal sacrificial ceremony and the *Sautrāmaṇi*, or ceremony in which liquors are also offered. The boys said, "We can take your food at the present stage of your ceremony, for now it will not be prohibitory. So you can deliver us the foodstuff."

Although the companions of Lord Kṛṣṇa and Balarāma were simple cowherd boys, they were in a position to dictate even to the high class *brāhmaṇas* engaged in the Vedic rituals of sacrifices. But the *smārta brāhmaṇas,* who were simply sacrificial-minded, could not understand the dictation of the transcendental devotees of the Lord. They could not even appreciate the begging of the Supreme Lord, Kṛṣṇa and Balarāma. Although they heard all the arguments on behalf of Kṛṣṇa and Balarāma, they did not care for them, and they refused to speak to the boys. Despite being highly elevated in the knowledge of Vedic sacrificial rites, all such nondevotee *brāhmanas*, although they think of themselves as very highly elevated, are ignorant, foolish persons. All their activities are useless because they do not know the purpose of the *Vedas,* as it is explained in the *Bhagavad-gītā*: to understand Kṛṣṇa. In spite of their advancement in Vedic knowledge and rituals, they do not understand Kṛṣṇa; therefore their knowledge of the *Vedas* is superficial. Lord Caitanya, therefore, gave His valuable opinion that a person does not have to be born in a *brāhmaṇa* family; if he knows Kṛṣṇa or the science of Kṛṣṇa consciousness, he is more than a *brāhmaṇa,* and he is quite fit to become spiritual master.

There are various details to be observed in the performance of sacrifices, and they are known collectively as *deśa.* They are as follows: *kāla* means the time, *pṛthak dravya,* the different detailed paraphernalia, *mantra,* hymns, *tantra,* scriptural evidences, *agni,* fire, *ṛtvij,* learned performers of sacrifices, *devatā,* the demigods, *vajamāna,* the performer of the sacrifices, *kratu,* the sacrifice itself, and *dharma,* the procedures. All these are for satisfying Kṛṣṇa. It is confirmed that He is the actual enjoyer of all sacrifices because He is directly the Supreme Personality of Godhead and the Supreme Absolute Truth, beyond the conception or speculation of material senses. He is present just like an ordinary human boy. But for persons who identify themselves with this body, it is very difficult to understand Him. The *brāhmaṇas* were very interested in the comforts of this material body and in elevation to the higher planetary residences called *svarga-vāsa.* They were therefore completely unable to understand the position of Kṛṣṇa.

When the boys saw that the *brāhmaṇas* would not speak to them, they became very disappointed. They then returned to Lord Kṛṣṇa and Balarāma and explained everything that had happened. After hearing their statements, the Supreme Personality began to smile. He told them that they should not be sorry for being refused by the *brāhmaṇas* because that is the way of begging. He convinced them that while one is engaged in collecting or begging, one should not think that he will be successful everywhere. He may be unsuccessful in some places, but that should not be cause for disappointment. Lord Kṛṣṇa then asked all the boys to go again, but this time to the wives of those *brāhmaṇas* engaged in sacrifices. He also informed them that these wives were great devotees. "They are always absorbed in thinking of Us. Go there and ask for some food in My name and the name of Balarāma, and I am sure that they will deliver you as much food as you desire."

Carrying out Kṛṣṇa's order, the boys immediately went to the wives of the *brāhmaṇas.* They found the wives sitting inside their house. They were very beautifully decorated with ornaments. After offering them all respectful obeisances, the boys said, "Dear mothers, please accept our humble obeisances and hear our statement. May we inform you that Lord Kṛṣṇa and Balarāma are nearby. They have come here with the cows, and you may know also that we have come here under Their instructions. All of us are very hungry; therefore, we have come to you for some food. Please give us something to eat for Kṛṣṇa, Balarāma and ourselves."

Immediately upon hearing this, the wives of the *brāhmaṇas* became anxious for Kṛṣṇa and Balarāma. These reactions were spontaneous. They did not have to be convinced of the importance of Kṛṣṇa and Balarāma; immediately upon hearing Their names, they became very anxious to see Them. Being advanced by thinking of Kṛṣṇa constantly, they were performing the greatest form of mystic meditation. All the wives then became very busily engaged in filling up different pots with nice foodstuff. Due to the performance of the sacrifice, the various food was all very palatable. After collecting a feast, they prepared to go to Kṛṣṇa, their most lovable object, exactly in the way rivers flow to the sea.

For a long time the wives had been anxious to see Kṛṣṇa. However, when they were preparing to leave home to go see Him, their husbands, fathers, sons and relatives asked them not to go. But the wives did not comply. When a devotee is called by the attraction of Kṛṣṇa, he does not care for bodily ties. The women entered the forest of Vṛndāvana on the bank of the Yamunā, which was verdant with vegetation and newly grown vines and flowers. Within that forest, they saw Kṛṣṇa and Balarāma engaged in tending the cows, along with Their very affectionate boy friends.

The *brāhmaṇas'* wives saw Kṛṣṇa putting on a garment glittering like gold. He wore a nice garland of forest flowers and a peacock feather on His head. He was also painted with the minerals found in Vṛndāvana, and He looked exactly like a dancing actor on a theatrical stage. They saw Him keeping one hand on the shoulder of His friend, and in His other hand, He was holding a lotus flower. His ears were decorated with lilies, He wore marks of *tilaka,* and He was smiling charmingly. With their very eyes, the wives of the *brāhmaṇas* saw the Supreme Personality of Godhead, of whom they had heard so much, who was so dear to them, and in whom their minds were always absorbed. Now they saw Him eye to eye and face to face, and Kṛṣṇa entered within their hearts through their eyes.

They began to embrace Kṛṣṇa to their hearts' content, and the distress of separation was mitigated immediately. They were just like great sages who, by their advancement of knowledge, merge into the existence of the Supreme. As the Supersoul living in everyone's heart, Lord Kṛṣṇa could understand their minds; they had come to Him despite all the protests of their relatives, fathers, husbands, brothers, and all the duties of household affairs. They came just to see Him who was their life and soul. They were actually following Kṛṣṇa's instruction in the *Bhagavad-gītā:* one should surrender to Him, giving up all varieties of occupational and religious duties. The wives of the *brāhmaṇas* actually carried out the instruction of the *Bhagavad-gītā* in total. He therefore began to speak to them, smiling very magnificently. It should be noted in this connection that when Kṛṣṇa entered into the wives' hearts and when they embraced Him and felt the transcendental bliss of being merged with Him, the Supreme Lord Kṛṣṇa did not lose His identity, nor did the individual wives lose theirs. The individuality of both the Lord and the wives remained, yet they felt oneness in existence. When a lover submits to his lover without any pinch of personal consideration, that is called oneness. Lord Caitanya has taught us this feeling of oneness in His *Śikṣāṣṭaka:* Kṛṣṇa may act freely, doing whatever He likes, but the devotee should always be in oneness or in agreement with His desires. That oneness was exhibited by the wives of the *brāhmaṇas* in their love for Kṛṣṇa.

Kṛṣṇa welcomed them with the following words: "My dear wives of the *brāhmaṇas,* you are all very fortunate and welcomed here. Please let Me know what I can do for you. Your coming here, neglecting all the restrictions and hindrances of relatives, fathers, brothers and husbands, in order to see Me, is completely befitting. One who does this actually knows his self interest, because rendering transcendental loving service unto Me, without motive or restriction, is actually auspicious for the living entities."

Lord Kṛṣṇa here confirms that the highest perfectional stage of the conditional soul is surrender to Him. One must give up all other responsibilities. This complete surrender unto the Supreme Personality of Godhead is the most auspicious path for the conditioned soul because the Supreme Lord is the supreme objective of love. Everyone is loving Kṛṣṇa ultimately, but realization is according to the advancement of his knowledge. One comes to understand that his self is the spirit soul, and the spirit soul is nothing but a part and parcel of the Supreme Lord; therefore the Supreme Lord is the ultimate goal of love, and thus one should surrender unto Him. This surrender is considered auspicious for the conditioned soul. Our life, property, home, wife, children, house, country, society and all paraphernalia which are very dear to us are expansions of the Supreme Personality of Godhead. He is the central object of love because He gives us all bliss, expanding Himself in so many ways according to our different situations, namely bodily, mental or spiritual.

"My dear wives of the *brāhmaṇas,"* Kṛṣṇa said. "You can now return to your homes. Engage yourselves in sacrificial activities and be engaged in the service of your husbands and household affairs so that your husbands will be pleased with you, and the sacrifice which they have begun will be properly executed. After all, your husbands are householders, and without your help how can they execute their prescribed duties?"

The wives of the *brāhmaṇas* replied, "Dear Lord, this sort of instruction does not befit You. Your eternal promise is that You will always protect Your devotees, and now You must fulfill this promise. Anyone who comes and surrenders unto You never goes back to the conditioned life of material existence. We expect that You will now fulfill Your promise. We have surrendered unto Your lotus feet, which are covered by the *tulasī* leaves, so we have no more desire to return to the company of our so-called relatives, friends, and society and give up the shelter of Your lotus feet. And what shall we do, returning home? Our husbands, brothers, fathers, sons, mothers and our friends do not expect to see us because we have already left them all. Therefore we have no shelter to return to. Please, therefore, do not ask us to return home, but arrange for our stay under Your lotus feet so that we can eternally live under Your protection."

The Supreme Personality of Godhead replied, "My dear wives, rest assured that your husbands will not neglect you on your return, nor will your brothers, sons, or fathers refuse to accept you. Because you are My pure devotees, not only your relatives but also people in general, as well as the demigods, will be satisfied with you." Kṛṣṇa is situated as the Supersoul in everyone's heart. So if someone becomes a pure devotee of Lord Kṛṣṇa, he immediately becomes pleasing to everyone. The pure devotee of Lord Kṛṣṇa is never inimical to anyone. A sane person cannot be an enemy of a pure devotee. "Transcendental love for Me does not depend upon bodily connection," Kṛṣṇa said further, "but anyone whose mind is always absorbed in Me will surely, very soon, come to Me for My eternal association."

After being instructed by the Supreme Personality of Godhead, all the wives again returned home to their respective husbands. Pleased to see their wives back home, the *brāhmaṇas* executed the performances of sacrifices by sitting together, as it is enjoined in the *śāstras*. According to Vedic principle, religious rituals must be executed by the husband and wife together. When the *brāhmaṇas'* wives returned, the sacrifice was duly and nicely executed. One of the *brāhmaṇas'* wives, however, who was forcibly checked from going to see Kṛṣṇa, began to remember Him as she heard of His bodily features. Being completely absorbed in His thought, she gave up her material body conditioned by the laws of nature.

Śrī Govinda, the ever-joyful Personality of Godhead, revealed His transcendental pastimes, appearing just like an ordinary human being, and enjoyed the food offered by the wives of the *brāhmaṇas.* In this way, He attracted common persons to Kṛṣṇa consciousness. He attracted to His words and beauty all the cows, cowherd boys and damsels in Vṛndāvana.

After the return of their wives from Kṛṣṇa, the *brāhmaṇas* engaged in the performance of sacrifices began to regret their sinful activities in refusing food to the Supreme Personality of Godhead. They could finally understand their mistake; engaged in the performance of Vedic rituals, they had neglected the Supreme Personality of Godhead who had appeared just like an ordinary human being and asked for some food. They began to condemn themselves after seeing the faith and devotion of their wives. They regretted very much that, although their wives were elevated to the platform of pure devotional service, they themselves could not understand even a little bit of how to love and offer transcendental loving service to the Supreme Soul. They began to talk among themselves. "To hell with our being born *brāhmaṇas!* To hell with our learning all Vedic literatures! To hell with our performing great sacrifices and observing all the rules and regulations! To hell with our family! To hell with our expert service in performing the rituals exactly to the description of scriptures! To hell with it all, for we have not developed transcendental loving service to the Supreme Personality of Godhead, who is beyond the speculation of the mind, body and senses."

The learned *brāhmaṇas,* expert in Vedic ritualistic performances, were properly regretful, because without developing Kṛṣṇa consciousness, all discharge of religious duties is simply a waste of time and energy. They continued to talk among themselves; "The external energy of Kṛṣṇa is so strong that it can create illusion to overcome even the greatest mystic *yogī.* Although we expert *brāhmaṇas* are considered to be the teachers of all other sections of human society, we also have been illusioned by the external energy. Just see how fortunate these women are who have so devotedly dedicated their lives to the Supreme Personality of Godhead, Kṛṣṇa. They could easily give up their family connection, which is so difficult to do. Family life is just like a dark well for the continuation of material miseries."

Women in general, being very simple in heart, can very easily take to Kṛṣṇa consciousness, and when they develop love of Kṛṣṇa they can easily get liberation from the clutches of *māyā,* which is very difficult for even so-called intelligent and learned men to surpass. According to Vedic injunction, women are not allowed to undergo the purificatory process of initiation by the sacred thread, nor are they allowed to live as *brahmacāriṇī* in the *āśrama* of the spiritual master; nor are they advised to undergo the strict disciplinary procedure; nor are they very much expert in discussing philosophy or self-realization. And by nature they are not very pure; nor are they very much attached to auspicious activities. "But how wonderful it is that they have developed transcendental love for Kṛṣṇa, the Lord of all mystic *yogīs!*" the *brāhmaṇas* exclaimed. "They have surpassed all of us in firm faith and devotion unto Kṛṣṇa. Being too attached to the materialistic way of life, although we are considered to be masters in all purificatory processes, we did not actually know what the goal is. Even though we were reminded of Kṛṣṇa and Balarāma by the cowherd boys, we disregarded Them. We think now that it was simply a trick of mercy upon us by the Supreme Personality of Godhead that He sent His friends to beg foodstuff from us. Otherwise, He had no need to send them. He could have satisfied their hunger then and there just by willing to do so."

If someone denies Kṛṣṇa's self-sufficiency on hearing that He was tending the cows for livelihood, or if someone doubts His not being in need of the foodstuff, thinking that He was actually hungry, then one should understand that the goddess of fortune is always engaged in His service. In this way the goddess can break her faulty habit of restlessness. In Vedic literatures like *Brahma-saṁhitā* it is stated that Kṛṣṇa is served in His abode with great respect by not only one goddess of fortune but many thousands. Therefore it is simply illusion for one to think that Kṛṣṇa begged food from the *brāhmaṇas.* It was actually a trick to show them the mercy of accepting Him in pure devotional service. The Vedic ceremonial paraphernalia, the suitable place, suitable time, different grades of articles for performing ritualistic ceremonies, the Vedic hymns, the priest who is able to perform such sacrifice, the fire and the demigods, the performer of the sacrifice and the religious principles are all meant for understanding Kṛṣṇa, for Kṛṣṇa is the Supreme Personality of Godhead. He is the Supreme Lord Viṣṇu, and the Lord of all mystic *yogīs.*

"Because He has appeared as a child in the dynasty of the Yadus, we were so foolish that we could not understand that He is the Supreme Personality of Godhead," the *brāhmaṇas* said. "But on the other hand, we are very proud because we have such exalted wives who have developed pure transcendental service of the Lord without being shackled by our rigid position. Let us therefore offer our respectful obeisances unto the lotus feet of Lord Kṛṣṇa, under whose illusory energy, called *māyā,* we are absorbed in fruitive activities. We therefore pray to the Lord to be kind enough to excuse us because we are simply captivated by His external energy. We transgressed His order without knowing His transcendental glories."

The *brāhmaṇas* repented for their sinful activities. They wanted to go personally to offer their obeisances unto Him, but being afraid of Kaṁsa, they could not go. In other words, it is very difficult for one to surrender fully unto the Personality of Godhead without being purified by devotional service. The example of the learned *brāhmaṇas* and their wives is vivid. The wives of the *brāhmaṇas*, because they were infused by pure devotional service, did not care for any kind of opposition. They immediately went to Kṛṣṇa. But although the *brāhmaṇas* had come to know the supremacy of the Lord and were repenting, they were still afraid of King Kaṁsa because they were too addicted to fruitive activities.

*Thus ends the Bhaktivedanta purport of the Twenty-third Chapter of* Kṛṣṇa, *"Delivering the Wives of the Brāhmaṇas Who Performed Sacrifices."*

# 24 / Worshiping Govardhana Hill

While engaged with the *brāhmaṇas* who were too involved in the performance of Vedic sacrifices, Kṛṣṇa and Balarāma also saw that the cowherd men were preparing a similar sacrifice in order to pacify Indra, the King of heaven, who is responsible for supplying water. As stated in the *Caitanya-caritāmṛta,* a devotee of Kṛṣṇa has strong and firm faith in the understanding that if he is simply engaged in Kṛṣṇa consciousness and Kṛṣṇa's transcendental loving service, then he is freed from all other obligations. A pure devotee of Lord Kṛṣṇa doesn't have to perform any of the ritualistic functions enjoined in the *Vedas*; nor is he required to worship any demigods. Being a devotee of Lord Kṛṣṇa, one is understood to have performed all kinds of Vedic rituals and all kinds of worship to the demigods. Just by performing the Vedic ritualistic ceremonies or worshiping the demigods, one does not develop devotional service for Kṛṣṇa. But one who is engaged fully in the service of the Lord has already finished all Vedic injunctions.

Kṛṣṇa ordered a stop to all such activities by His devotees, for He wanted to firmly establish exclusive devotional service during His presence in Vṛndāvana. Kṛṣṇa knew that the cowherd men were preparing for the Indra sacrifice because He is the omniscient Personality of Godhead, but as a matter of etiquette, he began to inquire with great honor and submission from elder personalities like Mahārāja Nanda and others.

Kṛṣṇa asked His father, "My dear father, what is this arrangement going on for a great sacrifice? What is the result of such sacrifice, and for whom is it meant? How is it performed? Will you kindly let Me know? I am very anxious to know this procedure, so please explain to Me the purpose of this sacrifice." Upon this inquiry, His father, Nanda Mahārāja, remained silent, thinking that his young boy would not be able to understand the intricacies of performing the *yajña*. Kṛṣṇa, however, persisted: "My dear father, for those who are liberal and saintly, there is no secrecy. They do not think anyone to be a friend or enemy because they are always open to everyone. And even for those who are not so liberal, nothing should be secret for the family members and friends, although secrecy may be maintained for persons who are inimical. Therefore you cannot keep any secrets from Me. All persons are engaged in fruitive activities. Some know what these activities are, and they know the result, and some execute activities without knowing the purpose or the result. A person who acts with full knowledge gets the full result; one who acts without knowledge does not get such a perfect result. Therefore, please let Me know the purpose of the sacrifice which you are going to perform. Is it according to Vedic injunction? Or is it simply a popular ceremony? Kindly let Me know in detail about the sacrifice."

On hearing this inquiry from Kṛṣṇa, Mahārāja Nanda replied, "My dear boy, this ceremonial performance is more or less traditional. Because rainfall is due to the mercy of King Indra and the clouds are his representatives, and because water is so important for our living, we must show some gratitude to the controller of this rainfall, Mahārāja Indra. We are arranging, therefore, to pacify King Indra, because he has very kindly sent us clouds to pour down sufficient quantity of rain for successful agricultural activities. Water is very important; without rainfall we cannot farm or produce grains. We cannot live if there is no rainfall. It is necessary for successful religious ceremonies, economic development, and, ultimately, liberation. Therefore we should not give up the traditional ceremonial function; if one gives it up, being influenced by lust, or greed or fear, then it does not look very good for him."

After hearing this, Kṛṣṇa, the Supreme Personality of Godhead, in the presence of His father and all the cowherd men of Vṛndāvana, spoke in such a way as to make heavenly King Indra very angry. He suggested that they forego the sacrifice. His reasons for discouraging the sacrifice performed to please Indra were twofold. First, as stated in the *Bhagavad-gītā,* there is no need to worship the demigods for any material advancement; all results derived from worshiping the demigods are simply temporary, and only those who are less intelligent are interested with temporary results. Secondly, whatever temporary result one derives from worshiping the demigods is actually granted by the permission of the Supreme Personality of Godhead. It is clearly stated in the *Bhagavad-gītā, mayaiva vihitān hi tān.* Whatever benefit is supposed to be derived from the demigods is actually bestowed by the Supreme Personality of Godhead. Without the permission of the Supreme Personality of Godhead, one cannot bestow any benefit upon others. But sometimes the demigods become puffed up by the influence of material nature; thinking themselves as all in all, they try to forget the supremacy of the Supreme Personality of Godhead. In the *Śrīmad-Bhāgavatam,* it is clearly stated that in this instance Kṛṣṇa wanted to make King Indra angry. Kṛṣṇa's advent was especially meant for the annihilation of the demons and protection of the devotees. King Indra was certainly a devotee, not a demon, but because he was puffed up, Kṛṣṇa wanted to teach him a lesson. He first tried to make Indra angry by stopping the Indra Pūjā which was arranged by the cowherd men in Vṛndāvana.

With this purpose in mind, Kṛṣṇa began to talk as if He were an atheist supporting the philosophy of *karma-mīmāṁsā.* Advocates of this type of philosophy do not accept the supreme authority of the Personality of Godhead. They put forward the argument that if anyone works nicely, the result is sure to come. Their opinion is that even if there is a God who gives man the result of his fruitive activities, there is no need to worship Him because unless man works He cannot bestow any good result. They say that instead of worshiping a demigod or God, people should give attention to their own duties, and thus the good result will surely come. Lord Kṛṣṇa began to speak to His father according to these principles of the *karma-mīmāṁsā* philosophy. "My dear father," He said, "I don't think you need to worship any demigod for the successful performance of your agricultural activities. Every living being is born according to his past *karma* and leaves this life simply taking the result of his present *karma.* Everyone is born in different types or species of life according to his past activities, and he gets his next birth according to the activities of this life. Different grades of material happiness and distress, comforts and disadvantages of life, are different results of different kinds of activities, either from the past or present life."

Mahārāja Nanda and other elderly members argued that without satisfying the predominating god, one cannot derive any good result simply by material activities. This is actually the fact. For example, it is sometimes found that, in spite of first-class medical help and treatment by a first-class physician, a diseased person dies. It is concluded, therefore, that first-class medical treatment or the attempts of a first-class physician are not in themselves the cause for curing a patient; there must be the hand of the Supreme Personality of Godhead. Similarly, a father's and mother's taking care of their children is not the cause of the children's comfort. Sometimes it is found that in spite of all care by the parents, the children go bad or succumb to death. Therefore material causes are not sufficient for results.

There must be the sanction of the Supreme Personality of Godhead. Nanda Mahārāja therefore advocated that, in order to get good results for agricultural activities, they must satisfy Indra, the superintending deity of the rain supply. Lord Kṛṣṇa nullified this argument, saying that the demigods give results only to persons who have executed their prescribed duties. The demigods cannot give any good results to the person who has not executed the prescribed duties; therefore demigods are dependent on the execution of duties and are not absolute in awarding good results to anyone.

"My dear father, there is no need to worship the demigod Indra," Lord Kṛṣṇa said. "Everyone has to achieve the result of his own work. We can actually see that one becomes busy according to the natural tendency of his work; and according to that natural tendency, all living entities—either human beings or demigods—achieve their respective results. All living entities achieve higher or lower bodies and create enemies, friends or neutral parties only because of their different kinds of work. One should be careful to discharge duties according to his natural instinct and not divert attention to the worship of various demigods. The demigods will be satisfied by proper execution of all duties, so there is no need to worship them. Let us, rather, perform our prescribed duties very nicely. Actually one cannot be happy without executing his proper prescribed duty. One who does not, therefore, properly discharge his prescribed duties, is compared with an unchaste woman. The proper prescribed duty of the *brāhmaṇas* is the study of the *Vedas;* the proper duty of the royal order, the *kṣatriyas,* is engagement in protecting the citizens; the proper duty of the *vaiśya* community is agriculture, trade and protection of the cows; and the proper duty of the *śūdras* is service to the higher classes, namely the *brāhmaṇas, kṣatriyas,* and *vaiśyas.* We belong to the *vaiśya* community, and our proper duty is to farm, or to trade with the agricultural produce, to protect cows, or take to banking."

Kṛṣṇa identified Himself with the *vaiśya* community because Nanda Mahārāja was protecting many cows, and Kṛṣṇa was taking care of them. He enumerated four kinds of business engagements for the *vaiśya* community, namely agriculture, trade, protection of cows and banking. Although the *vaiśyas* can take to any of these occupations, the men of Vṛndāvana were engaged primarily in the protection of cows.

Kṛṣṇa further explained to His father: "This cosmic manifestation is going on under the influence of three modes of material nature—goodness, passion, and ignorance. These three modes are the causes of creation, maintenance, and destruction. The cloud is caused by the action of the mode of passion; therefore it is the mode of passion which causes the rainfall. And after the rainfall, the living entities derive the result—success in agricultural work. What, then, has Indra to do in this affair? Even if you do not please Indra, what can he do? We do not derive any special benefit from Indra. Even if he is there, he pours water on the ocean also, where there is no need of water. So he is pouring water on the ocean or on the land; it does not depend on our worshiping him. As far as we are concerned, we do not need to go to another city or village or foreign country. There are palatial buildings in the cities, but we are satisfied living in this forest of Vṛndāvana. Our specific relationship is with Govardhana Hill and Vṛndāvana forest and nothing more. I therefore request you, My dear father, to begin a sacrifice which will satisfy the local *brāhmaṇas* and Govardhana Hill, and let us have nothing to do with Indra."

After hearing this statement by Kṛṣṇa, Nanda Mahārāja replied, "My dear boy, since You are asking, I shall arrange for a separate sacrifice for the local *brāhmaṇas* and Govardhana Hill. But for the present let me execute this sacrifice known as *Indra-yajña.*"

But Kṛṣṇa replied, "My dear father, don't delay. The sacrifice you propose for Govardhana and the local *brāhmaṇas* will take much time. Better take the arrangement and paraphernalia you have already made for sacrificing Indra-yajña and immediately engage it to satisfy Govardhana Hill and the local *brāhmaṇas.*"

Mahārāja Nanda finally relented. The cowherd men then inquired from Kṛṣṇa how He wanted the *yajña* performed, and Kṛṣṇa gave them the following directions. "Prepare very nice foodstuffs of all descriptions from the grains and ghee collected for the *yajña.* Prepare rice, dahl, then halavah, *pākorā, puri* and all kinds of milk preparations like sweet rice, sweetballs, *sandeśa, rasagullā* and *lāḍḍu* and invite the learned *brāhmaṇas* who can chant the Vedic hymns and offer oblations to the fire. The *brāhmaṇas* should be given all kinds of grains in charity. Then decorate all the cows and feed them well. After performing this, give money in charity to the *brāhmaṇas.* As far as the lower animals are concerned, such as the dogs, and the lower grades of people, such as the *cāṇḍālas,* or the fifth class of men who are considered untouchable, they also may be given sumptuous *prasādam.* After giving nice grasses to the cows, the sacrifice known as *Govardhana Pūjā* may immediately begin. This sacrifice will very much satisfy Me."

In this statement, Lord Kṛṣṇa practically described the whole economy of the *vaiśya* community. In all communities of human society, and in the animal kingdom, among the cows, dogs, goats, etc., everyone has his part to play. Each is to work in cooperation for the total benefit of all society, which includes not only animate objects but also inanimate objects like hills and land. The *vaiśya* community is specifically responsible for the economic improvement of the society by producing grains, by giving protection to the cows, by transporting food when needed, and by banking and finance.

From this statement we learn also that the cats and dogs, although not so important, are not to be neglected. Cow protection is actually more important than protection of cats and dogs. Another hint we get from this statement is that the *cāṇḍālas* or the untouchables are also not to be neglected by the higher classes. Everyone is important, but some are directly responsible for the advancement of human society, and some are only indirectly responsible. However, when Kṛṣṇa consciousness is there, then everyone's total benefit is taken care of.

The sacrifice known as Govardhana Pūjā is observed in the Kṛṣṇa consciousness movement. Lord Caitanya has recommended that since Kṛṣṇa is worshipable, so His land, Vṛndāvana and Govardhana Hill, are also worshipable. To confirm this statement, Lord Kṛṣṇa said that Govardhana Pūjā is as good as worship of Him. From that day, the Govardhana Pūjā has been still going on and is known as *Annakūṭa.* In all the temples of Vṛndāvana or outside of Vṛndāvana, huge quantities of food are prepared in this ceremony and are very sumptuously distributed to the general population. Sometimes the food is thrown to the crowds, and they enjoy collecting it off the ground. From these instances, we can understand that *prasādam* offered to Kṛṣṇa never becomes polluted or contaminated, even if it is thrown on the ground. The people, therefore, collect it and eat with great satisfaction.

The Supreme Personality of Godhead, Kṛṣṇa, therefore advised the cowherd men to stop the Indra-yajña and begin the Govardhana Pūjā in order to chastise Indra who was very much puffed up at being the supreme controller of the heavenly planets. The honest and simple cowherd men headed by Nanda Mahārāja accepted Kṛṣṇa's proposal and executed in detail everything He advised. They performed Govardhana worship and circumambulation of the hill. (Following the inauguration of Govardhana Pūjā, people in Vṛndāvana still dress nicely and assemble near Govardhana Hill to offer worship and circumambulate the hill, leading their cows all around.) According to the instruction of Lord Kṛṣṇa, Nanda Mahārāja and the cowherd men called in learned *brāhmaṇas* and began to worship Govardhana Hill by chanting Vedic hymns and offering *prasādam.* The inhabitants of Vṛndāvana assembled together, decorated their cows and gave them grass. Keeping the cows in front, they began to circumambulate Govardhana Hill. The *gopīs* also dressed themselves very luxuriantly and sat in bull-driven carts, chanting the glories of Kṛṣṇa's pastimes. Assembled there to act as priests for Govardhana Pūjā, the *brāhmaṇas* offered their blessings to the cowherd men and their wives, the *gopīs*. When everything was complete, Kṛṣṇa assumed a great transcendental form and declared to the inhabitants of Vṛndāvana that He was Himself Govardhana Hill in order to convince the devotees that Govardhana Hill and Kṛṣṇa Himself are identical. Then Kṛṣṇa began to eat all the food offered there. The identity of Kṛṣṇa and Govardhana Hill is still honored, and great devotees take rocks from Govardhana Hill and worship them exactly as they worship the Deity of Kṛṣṇa in the temples. Devotees therefore collect small rocks or pebbles from Govardhana Hill and worship them at home, because this worship is as good as Deity worship. The form of Kṛṣṇa who began to eat the offerings was separately constituted, and Kṛṣṇa Himself along with other inhabitants of Vṛndāvana began to offer obeisances to the Deity as well as Govardhana Hill. In offering obeisances to the huge form of Kṛṣṇa Himself and Govardhana Hill, Kṛṣṇa declared, "Just see how Govardhana Hill has assumed this huge form and is favoring us by accepting all the offerings." Kṛṣṇa also declared at that meeting, "One who neglects the worship of Govardhana Pūjā, as I am personally conducting it, will not be happy. There are many snakes on Govardhana Hill, and persons neglecting the prescribed duty of Govardhana Pūjā will be bitten by these snakes and killed. In order to assure the good fortune of the cows and themselves, all people of Vṛndāvana near Govardhana must worship the hill, as prescribed by Me."

Thus performing the Govardhana Pūjā sacrifice, all the inhabitants of Vṛndāvana followed the instructions of Kṛṣṇa, the son of Vasudeva, and afterwards they returned to their respective homes.

*Thus ends the Bhaktivedanta purport of the Twenty-fourth Chapter of* Kṛṣṇa, *"Worshiping Govardhana Hill."*

# 25 / Devastating Rainfall in Vṛndāvana

When Indra understood that the sacrifice offered by the cowherd men in Vṛndāvana was stopped by Kṛṣṇa, he became angry, and he vented his anger upon the inhabitants of Vṛndāvana, who were headed by Nanda Mahārāja, although Indra knew perfectly well that Kṛṣṇa was personally protecting them. As the director of different kinds of clouds, Indra called for the *sāṁvartaka.* This cloud is invited when there is a need to devastate the whole cosmic manifestation. The *sāṁvartaka* was ordered by Indra to go over Vṛndāvana and inundate the whole area with an extensive flood. Demonically, Indra thought himself to be the all-powerful supreme personality. When demons become very powerful, they defy the supreme controller, Personality of Godhead. Indra, though not a demon, was puffed up by his material position, and he wanted to challenge the supreme controller. He thought himself, at least for the time being, as powerful as Kṛṣṇa. Indra said, "Just see the impudence of the inhabitants of Vṛndāvana! They are simply inhabitants of the forest, but being infatuated with their friend Kṛṣṇa, who is nothing but an ordinary human being, they have dared to defy the demigods."

Kṛṣṇa has declared in the *Bhagavad-gītā* that the worshipers of the demigods are not very intelligent. He has also declared that one has to give up all kinds of worship and simply concentrate on Kṛṣṇa consciousness. Kṛṣṇa's invoking the anger of Indra and later on chastising him is a clear indication to His devotee that those who are engaged in Kṛṣṇa consciousness have no need to worship any demigod, even if it is found that the demigod has become angry. Kṛṣṇa gives His devotees all protection, and they should completely depend on His mercy.

Indra cursed the action of the inhabitants of Vṛndāvana and said, "By defying the authority of the demigods, the inhabitants of Vṛndāvana will suffer in material existence. Having neglected the sacrifice to the demigods, they cannot cross over the impediments of the ocean of material misery." Indra further declared, "These cowherd men in Vṛndāvana have neglected my authority on the advice of this talkative boy who is known as Kṛṣṇa. He is nothing but a child, and by believing this child, they have enraged me." Thus he ordered the *sāṁvartaka* cloud to go and destroy the prosperity of Vṛndāvana. "The men of Vṛndāvana," said Indra, "have become too puffed up over their material opulence and their confidence in the presence of their tiny friend, Kṛṣṇa. He is simply talkative, childish, and unaware of the complete cosmic situation, although He is thinking Himself very advanced in knowledge. Because they have taken Kṛṣṇa so seriously, they must be punished, and so I have ordered the *sāṁvartaka* cloud to go there and inundate the place. They should be destroyed with their cows."

It is indicated here that in the villages or outside the towns, the inhabitants must depend on the cows for their prosperity. When the cows are destroyed, the people are destitute of all kinds of opulences. When King Indra ordered the *sāṁvartaka* and companion clouds to go to Vṛndāvana, the clouds were afraid of the assignment. But King Indra assured them, "You go ahead, and I will also go, riding on my elephant, accompanied by great storms. And I shall apply all my strength to punish the inhabitants of Vṛndāvana."

Ordered by King Indra, all the dangerous clouds appeared above Vṛndavana and began to pour water incessantly, with all their strength and power. There was constant lightning and thunder, blowing of severe wind and incessant falling of rain. The rainfall seemed to fall like piercing sharp arrows. By pouring water as thick as pillars, without cessation, the clouds gradually filled all the lands in Vṛndāvana with water, and there was no visible distinction between higher and lower land. The situation was very dangerous, especially for the animals. The rainfall was accompanied by great winds, and every living creature in Vṛndāvana began to tremble from the severe cold. Unable to find any other source of deliverance, they all approached Govinda to take shelter at His lotus feet. The cows especially, being much aggrieved from the heavy rain, bowed down their heads, and taking their calves underneath their bodies, they approached the Supreme Personality of Godhead to take shelter of His lotus feet. At that time all the inhabitants of Vṛndāvana began to pray to Lord Kṛṣṇa. "Dear Kṛṣṇa," they prayed, "You are all-powerful, and You are very affectionate to Your devotees. Now please protect us who have been much harassed by angry Indra."

Upon hearing their prayer, Kṛṣṇa could also understand that Indra, being bereft of his sacrificial honor, was pouring down rain that was accompanied by heavy pieces of ice and strong winds, although all this was out of season. Kṛṣṇa understood that this was a deliberate exhibition of anger by Indra. He therefore concluded, "This demigod who thinks himself supreme has shown his great power, but I shall answer him according to My position, and I shall teach him that he is not autonomous in managing universal affairs. I am the Supreme Lord over all, and I shall thus take away his false prestige which has risen from his power. The demigods are My devotees, and therefore it is not possible for them to forget My supremacy, but somehow or other he has become puffed up with material power and thus is now maddened. I shall act in such a way to relieve him of this false prestige. I shall give protection to My pure devotees in Vṛndāvana, who are at present completely at My mercy and whom I have taken completely under My protection. I will save them by My mystic power."

Thinking in this way, Lord Kṛṣṇa immediately picked up Govardhana Hill with one hand, exactly as a child picks up a mushroom from the ground. Thus He exhibited His transcendental pastime of lifting Govardhana Hill. Lord Kṛṣṇa then began to address His devotees, "My dear brothers, My dear father, My dear inhabitants of Vṛndāvana, you can now safely enter under the umbrella of Govardhana Hill, which I have just lifted. Do not be afraid of the hill and think that it will fall from My hand. You have been too much afflicted from the heavy rain and strong wind; therefore I have lifted this hill, which will protect you exactly like a huge umbrella. I think this is a proper arrangement to relieve you from your immediate distress. Be happy along with your animals underneath this great umbrella." Being assured by Lord Kṛṣṇa, all the inhabitants of Vṛndāvana entered beneath the great hill and appeared to be safe along with their property and animals.

The inhabitants of Vṛndāvana and their animals remained there for one week without being disturbed by hunger, thirst or any other discomforts. They were simply astonished to see how Kṛṣṇa was holding up the mountain with the little finger of His left hand. Seeing the extraordinary mystic power of Kṛṣṇa, Indra, the King of heaven, was thunderstruck and baffled in his determination. He immediately called for all the clouds and asked them to desist. When the sky became completely cleared of all clouds and there was sunrise again, the strong winds stopped. At that time Kṛṣṇa, the Supreme Personality of Godhead, known now as the lifter of Govardhana Hill, said, "My dear cowherd men, now you can leave and take your wives, children, cows and valuables, because everything is ended. The inundation has gone down, along with the swelling waters of the river."

All the men loaded their valuables on carts and slowly left with their cows and other paraphernalia. After they had cleared out everything, Lord Kṛṣṇa very slowly replaced Govardhana Hill exactly in the same position as it had been before. When everything was done, all the inhabitants of Vṛndāvana approached Kṛṣṇa and embraced Him with great ecstasy. The *gopīs*, being naturally very affectionate to Kṛṣṇa, began to offer Him curd mixed with their tears, and they poured incessant blessings upon Him. Mother Yaśodā, mother Rohiṇī, Nanda, and Balarāma, who is the strongest of the strong, embraced Kṛṣṇa one after another and, from spontaneous feelings of affection, blessed Him over and over again. In the heavens, different demigods from different planetary systems, such as Siddhaloka, Gandharvaloka and Cāraṇaloka, also began to show their complete satisfaction. They poured showers of flowers on the surface of the earth and sounded different conchshells. There was beating of drums, and being inspired by godly feelings, residents of Gandharvaloka began to play on their tambouras to please the Lord. After this incident, the Supreme Personality of Godhead, surrounded by His dear friends and animals, returned to His home. As usual, the *gopīs* began to chant the glorious pastimes of Lord Kṛṣṇa with great feeling, for they were chanting from the heart.

*Thus ends the Bhaktivedanta purport of the Twenty-fifth Chapter of* Kṛṣṇa, *"Devastating Rainfall in Vṛndāvana."*

# 26 / Wonderful Kṛṣṇa

Without understanding the intricacies of Kṛṣṇa, the Supreme Personality of Godhead, and without knowing His uncommon spiritual opulences, the innocent cowherd boys and men of Vṛndāvana began to discuss the wonderful activities of Kṛṣṇa which surpass the activities of all men.

One of them said, "My dear friends, considering His wonderful activities, how is it possible that such an uncommon boy would come and live with us in Vṛndāvana? It is really not possible. Just imagine! He is now only seven years old! How was it possible for Him to lift Govardhana Hill in one hand and hold it up just like the king of elephants holds a lotus flower? To lift a lotus flower is a most insignificant thing for an elephant, and similarly Kṛṣṇa lifted Govardhana Hill without exertion. When He was simply a small baby and could not even see properly, He killed a great demon, Pūtanā. While sucking her breast, He also sucked out her life-air. Kṛṣṇa killed the Pūtanā demon exactly as eternal time kills a living creature in due course. When He was only three months old, He was sleeping underneath a hand-driven cart. Being hungry for His mother's breast, He began to cry and throw His legs upwards. And from the kicking of his small feet the cart immediately broke apart and fell to pieces. When He was only one year old, He was carried away by the Tṛṇāvarta demon disguised as a whirlwind, and although He was taken very high in the sky, He simply hung on the neck of the demon and forced him to fall from the sky and immediately die. Once His mother, being disturbed by His stealing butter, tied Him to a wooden mortar, and the child pushed it towards a pair of trees known as *yamala arjuna* and caused them to fall. Once, when He was engaged in tending the calves in the forest along with His elder brother, Balarāma, a demon named Bakāsura appeared, and Kṛṣṇa at once bifurcated the demon's beaks. When the demon known as Vatsāsura entered among the calves tended by Kṛṣṇa with a desire to kill Him, He immediately detected the demon, killed him, and threw him into a tree. When Kṛṣṇa, along with His brother, Balarāma, entered the Tālavana forest, the demon known as Dhenukāsura, in the shape of an ass, attacked Them and was immediately killed by Balarāma, who caught his hind legs and threw him in a palm tree. Although the Dhenukāsura demon was assisted by his cohorts, also in the shape of asses, all were killed, and the Tālavana forest was then open for the use of the animals and inhabitants of Vṛndāvana. When Pralambāsura entered amongst His cowherd boy friends, He caused his death by Balarāma. Thereafter, Kṛṣṇa saved His friends and cows from the severe forest fire, and He chastised the Kāliya serpent in the lake of Yamunā and forced him to leave the vicinity of the Yamunā River; He thereby made the water of the Yamunā poisonless."

Another one of the friends of Nanda Mahārāja said, "My dear Nanda, we do not know why we are so attracted by your son Kṛṣṇa. We want to forget Him, but this is impossible. Why are we so naturally affectionate toward Him? Just imagine how wonderful it is! On one hand He is only a boy of seven years old, and on the other hand there is a huge hill like Govardhana Hill, and He lifted it so easily! O Nanda Mahārāja, we are now in great doubt—your son Kṛṣṇa must be one of the demigods. He is not at all an ordinary boy. Maybe He is the Supreme Personality of Godhead."

On hearing the praises of the cowherd men in Vṛndāvana, King Nanda said, "My dear friends, in reply to you I can simply present the statement of Gargamuni so that your doubts may be cleared. When he came to perform the name-giving ceremony, he said that this boy descends in different periods of time in different colors and that this time He has appeared in Vṛndāvana in a dark color and is known as Kṛṣṇa. Previously, He has white color, then red color, then yellow color. He also said that this boy was once the son of Vasudeva, and everyone who knows of His previous birth calls Him Vāsudeva. Actually he said that my son has many varieties of names, according to His different qualities and activities. Gargācārya assured me that this boy will be all-auspicious for my family and that He will be able to give transcendental blissful pleasure to all the cowherd men and cows in Vṛndāvana. Even though we will be put into various kinds of difficulties, by the grace of this boy we will be very easily freed from them. He also said that formerly this boy saved the world from an unregulated condition, and He saved all honest men from the hands of the dishonest. He also said that any fortunate man who becomes attached to this boy, Kṛṣṇa, is never vanquished or defeated by his enemy. On the whole, He is exactly like Lord Viṣṇu, who always takes the side of the demigods, who are consequently never defeated by the demons.

Gargācārya thus concluded that my child will grow to be exactly like Viṣṇu in transcendental beauty, qualification, activities, influence and opulence, and so we should not be very astonished by His wonderful activities. After telling me this, Gargācārya returned home, and since then we have been continually seeing the wonderful activities of this child. According to the version of Gargācārya, I consider that He must be Nārāyaṇa Himself, or maybe a plenary portion of Nārāyaṇa."

When all the cowherd men very attentively heard the statements of Gargācārya through Nanda Mahārāja, they better appreciated the wonderful activities of Kṛṣṇa and became very jubilant and satisfied. They began to praise Nanda Mahārāja, because by consulting him their doubts about Kṛṣṇa were cleared. They said, "Let Kṛṣṇa, who is so kind, beautiful and merciful, protect us. When angry Indra sent torrents of rain, accompanied by showers of ice blocks and high wind, He immediately took compassion upon us and saved us and our families, cows and valuable possessions by picking up the Govardhana Hill, just as a child picks up a mushroom. He saved us so wonderfully. May He continue to mercifully glance over us and our cows. May we live peacefully under the protection of wonderful Kṛṣṇa."

*Thus ends the Bhaktivedanta purport of the Twenty-sixth Chapter of* Kṛṣṇa, *"Wonderful Kṛṣṇa."*

# 27 / Prayers by Indra, the King of Heaven

When Kṛṣṇa saved the inhabitants of Vṛndāvana from the wrath of Indra by lifting Govardhana Hill, a *surabhi* cow from Goloka Vṛndāvana, as well as King Indra from the heavenly planet, appeared before Him. Indra, the King of heaven, was conscious of his offence before Kṛṣṇa; therefore he stealthily appeared before Him from a secluded place. He immediately fell down at the lotus feet of Kṛṣṇa, although his own crown was dazzling like sunshine. Indra knew about the exalted position of Kṛṣṇa because Kṛṣṇa is the master of Indra, but he could not believe that Kṛṣṇa could come down and live in Vṛndāvana among the cowherd men. When Kṛṣṇa defied the authority of Indra, Indra became angry because he thought that he was all in all within this universe and that no one was as powerful as he. But after this incident, his false puffed up prestige was destroyed. Being conscious of his subordinate position, he appeared before Kṛṣṇa with folded hands and began to offer the following prayers.

"My dear Lord," Indra said, "being puffed up by my false prestige, I thought that You had offended me by not allowing the cowherd men to perform the Indra-*yajña,* and I thought that You wanted to enjoy the offerings that were arranged for the sacrifice. I thought that in the name of a Govardhana sacrifice, You were taking my share of profit, and therefore I mistook Your position. Now by Your grace I can understand that You are the Supreme Lord, Personality of Godhead, and that You are transcendental to all the material qualities. Your transcendental position is *viśuddha-sattvam,* which is above the platform of the material mode of goodness, and Your transcendental abode is beyond the disturbance of the material qualities. Your name, fame, form, quality and pastimes are all beyond this material nature, and they are never disturbed by the three material modes. Your abode is accessible only for one who undergoes severe austerities and penances and who is completely freed from the onslaught of material qualities like passion and ignorance. If someone thinks that when You come within this material world You accept the modes of material nature, he is mistaken. The webs of the material qualities are never able to touch You, and You certainly do not accept them when You are present within this world. Your Lordship is never conditioned by the laws of material nature.

"My dear Lord, You are the original father of this cosmic manifestation. You are the supreme spiritual master of this cosmic world, and You are the original proprietor of everything. As eternal time, You are competent to chastise offenders. Within this material world there are many fools like myself who consider themselves to be the Supreme Lord or the all in all within the universe. You are so merciful that without punishing their offenses, You devise means so that their false prestige is subdued and they can know that You, and none else, are the Supreme Personality of Godhead.

"My dear Lord, You are the supreme father, the supreme spiritual master and supreme king. Therefore, You have the right to chastise all living entities whenever there is any discrepancy in their behavior. The father, the spiritual master, and the supreme executive officer of the state are always well-wishers of their sons, their students and their citizens respectively. As such, the well-wishers have the right to chastise their dependents. By Your own desire You appear auspiciously on the earth in Your eternal varieties of forms; You come to glorify the earthly planet and specifically to chastise persons who are falsely claiming to be God. In the material world there is regular competition between different types of living entities to become supreme leaders of society, and after being frustrated in achieving the supreme positions of leadership, foolish persons claim to be God, the Supreme Personality. There are many such foolish personalities in this world, like me, but in due course of time, when they come to their senses, they surrender unto You and again engage themselves properly by rendering service unto You. And that is the purpose of Your chastising persons envious of You.

"My dear Lord, I committed a great offense unto Your lotus feet, being falsely proud of my material opulences, not knowing Your unlimited power. Therefore, my Lord, kindly excuse me, because I am fool number one. Kindly give me Your blessings so that I may not act so foolishly again. If You think, my Lord, that the offence is very great and cannot be excused, then I appeal to You that I am Your eternal servant; Your appearance in this world is to give protection to Your eternal servants and to destroy the demons who maintain great military strength just to burden the very existence of the earth. As I am Your eternal servant, kindly excuse me.

"My dear Lord, You are the Supreme Personality of Godhead. I offer my respectful obeisances unto You because You are the Supreme Person and the Supreme Soul. You are the son of Vasudeva, and You are the Supreme Lord, Kṛṣṇa, the master of all pure devotees. Please accept my prostrated obeisances. You are the personification of supreme knowledge. You can appear anywhere according to Your desire in any one of Your eternal forms. You are the root of all creation and the Supreme Soul of all living entities. Due to my gross ignorance, I created great disturbance in Vṛndāvana by sending torrents of rain and heavy hailstorm. I acted out of severe anger caused by Your stopping the sacrifice which was to be held to satisfy me. But my dear Lord, You are so kind to me that You have bestowed Your mercy upon me by destroying all my false pride. I therefore take shelter unto Your lotus feet. My dear Lord, You are not only the supreme controller, but also the spiritual master of all living entities."

Thus praised by Indra, Lord Kṛṣṇa, the Supreme Personality of Godhead, smiling beautifully, said, "My dear Indra, I have stopped your sacrifice just to show My causeless mercy and to revive your memory that I am your eternal master. I am not only your master, but I am the master of all the other demigods as well. You should always remember that all your material opulences are due to My mercy. Everyone should always remember that I am the Supreme Lord. I can show anyone My favor, and I can chastise anyone, because no one is superior to Me. If I find someone overpowered by false pride, in order to show him My causeless mercy, I withdraw all his opulences."

It is noteworthy that Kṛṣṇa sometimes removes all opulences in order to facilitate a rich man's becoming a surrendered soul to Him. This is a special favor of the Lord's. Sometimes it is seen that a person is very opulent materially, but due to his devotional service to the Lord, he may be reduced to poverty. One should not think, however, that because he worshiped the Supreme Lord he became poverty-stricken. The real purport is that when a person is a pure devotee, but at the same time, by miscalculation, he wants to lord it over material nature, the Lord shows His special mercy by taking away all material opulences until at last he surrenders unto the Supreme Lord.

After instructing Indra, Lord Kṛṣṇa asked him to return to his kingdom in the heavenly planet and to remember always that he is never the supreme but is always subordinate to the Supreme Personality of Godhead. He also advised him to remain as King of heaven, but to be careful of false pride.

After this, the transcendental *surabhi* cow, who also came with Indra to see Kṛṣṇa, offered her respectful obeisances unto Him and worshiped Him.

The *surabhi* offered her prayer as follows. "My dear Lord Kṛṣṇa, You are the most powerful of all mystic *yogīs* because You are the soul of the complete universe, and from You only all this cosmic manifestation has taken place. Therefore, although Indra tried his best to kill my descendant cows in Vṛndāvana, they remained under Your shelter, and You have protected them all so well. We do not know anyone else as the Supreme, nor do we go to any other god or demigods for protection. Therefore, You are our Indra, You are the Supreme Father of the whole cosmic manifestation, and You are the protector and elevator of all the cows, *brāhmaṇas,* demigods and others who are pure devotees of Your Lordship. O Supersoul of the universe, let us bathe You with our milk because You are our Indra. O Lord, You appear just to diminish the burden of impure activities on the earth."

In this way, Kṛṣṇa was bathed by the milk of the *surabhi* cows, and Indra was bathed by the water of the celestial Ganges through the trunk of his carrier elephant. After this, the heavenly King Indra, along with *surabhi* cows and all other demigods and their mothers, worshiped Lord Kṛṣṇa by bathing Him with Ganges water and the milk of the *surabhis.* Thus Govinda, Lord Kṛṣṇa, was pleased with all of them. The residents of all higher planetary systems, such as Gandharvaloka, Pitṛloka, Siddhaloka, and Cāraṇaloka, all combined and began to glorify the Lord by chanting His holy name. Their wives and damsels began to dance with great joy. They very much satisfied the Lord by incessantly pouring flowers from the sky. When everything was very nicely and joyfully settled, the cows overflooded the surface of the earth with their milk. The water of the rivers began to flow and give nourishment to the trees, producing fruits and flowers of different colors and taste. The trees began to pour drops of honey. The hills and mountains began to produce potent medicinal plants and valuable stones. Because of Kṛṣṇa's presence, all these things happened very nicely, and the lower animals, who were generally envious, were envious no longer.

After satisfying Kṛṣṇa, who is the Lord of all the cows in Vṛndāvana, who is known as Govinda, King Indra took His permission to return to his heavenly kingdom. He was surrounded by all kinds of demigods who passed with him through cosmic space. This great incident is a powerful example of how Kṛṣṇa consciousness can benefit the world. Even the lower animals forget their envious nature and become elevated to the qualities of the demigods.

*Thus ends the Bhaktivedanta purport of the Twenty-seventh Chapter of* Kṛṣṇa, *"Prayers by Indra, the King of Heaven."*

# 28 / Releasing Nanda Mahārāja from the Clutches of Varuṇa

The Govardhana Ceremony took place on the new moon day. After this, there were torrents of rain and hailstorms imposed by King Indra for seven days. Nine days of the waxing moon having passed, on the tenth day King Indra worshiped Lord Kṛṣṇa, and thus the matter was satisfactorily settled. After this, on the eleventh day of the full moon, there was *Ekādaśī.* Mahārāja Nanda observed fasting for the whole day, and just early in the morning of the *Dvādaśī,* the day after *Ekādaśī,* he went to take bath in the River Yamunā. He entered deep into the water of the river, but he was arrested immediately by one of the servants of Varuṇadeva. These servants brought Nanda Mahārāja before the demigod Varuṇa and accused him of taking a bath in the river at the wrong time. According to astronomical calculations, the time in which he took bath was considered demoniac. The fact was, Nanda Mahārāja wanted to take a bath in the River Yamunā early in the morning before the sunrise, but somehow or other he was a little too early, and he bathed at an inauspicious time. Consequently he was arrested.

When Nanda Mahārāja was taken away by Varuṇa's servants, his companions began to call loudly for Kṛṣṇa and Balarāma. Immediately Kṛṣṇa and Balarāma could understand that Nanda Mahārāja was taken by Varuṇa, and thus They went to the abode of Varuṇa, for They were pledged to give protection. The inhabitants of Vṛndāvana, the unalloyed devotees of the Lord, having no shelter other than the Supreme Personality of Godhead, naturally cried to Him for help, exactly like children who do not know anything but the protection of their parents. Demigod Varuṇa received Lord Kṛṣṇa and Balarāma with great respect and said, "My dear Lord, actually at this very moment, because of Your presence, I am materially defeated. Although I am the proprietor of all the treasures in the water, I know that such possessions do not make for a successful life.

But this moment, as I look at You, my life is made completely successful because by seeing You I no longer have to accept a material body. Therefore, O Lord, Supreme Personality of Godhead, Supreme Brahman and Supersoul of everything, let me offer my respectful obeisances unto You. You are the supreme transcendental personality; there is no possibility of imposing the influence of material nature upon You. I am very sorry that by being foolish, by not knowing what to do or what not to do, I have mistakenly arrested Your father, Nanda Mahārāja. So I beg Your pardon for the offence of my servants. I think that it was Your plan to show me Your mercy by Your personal presence here. My dear Lord Kṛṣṇa, Govinda, be merciful upon me—here is Your father. You can take him back immediately."

In this way Lord Kṛṣṇa, the Supreme Personality of Godhead, rescued His father and presented him before his friends with great jubilation. Nanda Mahārāja was surprised that, although the demigod was so opulent, he offered such respect to Kṛṣṇa. That was very astonishing to Nanda, and he began to describe the incident to his friends and relatives with great wonder.

Actually, although Kṛṣṇa was acting so wonderfully, Mahārāja Nanda and mother Yaśodā could not think of Him as the Supreme Personality of Godhead. Instead, they always accepted Him as their beloved child. Thus Nanda Mahārāja did not accept the fact that Varuṇa worshiped Kṛṣṇa because Kṛṣṇa was the Supreme Personality of Godhead; rather he took it that because Kṛṣṇa was such a wonderful child He was respected even by Varuṇa. The friends of Nanda Mahārāja, all the cowherd men, became eager to know if Kṛṣṇa were actually the Supreme Personality and if He were going to give them all salvation. When they were all thus consulting among themselves, Kṛṣṇa understood their minds, and in order to assure them of their destiny in the spiritual kingdom, He showed them the spiritual sky. Generally, ordinary persons are engaged simply in working hard in the material world, and they have no information that there is another kingdom or another sky, which is known as the spiritual sky, where life is eternal, blissful, and full of knowledge. As it is stated in the *Bhagavad-gītā,* a person returning to that spiritual sky never returns to this material world of death and suffering.

Kṛṣṇa, the Supreme Personality of Godhead, is always anxious to give information to the conditioned soul that there is a spiritual sky far, far beyond this material sky, transcendental to the innumerable universes created within the total material energy. Kṛṣṇa is, of course, always very kind to every conditioned soul, but, as stated in the *Bhagavad-gītā,* He is especially inclined to the devotees. Hearing their inquiries, Kṛṣṇa immediately thought that His devotees in Vṛndāvana should be informed of the spiritual sky and the Vaikuṇṭha planets therein. Within the material world, every conditioned soul is in the darkness of ignorance. This means that all conditioned souls are under the concept of this bodily existence.

Everyone is under the impression that he is of this material world, and with this concept of life, everyone is working in ignorance in different forms of life. The activities of the particular type of body are called *karma*, or fruitive action. All conditioned souls under the impression of the bodily concept are working according to their particular types of body. These activities are creating their future conditional life. Because they have very little information of the spiritual world, they do not generally take to spiritual activities, which are called *bhakti-yoga*. Those who successfully practice *bhakti-yoga*, after giving up this present body, go directly to the spiritual world and become situated in one of the Vaikuṇṭha planets. The inhabitants of Vṛndāvana are all pure devotees. Their destination after quitting the body is Kṛṣṇaloka. They even surpass the Vaikuṇṭhalokas. The fact is, those who are always engaged in Kṛṣṇa consciousness and mature, pure devotional service are given the chance, after death, to gain Kṛṣṇa's association in the universes within the material world. Kṛṣṇa's pastimes are continually going on, either in this universe or in another universe. Just as the sun globe is passing through many places across this earthly planet, so *Kṛṣṇa-līlā*, or the transcendental advent and pastimes of Kṛṣṇa, are also going on continually, either in this or another universe. The mature devotees, who have completely executed Kṛṣṇa consciousness, are immediately transferred to the universe where Kṛṣṇa is appearing. In that universe the devotees get their first opportunity to associate with Kṛṣṇa personally and directly. The training goes on, as we see in the Vṛndāvana *līlā* of Kṛṣṇa within this planet. Kṛṣṇa therefore revealed the actual feature of the Vaikuṇṭha planets so that the inhabitants of Vṛndāvana could know their destination.

Thus Kṛṣṇa showed them the eternal ever-existing spiritual sky which is unlimited and full of knowledge. Within this material world there are different gradations of forms, and according to the gradations, knowledge is proportionately manifested. For example, the knowledge in the body of a child is not as perfect as the knowledge in the body of an adult man. Everywhere there are different gradations of living entities, in aquatic animals, in the plants and trees, in the reptiles and insects, in birds and beasts and in the civilized and uncivilized human forms of life. Above the human form of life there are demigods, Cāraṇas and Siddhas on up to

Brahmaloka where Lord Brahmā lives, and among these demigods there are always different gradations of knowledge. But past this material world, in the Vaikuṇṭha sky, everyone is in full knowledge. All the living entities there are engaged in devotional service to the Lord, either in the Vaikuṇṭha planets or in Kṛṣṇaloka.

As it is confirmed in the *Bhagavad-gītā,* full knowledge means knowing Kṛṣṇa to be the Supreme Personality of Godhead. In the *Vedas* and *Bhagavad-gītā* it is also stated that in the *brahmajyoti* or spiritual sky there is no need of sunlight, moonlight, or electricity. All those planets are self-illuminating, and all of them are eternally situated. There is no question of creation and annihilation in the *brahmajyoti,* spiritual sky. *Bhagavad-gītā* also confirms that beyond the material sky there is another eternal spiritual sky where everything is eternally existing. Information of the spiritual sky can be had only from great sages and saintly persons who have already surpassed the influence of the three material modes of nature. Unless one is constantly situated on that transcendental platform, it is not possible to understand the spiritual nature.

Therefore it is recommended that one should take to *bhakti-yoga* and keep himself engaged twenty-four hours in Kṛṣṇa consciousness, which places one beyond the reach of the modes of material nature. One in Kṛṣṇa consciousness can easily understand the nature of the spiritual sky and Vaikuṇṭhaloka. The inhabitants of Vṛndāvana, being always engaged in Kṛṣṇa consciousness, could therefore very easily understand the transcendental nature of the Vaikuṇṭhalokas.

Thus Kṛṣṇa led all the cowherd men, headed by Nanda Mahārāja, to the lake where Akrūra was later shown the Vaikuṇṭha planetary system. They took their bath immediately and saw the real nature of the Vaikuṇṭhalokas. After seeing the spiritual sky and the Vaikuṇṭhalokas, all the men, headed by Nanda Mahārāja, felt wonderfully blissful, and coming out of the river, they saw Kṛṣṇa, who was being worshiped with excellent prayers.

*Thus ends the Bhaktivedanta purport of the Twenty-eighth Chapter of* Kṛṣṇa, *"Releasing Nanda Mahārāja from the Clutches of Varuṇa."*

# 29 / The Rāsa Dance: Introduction

In the *Śrīmad-Bhāgavatam* it is stated the *rāsa* dance took place on the full moon night of the *śarat* season. From the statement of previous chapters, it appears that the festival of Govardhana Pūjā was performed just after the dark moon night of the month of Kārttika, and thereafter the ceremony of *Bhrātṛdvitīya* was performed; then the wrath of Indra was exhibited in the shape of torrents of rain and hailstorm, and Lord Kṛṣṇa held up Govardhana Hill for seven days, up until the ninth day of the moon. Thereafter, on the tenth day, the inhabitants of Vṛndāvana were talking amongst themselves about the wonderful activities of Kṛṣṇa, and the next day, *Ekādaśī* was observed by Nanda Mahārāja. On the next day, *Dvādaśī,* Nanda Mahārāja went to take a bath in the Ganges and was arrested by the men of Varuṇa; then he was released by Lord Kṛṣṇa. Then Nanda Mahārāja, along with the cowherd men, was shown the spiritual sky.

In this way, the full moon night of *śarat* season came to an end. The full moon night of Āśvina is called *śārad-pūrṇimā.* It appears from the statement of *Śrīmad-Bhāgavatam* that Kṛṣṇa had to wait another year for such a moon before enjoying the *rāsa* dance with the *gopīs.* At the age of seven years, He lifted Govardhana Hill. Therefore, the *rāsa* dance took place during His eighth year.

From Vedic literature it appears that when a theatrical actor dances among many dancing girls, the group-dance is called a *rāsa* dance. When Kṛṣṇa saw the full moon night of the *śarat* season, He decorated Himself with various seasonal flowers, especially the *mallikā* flowers, which are very fragrant. He remembered the *gopīs'* prayers to goddess Kātyāyanī, wherein they prayed for Kṛṣṇa to be their husband. He thought that the full night of the *śarat* season was just suitable for a nice dance. So their desire to have Kṛṣṇa as their husband would then be fulfilled.

The words used in this connection in the *Śrīmad-Bhāgavatam* are *bhagavān api.* This means that although Kṛṣṇa is the Supreme Personality of Godhead, He has no desire that needs to be fulfilled because He is always full with six opulences. Yet He wanted to enjoy the company of the *gopīs. Bhagavān api* signifies that this is not like the ordinary dancing of young boys and young girls. The specific word used in the *Śrīmad-Bhāgavatam* is *yogamāyām upāśritaḥ,* which means that this dancing with the *gopīs* is on the platform of *yogamāyā,* not *mahāmāyā.* The dancing of young boys and girls within this material world is in the kingdom of *mahāmāyā,* or the external energy. The *rāsa* dance of Kṛṣṇa with the *gopīs* is on the platform of *yogamāyā.* The difference between the platform of *yogamāyā* and *mahāmāyā* is compared in the *Caitanya-caritāmṛta* to the difference between gold and iron. From the viewpoint of metallurgy, gold and iron are both metals, but the quality is completely different. Similarly, although the *rāsa* dance and Lord Kṛṣṇa's association with the *gopīs* appear like the ordinary mixing of young boys and girls, the quality is completely different. The difference is appreciated by great Vaiṣṇavas because they can understand the difference between love of Kṛṣṇa and lust.

On the *mahāmāyā* platform, dances take place on the basis of sense gratification. But when Kṛṣṇa called the *gopīs* by sounding His flute, the *gopīs* very hurriedly rushed towards the spot of *rāsa* dance with the transcendental desire of satisfying Kṛṣṇa. The author of *Caitanya-caritāmṛta,* Kṛṣṇadāsa Kavirāja Gosvāmī, has explained that lust means sense gratification, and love also means sense gratification—but for Kṛṣṇa. In other words, when activities are enacted on the platform of personal sense gratification, they are called material activities, but when they are enacted for the satisfaction of Kṛṣṇa, then they are spiritual activities. On any platform of activities, the principle of sense gratification is there. But on the spiritual platform, sense gratification is for the Supreme Personality of Godhead, Kṛṣṇa, whereas on the material platform it is for the performer. For example, on the material platform, when a servant serves a master, he is not trying to satisfy the senses of the master, but rather his own senses. The servant would not serve the master if the payment stopped. That means that the servant engages himself in the service of the master just to satisfy his senses. On the spiritual platform, the servitor of the Supreme Personality of Godhead serves Kṛṣṇa without payment, and he continues his service in all conditions. That is the difference between Kṛṣṇa consciousness and material consciousness.

It appears that Kṛṣṇa enjoyed the *rāsa* dance with the *gopīs* when He was eight years old. At that time, many of the *gopīs* were married, because in India, especially in those days, girls were married at a very early age. There are even many instances of a girl giving birth to a child at the age of twelve. Under the circumstances, all the *gopīs* who wanted to have Kṛṣṇa as their husband were already married. At the same time, they continued to hope that Kṛṣṇa would be their husband. Their attitude toward Kṛṣṇa was that of paramour love. Therefore, the loving affairs of Kṛṣṇa with the *gopīs* is called *parakīya-rasa.* A married man or a wife who desires another wife or husband is called *parakīya-rasa.*

Actually, Kṛṣṇa is the husband of everyone because He is the supreme enjoyer. The *gopīs* wanted Kṛṣṇa to be their husband, but factually there was no possibility of His marrying all the *gopīs.* But because they had that natural tendency to accept Kṛṣṇa as their supreme husband, the relationship between the *gopīs* and Kṛṣṇa is called *parakīya-rasa.* This *parakīya-rasa* is ever-existent in Goloka Vṛndāvana in the spiritual sky where there is no possibility of the inebriety which characterizes *parakīya-rasa* in the material world. In the material world, *parakīya-rasa* is abominable, whereas in the spiritual world it is present in the superexcellent relationship of Kṛṣṇa and the *gopīs.* There are many other relationships with Kṛṣṇa: master and servant, friends and friend, parent and son, and lover and beloved. Out of all these *rasas,* the *parakīya-rasa* is considered to be the topmost.

This material world is the perverted reflection of the spiritual world; it is just like the reflection of a tree on the bank of a reservoir of water: the topmost part of the tree is seen as the lowest part. Similarly, *parakīya-rasa,* when pervertedly reflected in this material world, is abominable. When people, therefore, imitate the *rāsa* dance of Kṛṣṇa with the *gopīs,* they simply enjoy the perverted, abominable reflection of the transcendental *parakīya-rasa.* There is no possibility of enjoying this transcendental *parakīya-rasa* within the material world. It is stated in the *Śrīmad-Bhāgavatam* that one should not imitate this *parakīya-rasa* even in dream or imagination. Those who do so drink the most deadly poison.

When Kṛṣṇa, the supreme enjoyer, desired to enjoy the company of the *gopīs* on that full moon night of the *śarat* season, exactly at that very moment, the moon, the lord of the stars, appeared in the sky, displaying its most beautiful features. The full moon night of the *śarat* season is the most beautiful night in the year. In India there is a great monument called Taj Mahal in Agra, a city in the Uttar Pradesh province, and the tomb is made of first-class marble stone. During the night of the full moon of the *śarat* season, many foreigners go to see the beautiful reflections of the moon on the tomb. Thus this full moon night is celebrated even today for its beauty.

When the full moon rose in the east, it tinged everything with a reddish color. With the rising of the moon, the whole sky appeared smeared by red *kuṅkuma.* When a husband long separated from his wife returns home, he decorates the face of his wife with red *kuṅkuma.* This long-expected moonrise of the *śarat* season was thus smearing the eastern sky.

The appearance of the moon increased Kṛṣṇa's desire to dance with the *gopīs.* The forests were filled with fragrant flowers. The atmosphere was cooling and festive. When Lord Kṛṣṇa began to blow His flute, the *gopīs* all over Vṛndāvana became enchanted. Their attraction to the vibration of the flute increased a thousand times due to the rising full moon, the red horizon, the calm and cool atmosphere, and the blossoming flowers. All these *gopīs* were by nature very much attracted to Kṛṣṇa's beauty, and when they heard the vibration of His flute, they became apparently lustful to satisfy the senses of Kṛṣṇa.

Immediately upon hearing the vibration of the flute, they all left their respective engagements and proceeded to the spot where Kṛṣṇa was standing. While they ran very swiftly, all their earrings swung back and forth. They all rushed toward the place known as Vaṁśīvaṭa. Some of them were engaged in milking cows, but they left their milking business half finished and immediately went to Kṛṣṇa. One of them had just collected milk and put it in a milk pan on the oven to boil, but she did not care whether the milk overboiled and spilled—she immediately left to go see Kṛṣṇa. Some of them were breast feeding their small babies, and some were engaged in distributing food to the members of their families, but they left all such engagements and immediately rushed towards the spot where Kṛṣṇa was playing His flute. Some were engaged in serving their husbands, and some were themselves engaged in eating, but neither caring to serve their husbands nor eat, they immediately left. Some of them wanted to decorate their faces with cosmetic ointments and to dress themselves very nicely before going to Kṛṣṇa, but unfortunately they could not finish their cosmetic decorations nor put on their dresses in the right way because of their anxiety to meet Kṛṣṇa immediately. Their faces were decorated hurriedly and were haphazardly finished; some even put the lower part of their dresses on the upper part of their bodies and the upper part on the lower part.

While all the *gopīs* were hurriedly leaving their respective places, their husbands, brothers and fathers were all struck with wonder to know where they were going. Being young girls, they were protected either by husbands, elderly brothers or fathers. All their guardians forbade them to go to Kṛṣṇa, but they disregarded them. When a person becomes attracted by

Kṛṣṇa and is in full Kṛṣṇa consciousness, he does not care for any worldly duties, even though very urgent. Kṛṣṇa consciousness is so powerful that it gives everyone relief from all material activities. Śrīla Rūpa Gosvāmī has written a very nice verse wherein one *gopī* advises another, "My dear friend, if you desire to enjoy the company of material society, friendship and love, then please do not go to see this smiling boy Govinda, who is standing on the bank of the Yamunā and playing His flute, His lips brightened by the beams of the full moonlight." Śrīla Rūpa Gosvāmī indirectly instructs that one who has been captivated by the beautiful smiling face of Kṛṣṇa has lost all attraction for material enjoyments. This is the test of advancement in Kṛṣṇa consciousness: a person advancing in Kṛṣṇa consciousness must lose interest in material activities and personal sense gratification.

Some of the *gopīs* were factually detained from going to Kṛṣṇa by their husbands and were locked up by force within their rooms. Being unable to go to Kṛṣṇa, they began to meditate upon His transcendental form by closing their eyes. They already had the form of Kṛṣṇa within their minds. They proved to be the greatest *yogīs;* as is stated in the *Bhagavad-gītā,* a person who is constantly thinking of Kṛṣṇa within his heart with faith and love is considered to be the topmost of all *yogīs.* Actually, a *yogī* concentrates his mind on the form of Lord Viṣṇu. That is real *yoga.* Kṛṣṇa is the original form of all Viṣṇu *tattvas.* The *gopīs* could not go to Kṛṣṇa personally, so they began to meditate on Him as perfect *yogīs.*

In the conditioned stage of the living entities, there are two kinds of results of fruitive activities: the conditioned living entity who is constantly engaged in sinful activities has suffering as his result, and he who is engaged in pious activities has material enjoyment as a result. In either case—material suffering or material enjoyment—the enjoyer or sufferer is conditioned by material nature.

The *gopī* associates of Kṛṣṇa, who assemble in the place where Kṛṣṇa is appearing, are from different groups. Most of the *gopīs* are eternal companions of Kṛṣṇa. As stated in the *Brahma-saṁhitā, ānanda-cin-maya-rasa-pratibhāvitābhiḥ:* in the spiritual world the associates of Kṛṣṇa, especially the *gopīs,* are the manifestation of the pleasure potency of Lord Kṛṣṇa. They are expansions of Śrīmatī Rādhārāṇī. But when Kṛṣṇa exhibits His transcendental pastimes within the material world in some of the universes, not only the eternal associates of Kṛṣṇa come, but also those who are being promoted to that status from this material world. The *gopīs* who joined Kṛṣṇa's pastimes within this material world were coming from the status of ordinary human beings. If they had been bound by fruitive action, they were fully freed from the reaction of *karma* by constant meditation on Kṛṣṇa. Their severe painful yearnings caused by their not being able to see Kṛṣṇa freed them from all sinful reactions, and their ecstacy of transcendental love for Kṛṣṇa in His absence was transcendental to all their reactions of material pious activities. The conditioned soul is subjected to birth and death, either by pious or sinful activities, but the *gopīs* who began to meditate on Kṛṣṇa transcended both positions and became purified and thus elevated to the status of the *gopīs* already expanded by His pleasure potency. All the *gopīs* who concentrated their minds on Kṛṣṇa in the spirit of paramour love became fully uncontaminated from all the fruitive reactions of material nature, and some of them immediately gave up their material bodies developed under the three modes of material nature.

Mahārāja Parīkṣit heard Śukadeva Gosvāmī explain the situation of the *gopīs* who assembled with Kṛṣṇa in the *rāsa* dance. When he heard that some of the *gopīs,* simply by concentrating on Kṛṣṇa as their paramour, became freed from all contamination of material birth and death, he said, "The *gopīs* did not know that Kṛṣṇa is the Supreme Personality of Godhead. They accepted Him as a beautiful boy and considered Him to be their paramour. So how was it possible for them to get freed from the material condition just by thinking of a paramour?" One should consider here that Kṛṣṇa and ordinary living beings are qualitatively one. The ordinary living beings, being part and parcel of Kṛṣṇa, are also Brahman, but Kṛṣṇa is the Supreme–Parabrahman. The question is, if it is possible for the devotee to get free from the material, contaminated stage simply by thinking of Kṛṣṇa, then why not others who are also thinking of someone? If one is thinking of a husband or son, or if anyone at all is thinking of another living entity, since all living entities are also Brahman, then why are they not all freed from the contaminated stage of material nature? This is a very intelligent question, because the atheists are always imitating Kṛṣṇa. In these days of Kaliyuga, there are many rascals who think themselves to be as great as Kṛṣṇa and who cheat people into believing that thinking of them is as good as thinking of Lord Kṛṣṇa. Parīkṣit Mahārāja, apprehending the dangerous condition of blind followers of demonic imitators, therefore asked this question, and fortunately it is recorded in the *Śrīmad-Bhāgavatam* to warn innocent people that thinking of an ordinary man and thinking of Kṛṣṇa are not the same.

Actually, even thinking of the demigods cannot compare with thinking of Kṛṣṇa. It is also warned in *Vaiṣṇava Tantra* that one who puts Viṣṇu, Nārāyaṇa, or Kṛṣṇa on the same level of the demigods is called *pāsaṇḍa,* or a rascal. On hearing this question of Mahārāja Parīkṣit, Śukadeva Gosvāmī replied, "My dear King, your question is already answered, even before this incident."

Because Parīkṣit Mahārāja wanted to clear up the situation, his spiritual master answered him very intelligently, "Why are you again asking the same subject matter which has already been explained to you? Why are you so forgetful?" A spiritual master is always in the superior position, so he has the right to chastise his disciple in this way. Śukadeva Gosvāmī knew that Mahārāja Parīkṣit asked the question not for his own understanding, but as a warning to the future innocent people who might think others to be equal to Kṛṣṇa.

Śukadeva Gosvāmī then reminded Parīkṣit Mahārāja about the salvation of Śiśupāla. Śiśupāla was always envious of Kṛṣṇa, and because of his envy Kṛṣṇa killed him. Since Kṛṣṇa is the Supreme Personality of Godhead, Śiśupāla gained salvation simply by seeing Him. If an envious person can get salvation simply by concentrating his mind on Kṛṣṇa, then what to speak of the *gopīs* who are so dear to Kṛṣṇa and always thinking of Him in love? There must be some difference between the enemies and the friends. If Kṛṣṇa's enemies could get freed from material contamination and become one with the Supreme, then certainly His dear friends like the *gopīs* are freed and with Him.

Besides that, in the *Bhagavad-gītā* Kṛṣṇa is called Hṛṣīkeśa. Śukadeva Gosvāmī also said that Kṛṣṇa is Hṛṣīkeśa, the Supersoul, whereas an ordinary man is a conditioned soul covered by the material body. Kṛṣṇa and Kṛṣṇa's body are the same because He is Hṛṣīkeśa. Any person making a distinction between Kṛṣṇa and Kṛṣṇa's body is fool number one. Kṛṣṇa is Hṛṣīkeśa and Adhokṣaja. These two particular words have been used by Parīkṣit Mahārāja in this instance. Hṛṣīkeśa is the Supersoul, and Adhokṣaja is the Supreme Personality of Godhead, transcendental to the material nature. Just to show favor to the ordinary living entities, out of His causeless mercy, He appears as He is. Unfortunately, foolish persons mistake Him to be another ordinary person, and so they become eligible to go to hell. Śukadeva Gosvāmī reconfirmed that Kṛṣṇa is the Supreme Personality of Godhead, imperishable, immeasurable, and free from all material contamination.

Sukadeva Gosvāmī continued to inform Mahārāja Parīkṣit that Kṛṣṇa is not an ordinary person. He is the Supreme Personality of Godhead, full of all spiritual qualities. He appears in this material world out of His causeless mercy, and whenever He appears, He appears as He is without change. This is also confirmed in the *Bhagavad-gītā*. There the Lord says that He appears in His spiritual potency. He does not appear under the control of this material potency. The material potency is under His control. In the *Bhagavad-gītā* it is stated that the material potency is working under His superintendence. It is also confirmed in the *Brahma-saṁhitā* that the material potency known as Durgā is acting just as a shadow which moves with the movement of the substance. The conclusion is that if one somehow or other becomes attached to Kṛṣṇa or attracted to Him, either because of His beauty, quality, opulence, fame, strength, renunciation or knowledge, or even through lust, anger or fear, or affection or friendship, then one's salvation and freedom from material contamination is assured.

In the *Bhagavad-gītā,* Eighteenth Chapter, the Lord also states that one who is engaged in preaching Kṛṣṇa consciousness is very dear to Him. A preacher has to face many difficulties in his struggle to preach pure Kṛṣṇa consciousness. Sometimes he has to suffer bodily injuries, and sometimes he has to meet death also. All this is taken as a great austerity on behalf of Kṛṣṇa. Kṛṣṇa therefore has said that such a preacher is very, very dear to Him. If Kṛṣṇa's enemies can expect salvation simply by concentrating their minds on Him, then what to speak of persons who are so dear to Kṛṣṇa? The conclusion should be that the salvation of those who are engaged in preaching Kṛṣṇa consciousness in the world is guaranteed in all circumstances. But such preachers never care for salvation, because factually one who is engaged in Kṛṣṇa consciousness, devotional service, has already achieved salvation. Śukadeva Gosvāmī therefore assured King Parīkṣit that he should always rest assured that one attracted by Kṛṣṇa attains liberation from material bondage because Kṛṣṇa is the transcendental master of all mystic power.

When all the *gopīs* assembled, as described, before Kṛṣṇa, He began to speak to them, welcoming them as well as discouraging them by word jugglery. Kṛṣṇa is the supreme speaker; He is the speaker of the *Bhagavad-gītā.* He can speak on the highest elevated subjects of philosophy, politics, economics—everything. And He also spoke before the *gopīs* who were so dear to Him. He wanted to enchant them by word jugglery, and thus He began to speak as follows.

"O ladies of Vṛndāvana," Kṛṣṇa said. "You are very fortunate, and you are very dear to Me. I am very pleased that you have come here, and I hope everything is well in Vṛndāvana. Now please order Me. What can I do for you? What is the purpose of coming here in this dead of night? Kindly take your seats and let Me know what I can do for you."

The *gopīs* had come to Kṛṣṇa to enjoy His company, to dance with Him, embrace Him and kiss Him, and when Kṛṣṇa began to receive them very officially, showing all kinds of etiquette, they were surprised. He was treating them as ordinary society women. Therefore they began to smile among themselves, and they very eagerly listened to Kṛṣṇa talk in that way. When He saw that they were smiling at Him, He said, "My dear friends, you must know now that it is the dead of night, and the forest is very dangerous. At this time all the ferocious jungle animals, the tigers, bears, jackals and wolves, are prowling in the forest. Therefore it is very dangerous for you. You cannot select a secure place now. Everywhere you go you will find that all these animals are loitering to find their prey. I think, therefore, that you are taking a great risk in coming here in the dead of night. Please turn back immediately, without delay."

When He saw that they continued to smile, He said, "I very much appreciate your bodily features. All of you have nice, very thin waists." All of the *gopīs* there were exquisitely beautiful. They are described by the word *sumadhyamā;* the standard of beauty of a woman is said to be *sumadhyamā* when the middle portion of the body is slender.

Kṛṣṇa wanted to impress on them that they were not old enough to take care of themselves. Actually, they required protection. It was not very wise for them to come in the dead of night to Kṛṣṇa. Kṛṣṇa also indicated that He was young and that they were young girls. "It does not look very well for young girls and boys to remain together in the dead of night." After hearing this advice, the *gopīs* did not seem very happy; therefore Kṛṣṇa began to stress the point in a different way.

"My dear friends, I can understand that you have left your homes without the permission of your guardians; therefore I think your mothers, your fathers, your elderly brothers or even your sons, and what to speak of your husbands, must be very anxious to find you. As long as you are here, they must be searching in different places, and their minds must be very agitated. So don't tarry. Please go back and make them peaceful."

When the *gopīs* appeared to be a little bit disturbed and angry from the free advice of Kṛṣṇa, they diverted their attention to looking at the beauty of the forest. At that time the whole forest was illuminated by the bright shining of the moon, and the air was blowing very silently over the blooming flowers, and the green leaves of the trees were moving in the breeze. Kṛṣṇa took the opportunity of their looking at the forest to advise them. "I think you have come out to see the beautiful Vṛndāvana forest on this night," He said, "but you must now be satisfied. So return to your homes without delay. I understand that you are all very chaste women, so now that you have seen the beautiful atmosphere of the Vṛndāvana forests, please return home and engage in the faithful service of your respective husbands. Some of you must have babies by this time, although you are very young. You must have left your small babies at home, and they must be crying. Please immediately go back home and just feed them with your breast milk. I can also understand that you have very great affection for Me, and out of that transcendental affection you have come here, hearing My playing on the flute. Your feelings of love and affection for Me are very appropriate because I am the Supreme Personality of Godhead. All living creatures are My parts and parcels, and naturally they are affectionate to Me. So this affection for Me is very much welcome, and I congratulate you for this. Now you can go back to your homes. Another thing I must explain to you is that for a chaste woman, service to the husband without duplicity is the best religious principle. A woman should be not only faithful and chaste to the husband, but affectionate to the friends of her husband, obedient to the father and mother of the husband, and affectionate to the younger brothers of the husband. And most importantly, the woman must take care of the children."

In this way, Kṛṣṇa explained the duty of a woman. He also stressed the point of serving the husband: "Even if he is not of very good character, or even if he is not very rich or fortunate, or even if he is old or invalid on account of continued diseases, whatever her husband's condition, a woman should not divorce her husband if she actually desires to be elevated to the higher planetary systems after leaving this body. Besides that, it is considered abominable in society if a woman is unfaithful and goes searching for another man. Such habits will deter a woman from being elevated to the heavenly planets, and the results of such habits are very degrading. A married woman should not search for a paramour, for this is not sanctioned by the Vedic principles of life. If you think that you are very much attached to Me and you want My association, I advise you not to personally try to enjoy Me. It is better for you to go home, simply talk about Me, think of Me, and by this process of constantly remembering Me and chanting My names, you will surely be elevated to the spiritual platform. There is no need to stand near Me. Please go back home."

The instruction given herein by the Supreme Personality of Godhead to the *gopīs* was not at all sarcastic. Such instructions should be taken very seriously by all honest women. The chastity of women is specifically stressed herein by the Supreme Personality of Godhead. Therefore this principle should be followed by any serious woman who wants to be elevated to a higher status of life. Kṛṣṇa is the center of all affection for all living creatures. When this affection is developed for Kṛṣṇa, then one surpasses and transcends all Vedic injunctions. This was possible for the *gopīs* because they saw Kṛṣṇa face to face. This is not possible for any women in the conditioned state. Unfortunately, by imitating the behavior of Kṛṣṇa with the *gopīs,* sometimes a rascal takes the position of Kṛṣṇa, following the philosophy of monism or oneness, and he very irresponsibly takes advantage of this *rāsa-līlā* to entice many innocent women and mislead them in the name of spiritual realization. As a warning, Lord Kṛṣṇa has herein hinted that what was possible for the *gopīs* is not possible for ordinary women. Although a woman can actually be elevated by advanced Kṛṣṇa consciousness, she should not be enticed by an imposter who says that he is Kṛṣṇa. She should concentrate her devotional activities in chanting and meditating upon Kṛṣṇa, as is advised herein. One should not follow the men called *sahajiyā,* the so-called devotees who take everything very lightly.

When Kṛṣṇa spoke in such a discouraging way to the *gopīs,* they became very sad, for they thought that their desire to enjoy *rāsa* dance with Kṛṣṇa would be frustrated. Thus they became full of anxiety. Out of great sadness, the *gopīs* began to breathe very heavily. Instead of looking at Kṛṣṇa face to face, they bowed their heads and looked to the ground, and they began to draw various types of curved lines on the ground with their toes. They were shedding heavy tears, and their cosmetic decorations were being washed from their faces. The water from their eyes mixed with the *kuṅkuma* of their breasts and fell to the ground. They could not say anything to Kṛṣṇa, but simply stood there silently. By their silence they expressed that their hearts were grievously wounded.

The *gopīs* were not ordinary women. In essence they were on an equal level with Kṛṣṇa. They are His eternal associates. As it is confirmed in the *Brahma-saṁhitā,* they are expansions of the pleasure potency of Kṛṣṇa, and as His potency they are nondifferent from Him. Although they were depressed by the words of Kṛṣṇa, they did not like to use harsh words against Him. Yet they wanted to rebuke Kṛṣṇa for His unkind words, and therefore they began to speak in faltering voices. They did not like to use harsh words against Kṛṣṇa because He was their dearmost, their heart and soul. The *gopīs* had only Kṛṣṇa within their hearts. They were completely surrendered and dedicated souls. Naturally, when they heard such unkind words, they tried to reply, but in the attempt torrents of tears fell from their eyes. Finally they managed to speak.

"Kṛṣṇa," they said, "You are very cruel! You should not talk like that. We are full-fledged surrendered souls. Please accept us, and don't talk in that cruel way. Of course, You are the Supreme Personality of Godhead, and You can do whatever You like, but it is not worthy of Your position to treat us in such a cruel way. We have come to You, leaving everything behind, just to take shelter of Your lotus feet. We know that You are completely independent and can do whatever You like, but we request You, don't reject us. We are Your devotees. You should accept us as Lord Nārāyaṇa accepts His devotees. There are many devotees of Lord Nārāyaṇa who worship Him for salvation, and He awards them salvation. Similarly, how can You reject us when we have no other shelter than Your lotus feet?

"O dear Kṛṣṇa," they continued, "You are the supreme instructor. There is no doubt about it. Your instructions to the women to be faithful to their husbands and to be merciful to their children, to take care of homely affairs and to be obedient to the elderly members of the family, are surely just according to the tenets of *śāstras.* But we know also that all these instructions of the *śāstras* may be observed perfectly by keeping oneself under the protection of Your lotus feet. Our husbands, friends, family members and children are all dear and pleasing to us only because of Your presence, for You are the Supersoul of all living creatures. Without Your presence, one is worthless. When You leave the body, the body immediately dies, and according to the injunction of the *śāstra,* a dead body must immediately be thrown in a river or burned. Therefore, ultimately You are the dearmost personality in this world. By placing our faith and love in Your personality, there is no chance of our being bereft of husband, friends, sons or daughters. If a woman accepts You as the supreme husband, then she will never be bereft of her husband, as in the bodily concept of life. If we accept You as our ultimate husband, then there is no question of being separated, divorced or widowed. You are the eternal husband, eternal son, eternal friend, and eternal master, and one who enters into a relationship with You is eternally happy. Since You are the teacher of all religious principles, Your lotus feet first have to be worshiped. Accordingly, the *śāstras* state, *ācārya-upāsanā:* the worship of Your lotus feet is the first principle. Besides that, as stated in the *Bhagavad-gītā,* You are the only enjoyer, You are the only proprietor, and You are the only friend. As such, we have come to You, leaving aside all so-called friends, society and love, and now You have become our enjoyer. Let us be everlastingly enjoyed by You. Be our proprietor, for that is Your natural claim, and be our supreme friend, for You are naturally so. Let us thus embrace You as the supreme beloved."

Then the *gopīs* told the lotus-eyed Kṛṣṇa, "Please do not discourage our long-cherished desires to have You as our husband. Any intelligent man who cares for his own self-interest reposes all his loving spirit in You. Persons who are simply misled by the external energy, who want to be satisfied by false concepts, try to enjoy themselves apart from You. The so-called husband, friend, son, daughter, or father and mother are all simply sources of material misery. No one is made happy in this material world by having a so-called father, mother, husband, son, daughter and friend. Although the father and mother are expected to protect the children, there are many children who are suffering for want of food and shelter. There are many good physicians, but when a patient dies, no physician can revive him. There are many means of protection, but when one is doomed, none of the protective measures can help, and without Your protection the so-called sources of protection simply become sources of continued distress. We therefore appeal to You, dear Lord of all lords, please do not kill our long-cherished desires to have You as our supreme husband.

"Dear Kṛṣṇa, as women, we are certainly satisfied when our hearts are engaged in the activities of family affairs, but our hearts have already been stolen by You. We can no longer engage them in family affairs. Besides that, You are asking us repeatedly to return home, and that is a very appropriate instruction, but unfortunately we have been stunned here. Our legs have no power to move a step from Your lotus feet. Therefore, if even at Your request we return home, what shall we do there? We have lost all our capacity to act without You. Instead of engaging our hearts in family affairs as women, we have now developed a different type of lust which is continually blazing in our hearts. Now we request You, dear Kṛṣṇa, to extinguish that fire with Your beautiful smile and the transcendental vibration emanating from Your lips. If You do not agree to do us this favor, we shall certainly be burned in the fire of separation. In that condition, we shall simply think of You and Your beautiful features and give up our bodies immediately. In that way we think it will be possible for us to reside at Your lotus feet in the next life. Dear Kṛṣṇa, if You say that if we go home our respective husbands will satisfy the lusty flame of our desire, we can only say that that is no longer possible. You have given us a chance to be enjoyed by You in the forest and have touched our breasts once in the past, which we accepted as a blessing, as did the goddesses of fortune, who are enjoyed in the Vaikuṇṭhalokas by You. Since we have tasted this transcendental enjoyment, we are no longer interested in going to anyone but You for the satisfaction of our lust. Dear Kṛṣṇa, the lotus feet of the goddess of fortune are always worshiped by the demigods, although she is always resting on Your chest in the

Vaikuṇṭha planets. She underwent great austerity and penance to have some shelter at Your lotus feet, which are always covered by *tulasī* leaves. Your lotus feet are the proper shelter of Your servitors, and the goddess of fortune, instead of abiding on Your chest, comes down and worships Your lotus feet. We have now placed ourselves under the dust of Your feet. Please do not reject us, for we are fully surrendered souls.

"Dear Kṛṣṇa, You are known as Hari. You destroy all the miseries of all living entities, specifically of those who have left their homes and family attachment and have completely taken to You. We have left our homes with the hope that we shall completely devote and dedicate our lives to Your service. We are simply begging to be engaged as Your servants. We do not wish to ask You to accept us as Your wives. Simply accept us as Your maidservants. Since You are the Supreme Personality of Godhead and like to enjoy the *parakīya-rasa* and are famous as a transcendental woman hunter, we have come to satisfy Your transcendental desires. We are also after our own satisfaction, for simply by looking at Your smiling face we have become very lusty. We have come before You decorated with all ornaments and dress, but until You embrace us, all our dresses and beautiful features remain incomplete. You are the Supreme Person, and if You complete our dressing attempt as the *puruṣa-bhūṣaṇa,* or the male ornament, then all our desires and bodily decorations are complete.

"Dear Kṛṣṇa, we have simply been captivated by seeing You with *tilaka* and with earrings and by seeing Your beautiful face covered with scattered hair and Your extraordinary smile. Not only that, but we are also attracted by Your arms, which always give assurance to the surrendered souls. And although we are also attracted by Your chest, which is always embraced by the goddess of fortune, we do not wish to take her position. We shall simply be satisfied by being Your maidservants. If You, however, accuse us of encouraging prostitution, then we can only ask where is that woman within these three worlds who is not captivated by Your beauty and the rhythmic songs vibrated by Your transcendental flute? Within these three worlds there is no distinction between men and women in relation to You because both men and women belong to the marginal potency or *prakṛti.* No one is actually the enjoyer or the male; everyone is meant to be enjoyed by You. There is no woman within these three worlds who cannot but deviate from her path of chastity once she is attracted to You because Your beauty is so sublime that not only men and women, but cows, birds, beasts and even trees, fruits and flowers—everyone and everything—become enchanted, and what to speak of ourselves? It is, however, definitely decided that as Lord Viṣṇu is always protecting the demigods from the onslaught of demons, so You have also advented in Vṛndāvana just to give the residents protection from all kinds of distress. O dear friend of the distressed, kindly place Your hand on our burning breasts as well as on our heads, because we have surrendered unto You as Your eternal maidservants. If You think, however, that Your lotus-like palms might be burned to ashes if placed on our burning breasts, let us assure You that Your palms will feel pleasure instead of pain, as the lotus flower, although very delicate and soft, enjoys the scorching heat of the sun."

Upon hearing the anxious plea of the *gopīs,* the Supreme Personality of Godhead began to smile, and being very kind to the *gopīs,* the Lord, although self-sufficient, began to embrace them and kiss them as they desired. When Kṛṣṇa, smiling, looked at the faces of the *gopīs,* the beauty of their faces became a hundred times enhanced. When He was enjoying them in their midst, He appeared just like the full moon surrounded by millions of shining stars. Thus the Supreme Personality of Godhead, surrounded by hundreds of *gopīs* and decorated with a flower garland of many colors, began to wander within the Vṛndāvana forest, sometimes singing to Himself and sometimes singing with the *gopīs.* In this way, both the Lord and the *gopīs* reached the cool sandy bank of the Yamunā where there were lilies and lotus flowers. In such a transcendental atmosphere, both the *gopīs* and Kṛṣṇa began to enjoy one another. While they were walking on the bank of the Yamunā, Kṛṣṇa would sometimes put His arms around a *gopī's* head, breast or waist. Pinching one another and joking and looking at one another, they enjoyed. When Kṛṣṇa touched the bodies of the *gopīs,* their lust to embrace Him increased. They all enjoyed these pastimes. Thus the *gopīs* were blessed with all mercy by the Supreme Personality of Godhead, for they enjoyed His company without a tinge of mundane sex life.

The *gopīs,* however, soon began to feel very proud, thinking themselves to be the most fortunate women in the universe by being favored by the company of Kṛṣṇa. Lord Kṛṣṇa, who is known as Keśava, could immediately understand their pride caused by their great fortune of enjoying Him personally, and in order to show them His causeless mercy and to curb their false pride, He immediately disappeared from the scene, exhibiting His opulence of renunciation. The Supreme Personality of Godhead is always full with six kinds of opulences, and this is an instance of the opulence of renunciation. This renunciation confirms Kṛṣṇa's total nonattachment. He is always self-sufficient and is not dependent on anything. This is the platform on which the transcendental pastimes are enacted.

*Thus ends the Bhaktivedanta purport of the Twenty-ninth Chapter of* Kṛṣṇa, *"The Rāsa Dance: Introduction."*

# 30 / Kṛṣṇa's Hiding from the Gopīs

When Kṛṣṇa suddenly disappeared from the company of the *gopīs,* they began to search for Him in every place. After not finding Him anywhere, they became afraid and almost mad after Him. They were simply thinking of the pastimes of Kṛṣṇa in great love and affection. Being absorbed in thought, they experienced loss of memory, and with dampened eyes they began to see the very pastimes of Kṛṣṇa, His beautiful talks with them, His embracing, kissing, and other activities. Being so attracted to Kṛṣṇa, they began to imitate His dancing, His walking and smiling, as if they themselves were Kṛṣṇa. Due to Kṛṣṇa's absence, they all became crazy; each one of them began to tell the others that she was Kṛṣṇa Himself. Soon they all began to assemble together and chant Kṛṣṇa's name very loudly, and they moved from one part of the forest to another searching for Him. Actually, Kṛṣṇa is all-pervasive; He is in the sky, and He is in the forest; He is within the heart, and He is always everywhere.

The *gopīs* therefore began to question the trees and plants about Kṛṣṇa. There were various types of big trees and small plants in the forest, and the *gopīs* began to address them. "Dear banyan tree, have you seen the son of Mahārāja Nanda passing this way, laughing and playing on His flute? He has stolen our hearts and has gone away. If you have seen Him, kindly inform us which way He has gone. Dear *aśoka* tree, dear *nāga* flower tree and *campaka* flower tree, have you seen the younger brother of Balarāma pass this way? He has disappeared because of our pride." The *gopīs* were aware of the reason for Kṛṣṇa's sudden disappearance. Thev could unaerstand that when they were enjoying Kṛṣṇa, they thought themselves to be the most fortunate women within the universe, and since they were feeling proud, Kṛṣṇa disappeared immediately just to curb their pride. Kṛṣṇa does not like His devotees to be proud of their service to Him. He accepts everyone's service, but He does not like one devotee to be prouder than others. If sometimes there are such feelings, Kṛṣṇa ends them by changing His attitude toward the devotee.

The *gopīs* then began to address the *tulasī* plants: "Dear *tulasī,* you are much beloved by Lord Kṛṣṇa because your leaves are always at His lotus feet. Dear *mālatī* flower, dear *mallikā* flower, dear jasmine flower, all of you must have been touched by Kṛṣṇa while He was passing this way after giving us transcendental enjoyment. Have you seen Mādhava passing this way? O mango trees, O trees of jack fruit, O pear trees and *asana* trees! O blackberries and *bael* trees and trees of *kadamba* flower–you are all very pious trees to be living on the bank of Yamunā. Kṛṣṇa must have passed through this way. Will you kindly let us know which way He has gone?

The *gopīs* then looked upon the ground they were traversing and began to address the earth, "Dear earthly planet, we do not know how many penances and austerities you have undergone to be now living with the footprints of Lord Kṛṣṇa upon you. You are very jolly; the hairs on your body are these jubilant trees and plants. Lord Kṛṣṇa must have been very much pleased with you, otherwise how could He have embraced you in the form of Varāha the boar? When you were submerged in water, He delivered you, taking the whole weight of your existence on His tusks."

After addressing the innumerable trees and plants, they turned their faces toward the beautiful deer who were looking on them very pleasingly. "It appears," they addressed the deer, "that Kṛṣṇa, who is the Supreme Nārāyaṇa Himself, must have passed through this way along with His companion, Lakṣmī, the goddess of fortune. Otherwise, how is it possible that the aroma of His garland, which is smeared with the red *kuṅkuma* from the breast of the goddess of fortune, can be perceived in the breeze blowing here? It appears that they must have passed through here and touched your bodies, and thus you are feeling so pleasant and are looking toward us with sympathy. Will you kindly, therefore, inform us which way Kṛṣṇa has gone? Kṛṣṇa is the well-wisher of Vṛndāvana. He is as kind to you as to us; therefore after leaving us, He must have been present in your company. O fortunate trees, we are thinking of Kṛṣṇa, the younger brother of Balarāma. While passing through here, with one hand resting on the shoulder of the goddess of fortune and the other hand whirling a lotus flower, He must have been very pleased to accept your obeisances, and He must have glanced at you with great pleasure.

Some of the *gopīs* then began to address their other *gopī* friends, "Dear friends, why don't you question these creepers who are so jubilantly embracing the big trees as if the trees were their husbands? It appears that the flowers of the creepers must have been touched by the nails of Kṛṣṇa. Otherwise, how could they feel so jubilant?"

After searching for Kṛṣṇa here and there, when the *gopīs* became fatigued, they began to talk like madwomen. They could only satisfy themselves by imitating the different pastimes of Kṛṣṇa. One of them imitated the demon, Pūtanā, and one of them imitated Kṛṣṇa and sucked her breast. One *gopī* imitated a hand-driven cart, and another *gopī* lay down beneath the cart and began to throw up her legs, touching the wheels of the cart, as Kṛṣṇa did to kill the demon Śakaṭāsura. They imitated child Kṛṣṇa, lying down on the ground, and one *gopī* became the demon Tṛṇāvarta and carried the small child Kṛṣṇa by force into the sky; and one of the *gopīs* began to imitate Kṛṣṇa while He was attempting to walk, ringing His ankle bells. Two *gopīs* imitated Kṛṣṇa and Balarāma, and many others imitated Their cowherd boy friends. One *gopī* assumed the form of Bakāsura, and another forced her to fall down as the demon Bakāsura did when he was killed; similarly, another *gopī* defeated Vatsāsura. Just as Kṛṣṇa used to call His cows by their different names, so the *gopīs* imitated Him, calling the cows by their respective names. One of the *gopīs* began to play on a flute, and another praised her the way Kṛṣṇa's boy friends praised Him while He played on His flute. One of the *gopīs* took another *gopī* on her shoulders, just as Kṛṣṇa used to take His boy friends. Absorbed in thoughts of Kṛṣṇa, the *gopī* who was carrying her friend began to boast that she was Kṛṣṇa herself: "All of you just see my movement!" One of the *gopīs* raised her hand with her covering garments and said, "Now don't be afraid of torrents of rain and severe hurricanes. I'll save you!" In this way she imitated the lifting of Govardhana Hill. One *gopī* forcibly put her feet on the head of another *gopī* and said, "You rascal Kāliya! I shall punish you severely. You must leave this place. I have descended on this earth to punish all kinds of miscreants!" Another *gopī* told her friends, "Just see! The flames of the forest fire are coming to devour us. Please close your eyes, and I shall immediately save you from this imminent danger."

In this way all the *gopīs* were madly feeling the absence of Kṛṣṇa. They enquired for Him from the trees and plants. In some places they found the imprints of the marks on the sole of His feet—namely the flag, the lotus flower, the trident, the thunderbolt, etc. After seeing those footprints, they exclaimed, "O here is the impression of the marks on the sole of Kṛṣṇa. All the marks, such as the flag, the lotus flower, the trident and the thunderbolt, are distinctly visible here." They began to follow the footprints, and shortly they saw another set of footprints beside them, and immediately they became very sorry. "Dear friends, just see! Whose are these other footprints? They are beside the footprints of the son of Mahārāja Nanda. It is certainly Kṛṣṇa passing through, resting His hand on some other *gopī,* exactly as an elephant goes side by side with his beloved mate. We must, therefore, understand that this particular *gopī* served Kṛṣṇa with greater affectionate love than ourselves. Because of this, although He has left us, He could not leave Her company. He has taken Her along with Him. Dear friends, just imagine how the dust of this place is transcendentally glorious. The dust of the lotus feet of Kṛṣṇa is worshiped even by Lord Brahmā and Lord Śiva, and the goddess of fortune, Lakṣmī. But at the same time, we are very sorry that this particular *gopī* has gone along with Kṛṣṇa, for She is sharing the nectar of Kṛṣṇa's kisses and leaving us aside to lament. O friends, just see! At this particular spot we do not see the footprints of that *gopī.* It appears that because there were some pin-pricks from the dried grass, Kṛṣṇa took Rādhārāṇī on His shoulder. O, She is so dear to Him! Kṛṣṇa must have picked some flowers in this spot to satisfy Rādhārāṇī, because here, where He stood erect to get the flowers from the high branches of the tree, we find only half the impression of His feet. Dear friends, just see how Kṛṣṇa must have sat down here with Rādhārāṇī and tried to set flowers in Her hair. You can be certain that both of Them sat together here. Kṛṣṇa is self-sufficient; He has nothing to enjoy from any other source, yet just to satisfy His devotee He has treated Rādhārāṇī exactly as a lusty boy treats his girl friend. Kṛṣṇa is so kind that He always tolerates the disturbances created by His girl friends."

In this way, all the *gopīs* began to point out the faults of the particular *gopī* who had been taken alone by Kṛṣṇa. They began to say that the chief *gopī,* Rādhārāṇī, who was taken alone by Kṛṣṇa, must be very proud of Her position, thinking Herself the greatest of the *gopīs.* "Yet how could Kṛṣṇa take Her away alone, leaving all of us aside, unless She be extraordinarily qualified and beautiful? She must have taken Kṛṣṇa in the deep forest and told Him, 'My dear Kṛṣṇa, I am now very tired. I cannot go any further. Please carry Me wherever You like.' When Kṛṣṇa was spoken to in this way, He might have told Rādhārāṇī, 'All right, better get on My shoulder.' But immediately Kṛṣṇa must have disappeared, and now Rādhārāṇī must be lamenting for Him, 'My dear lover, My dearest, You are so fine and so powerful. Where have You gone? I am nothing but Your most obedient maidservant. I am very much aggrieved. Please come and be with Me again.' Kṛṣṇa, however, is not coming to Her. He must be watching Her from a distant place and enjoying Her sorrow."

All the *gopīs* then went further and further into the forest, searching out Kṛṣṇa, but when they learned that actually Rādhārāṇī was left alone by Kṛṣṇa, they became very sorry. This is the test of Kṛṣṇa consciousness. In the beginning they were a little envious that Kṛṣṇa had taken Rādhārāṇī alone, leaving aside all other *gopīs,* but as soon as they knew that Kṛṣṇa had also left Rādhārāṇī and that She was alone lamenting for Him, they became more sympathetic to Her. The *gopīs* found Rādhārāṇī and heard everything from Her, about how She misbehaved with Kṛṣṇa and how She was proud and was insulted for Her pride. After hearing all this, they became actually very sympathetic. Then all the *gopīs,* including Rādhārāṇī, began to proceed further into the forest until they could no longer see the moonlight.

When they saw that it was getting gradually darker, they stopped. Their mind and intelligence became absorbed in the thoughts of Kṛṣṇa; they all imitated the activities of Kṛṣṇa and His speeches. Due to their heart and soul being completely given to Kṛṣṇa, they began to chant His glories, completely forgetting their family interests. In this way, all the *gopīs* assembled together on the bank of Yamunā, and expecting that Kṛṣṇa must return to them, they simply engaged in the chanting of the glories of Śrī Kṛṣṇa–Hare Kṛṣṇa, Hare Kṛṣṇa, Kṛṣṇa Kṛṣṇa, Hare Hare, Hare Rāma, Hare Rāma, Rāma Rāma, Hare Hare.

*Thus ends the Bhaktivedanta purport of the Thirtieth Chapter of* Kṛṣṇa, *"Kṛṣṇa's Hiding from the Gopīs"*

# 31 / Songs by the Gopīs

One *gopī* said, "My dear Kṛṣṇa, ever since You took Your birth in this land of Vrajabhūmi, everything appears to be glorious. The land of Vṛndāvana has become glorious, and it is as if the goddess of fortune is personally always existing here. But it is only we who are very unhappy, because we are searching for You, but cannot see You with our greatest effort. Our life is completely dependent upon You; therefore we request that You again come to us."

Another *gopī* said, "My dear Kṛṣṇa, You are the life and soul even of the lotus flower that grows on the water of lakes made transparent by the clear rains of autumn. Although the lotus flowers are so beautiful, without Your glance they fade away. Similarly, without You, we are also dying. Actually, we are neither Your wives nor slaves. You never spent any money for us, yet we are simply attracted by Your glance. Now, if we die without receiving Your glance, You'll be responsible for our deaths. Certainly the killing of women is a great sin, and if You do not come to see us and we die, You will suffer the reactions of sin. So please come see us. Do not think that one can be killed only by certain weapons. We are being killed by Your absence. You should consider how You are responsible for killing women. We are always grateful to You because You have protected us many times: from the poisonous water of Yamunā, from the serpent Kāliya, from Bakāsura, from the anger of Indra and his torrents of rain, from forest fire and so many other incidents. You are the greatest and most powerful of all. It is wonderful for You to protect us from so many dangers, but we are surprised that You are neglecting us at this moment. Dear Kṛṣṇa, dear friend, we know very well that You are not actually the son of mother Yaśodā or the cowherd man Nanda Mahārāja. You are the Supreme Personality of Godhead and the Supersoul of all living entities. You have, out of Your own causeless mercy, appeared in this world, requested by Lord Brahmā for the protection of the world. It is by Your kindness only that You have appeared in the dynasty of Yadu. O best in the dynasty of Yadu, if anyone afraid of this materialistic way of life takes shelter at Your lotus feet, You never deny him protection. Your movements are sweet, and You are independent, touching the goddess of fortune with one hand and in the other bearing a lotus flower. That is Your extraordinary feature. Please, therefore, come before us and bless us with the lotus flower in Your hand.

"Dear Kṛṣṇa, You are the killer of all the fears of the inhabitants of Vṛndāvana. You are the supremely powerful hero, and we know that You can kill the unnecessary pride of Your devotee as well as the pride of women like us simply by Your beautiful smile. We are simply Your maidservants and slaves; please, therefore, accept us by showing us Your lotus-like beautiful face.

"Dear Kṛṣṇa, actually we have become very lusty, having been touched by Your lotus feet. Your lotus feet certainly kill all kinds of sinful activities of devotees who have taken shelter there. You are so kind that even the ordinary animals take shelter under Your lotus feet. Your lotus feet are also the residence of the goddess of fortune, yet You dance on the head of the Kāliya serpent with them. Now we are requesting You to kindly place Your lotus feet on our breasts and pacify our lusty desires to touch You.

"O Lord, Your attractive eyes, like the lotus, are so nice and pleasing. Your sweet words are so fascinating that they please even the greatest scholars, who also become attracted to You. We are also attracted by Your speaking and by the beauty of Your face and eyes. Please, therefore, satisfy us by Your nectarean kisses. Dear Lord, words spoken by You or words describing Your activities are full of nectar, and simply by speaking or hearing Your words one can be saved from the blazing fire of material existence. Great demigods like Lord Brahmā and Lord Śiva are always engaged in chanting the glories of Your words. They do so to eradicate the sinful activities of all living entities in the material world. If one simply tries to hear Your transcendental words, he can very quickly be elevated to the platform of pious activities. For the Vaiṣṇavas, Your words give transcendental pleasure, and saintly persons who are engaged in distributing Your transcendental message all over the world are first-class charitable persons." (This is confirmed by Rūpa Gosvāmī also when he addressed Lord Caitanya as the most munificent incarnation because Lord Caitanya distributed the words of Kṛṣṇa and love of Kṛṣṇa free of charge all over the world.)

"Dear Kṛṣṇa," the *gopīs* continued, "You are very cunning. You can imagine how much we are distressed simply by remembering Your cunning smile, Your pleasing glance, Your walking with us in the forest of Vṛndāvana, and Your auspicious meditations. Your talks with us in lonely places were heart-warming. Now we are all aggrieved to remember Your behavior. Please save us. Dear Kṛṣṇa, certainly You know how much we are saddened when You go out of Vṛndāvana village to tend the cows in the forest. How we are afflicted simply to think that Your soft lotus feet are being pricked by the dry grass and the tiny stones in the forest! We are so attached to You that we always think simply of Your lotus feet.

"O Kṛṣṇa, when You return from the pasturing ground with the animals, we see Your face covered by Your curly hair and dusted by the hoof-dust of the cows. We see Your mildly smiling face, and our desire to enjoy You increases. O dear Kṛṣṇa, You are the supreme lover, and You always give shelter to surrendered souls. You fulfill everyone's desire; Your lotus feet are even worshiped by Lord Brahmā, the creator of the universe. To whomever worships Your lotus feet, You without a doubt always bestow Your benedictions. So kindly be pleased with us and keep Your lotus feet on our breasts and thus relieve our present distresses. Dear Kṛṣṇa, we are seeking Your kisses which You offer even to Your flute. The vibration of Your flute enchants the whole world and our hearts also. Kindly, therefore, return and kiss us with Your mouth of nectar."

When Lord Kṛṣṇa finally reappeared and assembled with the *gopīs*, He looked very beautiful, just befitting a person with all kinds of opulences. In the *Brahma-saṁhitā*, it is stated, *ānanda-cin-maya-rasa-pratibhāvitābhiḥ:* Kṛṣṇa alone is not particularly beautiful, but when His energy—especially His pleasure energy, represented by Rādhārāṇī—expands, He looks very magnificent. The Māyāvāda conception of the perfection of the Absolute Truth without potency is due to insufficient knowledge. Actually, outside the exhibition of His different potencies, the Absolute Truth is not complete. *Ānanda-cin-maya-rasa* means that His body is a transcendental form of eternal bliss and knowledge. Kṛṣṇa is always surrounded by different potencies, and therefore He is perfect and beautiful. We understand from *Brahma-saṁhitā* and *Skanda Purāṇa* that Kṛṣṇa is always surrounded by many thousands of goddesses of fortune. The *gopīs* are all goddesses of fortune, and Kṛṣṇa took them hand in hand on the bank of the Yamunā.

It is said in the *Skanda Purāṇa* that out of many thousands of *gopīs*, 16,000 are predominant; out of those 16,000 *gopīs*, 108 *gopīs* are especially prominent; and out of 108 *gopīs*, eight *gopīs* are still more prominent; out of eight *gopīs,* Rādhārāṇī and Candrāvalī are prominent; and out of these two *gopīs,* Rādhārāṇī is the most prominent.

When Kṛṣṇa entered the forest on the bank of the Yamunā, the moonlight dissipated the surrounding darkness. Due to the season, flowers like the *kunda* and *kadamba* were blooming, and a gentle breeze was carrying their aroma. Due to the aroma, the bees were also flying in the breeze, thinking that the aroma was honey. The *gopīs* made a seat for Kṛṣṇa by leveling the soft sand and placing cloths over it.

The *gopīs* who were gathered there were mostly all followers of the *Vedas.* In their previous births, during Lord Rāmacandra's advent, they were Vedic scholars who desired the association of Lord Rāmacandra in conjugal love. Rāmacandra gave them the benediction that they would be present for the advent of Lord Kṛṣṇa, and He would fulfill their desires. During Kṛṣṇa's advent, the Vedic scholars took birth in the shape of the *gopīs* in Vṛndāvana; as young *gopīs,* they got the association of Kṛṣṇa in fulfillment of their previous births' desire. The ultimate goal of their perfect desire was attained, and they were so joyous that they had nothing further to desire. This is confirmed in the *Bhagavad-gītā:* if one attains the Supreme Personality of Godhead, then he has no desire for anything. When the *gopīs* had Kṛṣṇa in their company, not only all their grief, but their lamenting in the absence of Kṛṣṇa was relieved. They felt they had no desire to be fulfilled. Fully satisfied in the company of Kṛṣṇa, they spread their cloths on the ground. These garments were made of fine linen and smeared with the red *kuṅkuma* which decorated their breasts. With great care they spread a sitting place for Kṛṣṇa. Kṛṣṇa was their life and soul, and they created a very comfortable seat for Him.

Sitting on the seat amongst the *gopīs,* Kṛṣṇa became more beautiful. Great *yogīs* like Lord Śiva, Lord Brahmā or even Lord Śeṣa and others always try to fix their attention upon Kṛṣṇa in their heart, but here the *gopīs* actually saw Kṛṣṇa seated before them on their cloths. In the society of the *gopīs,* Kṛṣṇa looked very beautiful. They were the most beautiful damsels within the three worlds, and they assembled together around Kṛṣṇa.

It may be asked herein how Kṛṣṇa seated Himself beside so many *gopīs* and yet sat alone. There is a significant word in this verse: *īśvara.* As it is stated in the *Bhagavad-gītā, īśvaraḥ sarva-bhūtānām. Īśvara* refers to the Supreme Lord as the Supersoul seated in everyone's heart. Kṛṣṇa also manifested this potency of expansion as Paramātmā in this gathering with the *gopīs.* Kṛṣṇa was sitting by the side of each *gopī,* unseen by the others. Kṛṣṇa was so kind to the *gopīs* that instead of sitting in their hearts to be appreciated in yogic meditation, He seated Himself by their sides. By seating Himself outside, He showed special favor to the *gopīs,* who were the selected beauties of all creation. Having gotten their most beloved Lord, the *gopīs* began to please Him by moving their eyebrows and smiling and also by suppressing their anger. Some of them took His lotus feet in their laps and began to massage Him. And while smiling, they confidentially expressed their suppressed anger and said, "Dear Kṛṣṇa, we are ordinary women of Vṛndāvana, and we do not know much about Vedic knowledge–what is right and what is wrong. We therefore put a question to You, and, since You are very learned, You can answer it properly. In dealing between lovers, we find that there are three classes of men. One class simply receives, another class reciprocates favorably, even if the lover is very contrary, and the third class neither acts contrary nor answers favorably in dealings of love. So out of these three classes, which do You prefer, or which do You call honest?"

In answer, Kṛṣṇa said, "My dear friends, persons who simply reciprocate the loving dealings of the other party are just like merchants. They give in loving affairs as much as they get from the other party. Practically there is no question of love. It is simply business dealing, and it is self-interested or self-centered. Better the second class of men, who love in spite of the opposite party's contrariness; even those without a tinge of loving affairs are better than the merchants. Sincere love can be seen when the father and mother love their children in spite of their children's neglect. The third class neither reciprocates nor neglects. They can be further divided into two classes. One is the self-satisfied, who do not require anyone's love. They are called *ātmārāma,* which means they are absorbed in the thought of the Supreme Personality of Godhead and so do not care whether one loves them or not. But another class are ungrateful men. They are called callous. The men in this group revolt against superior persons. For instance, a son, in spite of receiving all kinds of things from loving parents, may be callous and not reciprocate. Those in this class are generally known as *gurudruha,* which means they receive favors from the parents or the spiritual master and yet neglect them."

Kṛṣṇa indirectly answered the questions of the *gopīs,* even those questions which implied that Kṛṣṇa did not properly receive their dealings. In answer, Kṛṣṇa said that He, as the Supreme Personality of Godhead, is self-satisfied. He does not require anyone's love, but at the same time He said that He is not ungrateful.

"My dear friends," Kṛṣṇa continued, "you might be aggrieved by My words and acts, but you must know that sometimes I do not reciprocate my devotees' dealings with Me. It appears that my devotees are very much attached to Me, but sometimes I do not reciprocate their feelings properly in order to increase their love for Me more and more. If I can very easily be approached by them, they might think, 'Kṛṣṇa is so easily available.' So sometimes I do not respond. If a person has no money but after some time accumulates some wealth and then loses it, he will think of the lost property twenty-four hours a day. Similarly, in order to increase the love of My devotees, sometimes I appear to be lost to them, and instead of forgetting Me, they feel their loving sentiments for Me increase. My dear friends, do not think for a moment that I have been dealing with You just like ordinary devotees. I know what you are. You have forsaken all kinds of social and religious obligations; you have given up all connection with your parents. Without caring for social convention and religious obligations, you have come to Me and loved Me, and I am so much obliged to you that I cannot treat you as ordinary devotees. Do not think that I was away from you. I was near to you. I was simply seeing how much you were anxious for Me in My absence. So please do not try to find fault in Me. Because you consider Me so dear to you, kindly excuse Me if I have done anything wrong. I cannot repay your continual love for Me, even throughout the lifetimes of the demigods in the heavenly planets. It is impossible to repay you or show gratitude for your love; therefore please be satisfied by your own pious activities. You have displayed exemplary attraction for Me, overcoming the greatest difficulties arising from family connections. Please be satisfied with your highly exemplary character, for it is not possible for Me to repay your debt."

The exemplary character of devotional service manifested by the devotees of Vṛndāvana is the purest type of devotion. It is enjoined in authoritative *śāstra* that devotional service must be *ahaituka* and *apratihata.* This means that devotional service to Kṛṣṇa cannot be checked by political or religious convention. The stage of devotional service is always transcendental. The *gopīs* particularly showed pure devotional service towards Kṛṣṇa, so much so that Kṛṣṇa Himself remained indebted to them. Lord Caitanya thus said that the devotional service manifested by the *gopīs* in Vṛndāvana excelled all other methods of approaching the Supreme Personality of Godhead.

*Thus ends the Bhaktivedanta purport of the Thirty-first Chapter of* Kṛṣṇa, *"Songs by the Gopīs."*

# 32 / Description of the Rāsa Dance

Thus hearing the Supreme Personality of Godhead, Kṛṣṇa, speaking to pacify them, the *gopīs* became very much pleased. And not only by hearing His words, but also by touching the hands and legs of the Supreme Personality of Godhead, they became completely relieved from the great suffering of separation. After this, the Supreme Personality of Godhead began His *rāsa* dance. When one dances in the midst of many girls, it is called a *rāsa* dance. So Kṛṣṇa began to dance among the most beautiful and fortunate girls within the three worlds. The *gopīs* of Vṛndāvana, who were so attracted to Him, danced with Kṛṣṇa, hand in hand.

Kṛṣṇa's *rāsa* dance should never be compared with any kind of material dance, such as a ball dance or a society dance. The *rāsa* dance is a completely spiritual performance. In order to establish this fact, Kṛṣṇa, the supreme mystic, expanded Himself in many forms and stood beside each *gopī*. Placing His hands on the shoulders of the *gopīs* on both sides of Him, He began to dance in their midst. The mystic expansions of Kṛṣṇa were not perceived by the *gopīs* because Kṛṣṇa appeared alone to each of them. Each *gopī* thought that Kṛṣṇa was dancing with her alone. Above that wonderful dance flew many airplanes carrying the denizens of the heavenly planets, who were very anxious to see the wonderful dance of Kṛṣṇa with the *gopīs*. The Gandharvas and Kinnaras began to sing, and, accompanied by their respective wives, all the Gandharvas began to shower flowers on the dancers.

As the *gopīs* and Kṛṣṇa danced together, a very blissful musical sound was produced from the tinkling of their bells, ornaments and bangles. It appeared that Kṛṣṇa was a greenish sapphire locket in the midst of a golden necklace decorated with valuable stones. While Kṛṣṇa and the *gopīs* danced they displayed extraordinary bodily features. The movements of their legs, their placing their hands on one another, the movements of their eyebrows, their smiling, the movements of the breasts of the *gopīs* and their clothes, their earrings, their cheeks, their hair with flowers—as they sang and danced these combined together to appear like clouds, thunder, snow and lightning. Kṛṣṇa's bodily features appeared just like a group of clouds, their songs were like thunder, the beauty of the *gopīs* appeared to be just like lightning in the sky, and the drops of perspiration visible on their faces appeared like falling snow. In this way, both the *gopīs* and Kṛṣṇa fully engaged in dancing.

The necks of the *gopīs* became tinted with red due to their desire to enjoy Kṛṣṇa more and more. To satisfy them, Kṛṣṇa began to clap His hands in time with their singing. Actually the whole world is full of Kṛṣṇa's singing, but it is appreciated in different ways by different kinds of living entities. This is confirmed in the *Bhagavad-gītā: ye yathā māṁ prapadyante.* Kṛṣṇa is dancing, and every living entity is also dancing, but there is a difference in the dancing in the spiritual world and in the material world. This is expressed by the author of *Caitanya-caritāmṛta,* who says that the master dancer is Kṛṣṇa and everyone is His servant. Everyone is trying to imitate Kṛṣṇa's dancing. Those who are actually in Kṛṣṇa consciousness respond rightly to the dancing of Kṛṣṇa: they do not try to dance independently. But those in the material world try to imitate Kṛṣṇa as the Supreme Personality of Godhead. The living entities are dancing under the direction of Kṛṣṇa's *māyā* and are thinking that they are equal to Kṛṣṇa. But this is not a fact. In Kṛṣṇa consciousness, this misconception is absent, for a person in Kṛṣṇa consciousness knows that Kṛṣṇa is the supreme master and everyone is His servant. One has to dance to please Kṛṣṇa, not to imitate or to become equal to the Supreme Personality of Godhead. The *gopīs* wanted to please Kṛṣṇa, and therefore as Kṛṣṇa sang, they responded and encouraged Him by saying, "Well done, well done." Sometimes they presented beautiful music for His pleasure, and He responded by praising their singing.

When some of the *gopīs* became very tired from dancing and moving their bodies, they placed their hands on the shoulders of Śrī Kṛṣṇa. Then their hair loosened and flowers fell to the ground. When they placed their hands on Kṛṣṇa's shoulder, they became overwhelmed by the fragrance of His body which emanated from the lotus, other aromatic flowers, and the pulp of sandalwood. They became filled with attraction for Him, and they began to kiss one another. Some *gopīs* touched Kṛṣṇa cheek to cheek, and Kṛṣṇa began to offer them chewed betel nuts from His mouth, which they exchanged with great pleasure by kissing. And by accepting those betel nuts, the *gopīs* spiritually advanced.

The *gopīs* became tired after long singing and dancing. Kṛṣṇa was dancing beside them, and to alleviate their fatigue they took Śrī Kṛṣṇa's hand and placed it on their raised breasts. Kṛṣṇa's hand, as well as the breasts of the *gopīs*, are eternally auspicious; therefore when they combined, both of them became spiritually enhanced. The *gopīs* so enjoyed the company of Kṛṣṇa, the husband of the goddess of fortune, that they forgot that they had any other husband in the world, and upon being embraced by the arms of Kṛṣṇa and dancing and singing with Him, they forgot everything. The *Śrīmad-Bhāgavatam* thus describes the beauty of the *gopīs* while they were *rāsa* dancing with Kṛṣṇa. There were lotus flowers over both their ears, and their faces were decorated with sandalwood pulp. They wore *tilaka*, and there were drops of sweat on their smiling mouths. From their feet came the tinkling sound of ankle bells as well as bangles. The flowers within their hair were falling to the lotus feet of Kṛṣṇa, and He was very satisfied.

As stated in the *Brahma-saṁhitā*, all these *gopīs* are expansions of Kṛṣṇa's pleasure potency. Touching their bodies with His hands and looking at their pleasing eyes, Kṛṣṇa enjoyed the *gopīs* exactly as a child enjoys playing with the reflection of his body in a mirror. When Kṛṣṇa touched the different parts of their bodies, the *gopīs* felt surcharged with spiritual energy. They could not adjust their loosened clothes, although they tried to keep them properly. Their hair and garments became scattered, and their ornaments loosened as they forgot themselves in company with Kṛṣṇa.

While Kṛṣṇa was enjoying the company of the *gopīs* in the *rāsa* dance, the astonished demigods and their wives gathered in the sky. The moon, being afflicted with a sort of lust, began to watch the dance and became stunned with wonder. The *gopīs* had prayed to the goddess Kātyāyanī to have Kṛṣṇa as their husband. Now Kṛṣṇa was fulfilling their desire by expanding Himself in as many forms as there were *gopīs* and enjoying them exactly as a husband.

Śrīla Śukadeva Gosvāmī has remarked that Kṛṣṇa is self-sufficient—He is *ātmārāma*. He doesn't need anyone else for His satisfaction. Because the *gopīs* wanted Kṛṣṇa as their husband, He fulfilled their desire. When Kṛṣṇa saw that the *gopīs* were tired from dancing with Him, He immediately began to smear His hands over their faces so that their fatigue would be relieved. In order to reciprocate the kind hospitality of Kṛṣṇa, the *gopīs* began to look at Him lovingly. They were overjoyed by the auspicious touch of the hand of Kṛṣṇa. Their smiling cheeks shone with beauty, and they began to sing the glories of Kṛṣṇa with transcendental pleasure. As pure devotees, the more the *gopīs* enjoyed Kṛṣṇa's company, the more thev became enlightened with His glories, and thus they reciprocated wιth Him. They wanted to satisfy Kṛṣṇa by glorifying His transcendental pastimes. Kṛṣṇa is the Supreme Personality of Godhead, the master of all masters, and the *gopīs* wanted to worship Him for His unusual exhibition of mercy upon them.

Both the *gopīs* and Kṛṣṇa entered the water of the Yamunā just to relieve their fatigue from the *rāsa* dance. The lily flower garlands around the necks of the *gopīs* were strewn to pieces due to their embracing the body of Kṛṣṇa, and the flowers were reddish from being smeared with the *kuṅkuma* on their breasts. The bumblebees were humming about in order to get honey from the flowers. Kṛṣṇa and the *gopīs* entered the water of Yamunā just as an elephant enters a water tank with his many female companions. Both the *gopīs* and Kṛṣṇa forgot their real identity, playing in the water, enjoying each others' company and relieving the fatigue of *rāsa* dancing. The *gopīs* began to splash water on the body of Kṛṣṇa, all the while smiling, and Kṛṣṇa enjoyed this. As Kṛṣṇa was taking pleasure in the joking words and splashing water, the demigods in the heavenly planets began to shower flowers. The demigods thus praised the super-excellent *rāsa* dance of Kṛṣṇa, the supreme enjoyer, and His pastimes with the *gopīs* in the water of Yamunā.

After this, Lord Kṛṣṇa and the *gopīs* came out of the water and began to stroll along the bank of the Yamunā, where a nice breeze was blowing, carrying the aroma of different kinds of flowers over the water and land. While strolling on the bank of the Yamunā, Kṛṣṇa recited various kinds of poetry. He thus enjoyed the company of the *gopīs* in the soothing moonlight of autumn.

Sex desire is especially excited in the autumn season, but the wonderful thing about Kṛṣṇa's association with the *gopīs* is that there was no question of sex desire. It was, as clearly stated in the *Bhāgavata* description by Śukadeva Gosvāmī, *avaruddha-sauratah*, namely the sex impulse was completely controlled. There is a distinction between Lord Kṛṣṇa's dancing with the *gopīs* and the ordinary dancing of living entities within the material world. In order to clear up further misconceptions about the *rāsa* dance and the affairs of Kṛṣṇa and the *gopīs*, Mahārāja Parīkṣit, the hearer of *Śrīmad-Bhāgavatam*, told Śukadeva Gosvāmī, "Kṛṣṇa appeared on the earth to establish the regulative principles of religion and to curb the predominance of irreligion. But the behavior of Kṛṣṇa and the *gopīs* might encourage irreligious principles in the material world. I am simply surprised that He would act in such a way, enjoying the company of others' wives in the dead of night." This statement of Mahārāja Parīkṣit's was very much appreciated by Śukadeva Gosvamī. The answer anticipates the abominable acts of the Māyāvādī impersonalists who place themselves in the position of Kṛṣṇa and enjoy the company of young girls and women.

The basic Vedic injunctions never allow a person to enjoy sex with any woman except one's own wife. Kṛṣṇa's appreciation of the *gopīs* appeared to be distinctly in violation of these rules. Mahārāja Parīkṣit understood the total situation from Śukadeva Gosvāmī, yet to further clear the transcendental nature of Kṛṣṇa and the *gopīs* in *rāsa* dance, he expressed his surprise. This is very important in order to check the unrestricted association with women by the *prakṛta-sahajiyā.*

In his statement, Mahārāja Parīkṣit has used several important words which require clarification. The first word, *jugupsitam,* means abominable. The first doubt of Mahārāja Parīkṣit was as follows: Lord Kṛṣṇa is the Supreme Personality of Godhead who has advented Himself to establish religious principles. Why then did He mix with others' wives in the dead of night and enjoy dancing, embracing and kissing? According to the Vedic injunctions, this is not allowed. Also, when the *gopīs* first came to Him, He gave instructions to them to return to their homes. To call the wives of other persons or young girls and enjoy dancing with them is certainly abominable according to the *Vedas.* Why should Kṛṣṇa have done this?

Another word used here is *āptakāma.* Some may take it for granted that Kṛṣṇa was very lusty among young girls, but Parīkṣit Mahārāja said that this was not possible. He could not be lusty. First of all, from the material calculation He was only eight years old. At that age a boy cannot be lusty. *Āptakāma* means that the Supreme Personality of Godhead is self-satisfied. Even if He were lusty, He doesn't need to take help from others to satisfy His lusty desires. The next point is that, although not lusty Himself, He might have been induced by the lusty desires of the *gopīs.* But Mahārāja Parīkṣit then used another word, *yadu-pati,* which indicates that Kṛṣṇa is the most exalted personality in the dynasty of the Yadus. The kings in the dynasty of Yadu were considered to be the most pious, and their descendants were also like that. Having taken birth in that family, how could Kṛṣṇa have been induced, even by the *gopīs?* It is concluded, therefore, that it was not possible for Kṛṣṇa to do anything abominable. But Mahārāja Parīkṣit was in doubt as to *why* Kṛṣṇa acted in that way. What was the real purpose? Another word Mahārāja Parīkṣit used when he addressed Śukadeva Gosvāmī is *suvrata,* which means to take a vow to enact pious activities. Śukadeva Gosvāmī was an educated *brahmacārī,* and under the circumstances, it was not possible for him to indulge in sex. This is strictly prohibited for *brahmacārīs,* and what to speak of a *brahmacārī* like Śukadeva Gosvāmī. But because the circumstances of the *rāsa* dance were very suspect, Mahārāja Parīkṣit inquired for clarification from Śukadeva Gosvāmī. Śukadeva Gosvāmī immediately replied that transgressions of religious principles by the supreme controller testify to His great power. For example, fire can consume any abominable thing; that is the manifestation of the supremacy of fire. Similarly, the sun can absorb water from a urinal or from stool, and the sun is not polluted; rather, due to the influence of sunshine, the polluted, contaminated place becomes disinfected and sterilized.

One may also argue that since Kṛṣṇa is the supreme authority, His activities should be followed. In answer to this question, Śukadeva Gosvāmī has very clearly said that *īśvarāṇām,* or the supreme controller, may sometimes violate His instructions, but this is only possible for the controller Himself, not for the followers. Unusual and uncommon activities by the controller can never be imitated. Śukadeva Gosvāmī warned that the conditioned followers, who are not actually in control, should never even imagine imitating the uncommon activities of the controller. A Māyāvādī philosopher may falsely claim to be God or Kṛṣṇa, but he cannot actually act like Kṛṣṇa. He can persuade his followers to falsely imitate *rāsa* dance, but he is unable to lift Govardhana Hill. We have many experiences in the past of Māyāvādī rascals deluding their followers by posing themselves as Kṛṣṇa in order to enjoy *rāsa-līlā.* In many instances they were checked by the government, arrested and punished. In Orissa, Ṭhākur Bhaktivinode also punished a so-called incarnation of Viṣṇu, who was imitating *rāsa-līlā* with young girls. There were many complaints against him. At that time, Bhaktivinode Ṭhākur was magistrate, and the government deputed him to deal with that rascal, and he punished him very severely. The *rāsa-līlā* dance cannot be imitated by anyone. Śukadeva Gosvāmī warns that one should not even think of imitating it. He specifically mentions that if, out of foolishness, one tries to imitate Kṛṣṇa's *rāsa* dance, he will be killed, just like a person who wants to imitate Lord Śiva's drinking of an ocean of poison. Lord Śiva drank an ocean of poison and kept it within his throat. The poison made his throat turn blue; and therefore Lord Śiva is called Nīlakaṇṭa. But if any ordinary person tries to imitate Lord Śiva by drinking poison or smoking *gañja,* he is sure to be vanquished and will die within a very short time. Lord Śrī Kṛṣṇa's dealing with the *gopīs* was under special circumstances.

Most of the *gopīs* in their previous lives were great sages, expert in the studies of the *Vedas,* and when Lord Kṛṣṇa appeared as Lord Rāmacandra, they wanted to enjoy with Him. Lord Rāmacandra gave them the benediction that their desires would be fulfilled when He would appear as Kṛṣṇa. Therefore the desire of the *gopīs* to enjoy the appearance of Lord Kṛṣṇa was long cherished. So they approached goddess Kātyāyanī to have Kṛṣṇa as their husband. There are many other circumstances also which testify to the supreme authority of Kṛṣṇa and show that He is not bound to the rules and regulations of the material world. In special cases, He acts as He likes to favor His devotees. This is only possible for Him, because He is the supreme controller. People in general should follow the instructions of Lord Kṛṣṇa as given in the *Bhagavad-gītā* and should not even imagine imitating Lord Kṛṣṇa in the *rāsa* dance.

Kṛṣṇa's lifting of Govardhana Hill, His killing great demons like Pūtanā and others are all obviously extraordinary activities. Similarly, the *rāsa* dance is also an uncommon activity and cannot be imitated by any ordinary man. An ordinary person engaged in his occupational duty, like Arjuna, should execute his duty for the satisfaction of Kṛṣṇa; that is within his power. Arjuna was a fighter, and Kṛṣṇa wanted him to fight for His satisfaction. Arjuna agreed, although at first he was not willing to fight. Duties are required for ordinary persons. They should not jump up and try to imitate Kṛṣṇa and indulge in *rāsa-līlā* and thus bring about their ruin. One should know with certainty that Kṛṣṇa had no personal interest in whatever He did for the benediction of the *gopīs*. As stated in the *Bhagavad-gītā, na māṁ karmāṇi limpanti:* Kṛṣṇa never enjoys or suffers the result of His activities. Therefore it is not possible for Him to act irreligiously. He is transcendental to all activities and religious principles. He is untouched by the modes of material nature. He is the supreme controller of all living entities, either in human society, in the demigod society in heavenly planets, or in lower forms of life. He is the supreme controller of all living entities and of material nature; therefore, He has nothing to do with religious or irreligious principles.

Śukadeva Gosvāmī further concludes that the great sages and devotees, who are washed clean of all conditional life, can move freely even within the contamination of material nature by keeping Kṛṣṇa the Supreme Personality of Godhead within their hearts. In this way also they do not become subject to the laws of pleasure and pain in the modes of material nature. How, then, is it possible for Kṛṣṇa, who appears in His own internal potency, to be subjected to the laws of *karma?*

In the *Bhagavad-gītā* the Lord clearly says that whenever He appears He does so by His internal potency; He is not forced to accept a body by the laws of *karma* like an ordinary living entity. Every other living entity is forced to accept a certain type of body by his previous actions. But when Kṛṣṇa appears, He always appears in a body; it is not forced upon Him by the action of His past deeds. His body is a vehicle for His transcendental pleasure which is enacted by His internal potency. He has no obligation to the laws of *karma.* The Māyāvādī monist must accept a certain type of body, being forced by the laws of nature; therefore, his claim to be one with Kṛṣṇa or God is only theoretical. Such persons who claim to be equal with Kṛṣṇa and indulge in *rāsa-līlā* create a dangerous situation for the people in general. Kṛṣṇa, the Supreme Personality of Godhead, is already present as Supersoul within the bodies of the *gopīs* and their husbands. He is the guide of all living entities, as is confirmed in the *Kaṭha Upaniṣad, nityo nityānāṁ cetanaś cetanānām.* The Supersoul directs the individual soul to act, and the Supersoul is the actor and witness of all action.

It is confirmed in the *Bhagavad-gītā* that Kṛṣṇa is present in everyone's heart, and from Him come all action, remembrance and forgetfulness. He is the original person to be known by Vedic knowledge. He is the author of *Vedānta* philosophy, and He knows the *Vedānta* philosophy perfectly well. The so-called Vedāntists and Māyāvādīs cannot understand Kṛṣṇa as He is; they simply mislead followers by imitating the actions of Kṛṣṇa in an unauthorized way. Kṛṣṇa, the Supersoul of everyone, is already within the body of everyone; therefore if He sees someone or embraces someone there is no question of propriety.

Some ask that if Kṛṣṇa is self-sufficient, why should He at all manifest pastimes with the *gopīs* which are disturbing to the so-called moralists of the world? The answer is that such activities show special mercy to the fallen, conditioned souls. The *gopīs* are also expansions of His internal energy, but because Kṛṣṇa wanted to exhibit the *rāsa-līlā,* they also appeared as ordinary human beings. In the material world, pleasure is ultimately manifested in the sex attraction between man and woman. The man lives simply to be attracted by women, and the woman lives simply to be attracted by men. That is the basic principle of material life. As soon as these attractions are combined, people become more and more implicated in material existence. In order to show them special favor, Kṛṣṇa exhibited this *rāsa-līlā* dance. It is just to captivate the conditioned soul. Since they are very much attracted by sexology, they can enjoy the same life with Kṛṣṇa and thus become liberated from the material condition. In the Second Canto of *Śrīmad-Bhāgavatam,* Mahārāja Parīkṣit also explains that the pastimes and activities of Lord Kṛṣṇa are medicine for the conditioned souls. If they simply hear about Kṛṣṇa they become relieved from the material disease. They are addicted to material enjoyment and are accustomed to reading sex literature, but by hearing these transcendental pastimes of Kṛṣṇa with the *gopīs,* they will be relieved from material contamination.

How they should hear and from whom is also explained by Śukadeva Gosvāmī. The difficulty is that the whole world is full of Māyāvādīs, and when they become professional reciters of *Śrīmad-Bhāgavatam,* and when people, without knowing the effect of the Māyāvāda philosophy, hear from such persons, they become confused. Discussion of *rāsa-līlā* among people in general is not recommended because they are affected by the Māyāvāda philosophy, but if one who is advanced explains, and people hear from him, certainly the hearers will be gradually elevated to the position of Kṛṣṇa consciousness and liberated from materially contaminated life.

Another important point is that all the *gopīs* who danced with Kṛṣṇa were not in their material bodies. They danced with Kṛṣṇa in their spiritual bodies. All their husbands thought that their wives were sleeping by their sides. The so-called husbands of the *gopīs* were already enamored by the influence of the external energy of Kṛṣṇa; so by dint of this very energy they could not understand that their wives had gone to dance with Kṛṣṇa. What then is the basis of accusing Kṛṣṇa of dancing with others' wives? The bodies of the *gopīs,* which were their husbands', were lying in bed, but the spiritual parts and parcels of Kṛṣṇa were dancing with Him. Kṛṣṇa is the supreme person, the whole spirit, and He danced with the spiritual bodies of the *gopīs.* There is therefore no reason to accuse Kṛṣṇa in any way.

After the *rāsa* dance was over, the night turned into the *brāhma-muhūrta* (the night of Brahmā, a very, very long period, as mentioned in the *Bhagavad-gītā).* The *brāhma-muhūrta* takes place about one and a half hours before sunrise. It is recommended that one should rise from bed at that time and, after finishing daily ablutions, take to spiritual activities by performing *Maṅgala-ārātrika* and chanting the Hare Kṛṣṇa *mantra.* This period is very convenient for the execution of spiritual activities. When that auspicious moment arrived, Kṛṣṇa asked the *gopīs* to leave. Although they were not willing to quit His company, they were very obedient and dear to Him. As soon as Kṛṣṇa asked them to go home, they immediately left and returned home. Śukadeva Gosvāmī concludes this episode of *rāsa-līlā* by pointing out that if a person hears from the right source of the pastimes of Kṛṣṇa, who is Viṣṇu Himself, and the *gopīs,* who are expansions of His energy, then he will be relieved from the most dangerous type of disease, namely lust. If one actually hears *rāsa-līlā,* he will become completely freed from the lusty desire of sex life and elevated to the highest level of spiritual understanding. Generally, because they hear from Māyāvādīs and they themselves are Māyāvādīs, people become more and more implicated in sex life. The conditioned soul should hear the *rāsa-līlā* dance from an authorized spiritual master and be trained by him so that he can understand the whole situation; thus one can be elevated to the highest standard of spiritual life, otherwise one will be implicated. Material lust is a kind of heart disease, and to cure the material heart disease of the conditioned soul, it is recommended that one should hear, but not from the impersonalist rascals. If one hears from the right sources with right understanding, then his situation will be different.

Śukadeva Gosvāmī has used the word *śraddhānvita* for one who is trained in the spiritual life. *Śraddhā,* or faith, is the beginning. One who has developed his faith in Kṛṣṇa as the Supreme Personality of Godhead, the Supreme Spirit Soul, can both describe and hear. Śukadeva also uses the word *anuśṛṇuyāt.* One must hear from disciplic succession. *Anu* means following, and *anu* means always. So one must always follow the disciplic succession and not hear from any stray professional reciter, Māyāvādī or ordinary man. *Anuśṛṇuyāt* means that one must hear from an authorized person who is in the disciplic succession and is always engaged in Kṛṣṇa consciousness. When a person wants to hear in this way, then the effect will be sure. By hearing *rāsa-līlā,* one will be elevated to the highest position of spiritual life.

Śukadeva Gosvāmī uses two specific words, *bhaktim* and *parām. Bhaktim parām* means execution of devotional service above the neophyte stage. Those who are simply attracted to temple worship but do not know the philosophy of *bhakti* are in the neophyte stage. That sort of *bhakti* is not the perfectional stage. The perfectional stage of *bhakti,* or devotional service, is completely free from material contamination. The most dangerous aspect of contamination is lust or sex life. *Bhaktim parām* devotional service is so potent that the more one advances in this line, the more he loses his attraction for material life. One who is actually deriving benefit from hearing *rāsa-līlā* dance surely achieves the transcendental position. He surely loses all traces of lust in his heart.

Śrīla Viśvanātha Cakravartī Ṭhākur points out that according to *Bhagavad-gītā,* the Brahmā day and Brahmā night are periods of solar years expanding to 4,300,000 multiplied by 1,000. According to Viśvanātha Cakravartī Ṭhākur, the *rāsa* dance was performed during the long period of Brahmā's night, but the *gopīs* could not understand that. In order to fulfill their desire, Kṛṣṇa extended the night to cover such a great period of time. One may ask how this was possible, and Viśvanātha Cakravartī Ṭhākur reminds us that Kṛṣṇa, although bound by a small rope, could show His mother the whole universe within His mouth. How was this possible? The answer is that He can do anything for the pleasure of His devotees. Similarly, because the *gopīs* wanted to enjoy Kṛṣṇa, they were given the opportunity to associate with Him for a long period. This was done according to His promise. When Kṛṣṇa stole the garments of the *gopīs* while they were taking bath at Cirghat on Yamunā, Kṛṣṇa promised to fulfill their desire in some future night. In one night, therefore, they enjoyed the company of Kṛṣṇa as their beloved husband, but that night was not an ordinary night. It was a night of Brahmā, and lasted millions and millions of years. Everything is possible for Kṛṣṇa, for He is the supreme controller.

*Thus ends the Bhaktivedanta purport of the Thirty-second Chapter of* Kṛṣṇa, *"Description of the Rāsa Dance."*

# 33 / Vidyādhara Liberated and the Demon Śaṅkhāsura Killed

Once upon a time, the cowherd men of Vṛndāvana, headed by Nanda Mahārāja, desired to go to Ambikāvana to perform the *Śivarātri* performance. The *rāsa-līlā* was performed during the autumn, and after that the next big ceremony is *Holi* or the *Dolayātrā* ceremony. Between the *Dolayātrā* ceremony and the *rāsa-līlā* ceremony there is one important ceremony which is called *Śivarātri,* which is especially observed by the Śaivites, or devotees of Lord Śiva. But sometimes the Vaiṣṇavas also observe this ceremony because they accept Lord Śiva as the foremost Vaiṣṇava. But the function of *Śivarātri* is not observed very regularly by the *bhaktas,* or devotees of Kṛṣṇa. Under the circumstances, it is stated in *Śrīmad-Bhāgavatam* that the cowherd men headed by Nanda Mahārāja "once upon a time desired." That means that they were not regularly observing the *Śivarātri* function, but that once upon a time they wanted to go to Ambikāvana out of curiosity. Ambikāvana is situated somewhere in the Gujarat province. Ambikāvana is said to be situated on the river Sarasvatī, yet we do not find any Sarasvatī River in the Gujarat province; the only river there is Savarmati. In India, all the big places of pilgrimage are situated on nice rivers like the Ganges, Yamunā, Sarasvatī, Narmadā, Godāvarī, Kāverī, etc. Ambikāvana was situated on the bank of Sarasvatī, and all the cowherd men and Nanda Mahārāja went there.

They very devotedly began to worship the deity of Lord Śiva and Ambikā. It is the general practice that wherever there is a temple of Lord Śiva, there must be another temple of Ambikā (or Durgā) because Ambikā is the wife of Lord Śiva and is the most exalted of chaste women. She doesn't live outside the association of her husband. After reaching Ambikāvana, the cowherd men of Vṛndāvana first bathed themselves in the River Sarasvatī. If one goes to any place of pilgrimage, his first duty is to take a bath and sometimes to shave his head. That is the first business. After taking bath, they worshiped the Deities and then distributed charity in the holy places.

According to the Vedic system, charity is given to the *brāhmaṇas.* It is stated in the Vedic *śāstras* that only the *brāhmaṇas* and the *sannyāsīs* can accept charity. The cowherd men from Vṛndāvana gave cows decorated with golden ornaments and beautiful garlands. The *brāhmaṇas* are given charity because they are not engaged in any business profession. They are supposed to be engaged in brahminical occupations, as described in the *Bhagavad-gītā*—namely, they must be very learned and must perform austerity and penances. They must not only themselves be learned, but they must also teach others. *Brāhmaṇas* are not meant to be *brāhmaṇas* alone; they should create other *brāhmaṇas* also. If a man is found who agrees to become a *brāhmaṇa's* disciple, he is also given the chance to become a *brāhmaṇa.* The *brāhmaṇa* is always engaged in the worship of Lord Viṣṇu. Therefore the *brāhmaṇas* are eligible to accept all kinds of charity. But if the *brāhmaṇas* receive excess charity, they are to distribute it for the service of Viṣṇu. In the Vedic scripture, therefore, one is recommended to give in charity to the *brāhmaṇas,* and by so doing one pleases Lord Viṣṇu and all the demigods.

The pilgrims take bath, worship the Deity, and give in charity; they are also recommended to fast one day. They should go to a place of pilgrimage and stay there at least for three days. The first day is spent fasting, and at night they can drink a little water because water does not break the fast.

The cowherd men, headed by Nanda Mahārāja, spent that night on the bank of the Sarasvatī. They fasted all day and drank a little water at night. But while they were taking their rest, a great serpent from the nearby forest appeared before them and hungrily began to swallow up Nanda Mahārāja. Nanda began to cry helplessly, "My dear son, Kṛṣṇa, please come and save me from this danger! This serpent is swallowing me!" When Nanda Mahārāja cried for help, all the cowherd men got up and saw what was happening. They immediately took up burning logs and began to beat the snake to kill it. But in spite of being beaten with burning logs, the serpent was not about to give up swallowing Nanda Mahārāja.

At that time Kṛṣṇa appeared on the scene and touched the serpent with His lotus feet. Immediately upon being touched by the lotus feet of Kṛṣṇa, the serpent shed its reptilian body and appeared as a very beautiful demigod named Vidyādhara. His bodily features were so beautiful that he appeared to be worshipable. There was a luster and effulgence emanating from his body, and he was garlanded with a gold necklace. He offered obeisances to Lord Kṛṣṇa and stood before Him with great humility. Kṛṣṇa then asked the demigod, "You appear to be a very nice demigod and to be favored by the goddess of fortune. How is it that you performed such abominable activities, and how did you get the body of a serpent?" The demigod then began to narrate the story of his previous life.

"My dear Lord," he said, "in my previous life I was named Vidyādhara and was known all over the world for my beauty. Because I was a celebrated personality, I used to travel all over in my airplane. While traveling, I saw a great sage named Āṅgirā. He was very ugly, and because I was very proud of my beauty, I laughed at him. Due to this sinful action, I was condemned by the great sage to assume the form of a serpent."

One should note here that before being favored by Kṛṣṇa, a person is always under the modes of material nature, however elevated he may be materially. Vidyādhara was a materially elevated demigod, and he was very beautiful. He also held a great material position and was able to travel all over by airplane. Yet he was condemned to become a serpent in his next life. Any materially elevated person can be condemned to an abominable species of life if he is not careful. It is a misconception that after reaching the human body one is never degraded. Vidyādhara himself states that even though he was a demigod, he was condemned to become a serpent. But because he was touched by the lotus feet of Kṛṣṇa, he immediately came to Kṛṣṇa consciousness. He admitted, however, that in his previous life he was actually sinful. A Kṛṣṇa conscious person knows that he is always the servant of the servant of Kṛṣṇa; he is most insignificant, and whatever good he does is by the grace of Kṛṣṇa and the spiritual master.

The demigod Vidyādhara continued to speak to Śrī Kṛṣṇa. "Because I was very proud of the exquisite beauty of my body," he said, "I derided the ugly features of the great sage Āṅgirā. He cursed me for my sin, and I became a snake. Now I consider that this curse by the sage was not at all a curse; it was a great benediction for me. Had he not cursed me, I would not have assumed the body of a serpent and would not have been kicked by Your lotus feet and thus freed from all material contamination."

In material existence, four things are very valuable: to be born in a decent family, to be very rich, to be very learned, and to be very beautiful. These are considered to be material assets. Unfortunately, without Kṛṣṇa consciousness, these material assets sometimes become sources of sin and degradation. Despite Vidyādhara's being a demigod and having a beautiful body, he was condemned to the body of a snake due to pride. A snake is considered to be the most cruel and envious living entity, but those who are human beings and are envious of others are considered to be even more vicious than snakes. The snake can be subdued or controlled by charming *mantras* and herbs, but a person who is envious cannot be controlled by anyone.

"My dear Lord," Vidyādhara continued, "Now since I think I have become freed from all kinds of sinful activities, I am asking Your permission to return to my abode, the heavenly planet." This request indicates that persons who are attached to fruitive activities, desiring promotion to the comforts of higher planetary systems, cannot achieve their ultimate goal of life without the sanction of the Supreme Personality of Godhead. It is also stated in the *Bhagavad-gītā* that the less intelligent want to achieve material benefits and therefore worship different kinds of demigods, but they actually get the benediction from the demigods through the permission of Lord Viṣṇu, or Kṛṣṇa. Demigods have no power to bestow material profit. Even if one is attached to material benediction, he can worship Kṛṣṇa the Supreme Personality of Godhead and ask Him. Kṛṣṇa is completely able to give even material benediction. There is a difference, however, in asking material benediction from the demigods and from Kṛṣṇa. Dhruva Mahārāja worshiped the Supreme Personality of Godhead for material benediction, but when he actually achieved the favor of the Supreme Lord and saw Him, he was so satisfied that he refused to accept any material benediction. The intelligent person does not ask favors from or worship the demigods; he directly becomes Kṛṣṇa conscious, and if he has any desire for material benefit, he asks Kṛṣṇa, not the demigods.

Vidyādhara, awaiting permission of Kṛṣṇa to return to the heavenly planets, said, "Now because I am touched by Your lotus feet, I am relieved from all kinds of material pangs. You are the most powerful of all mystics. You are the original Supreme Personality of Godhead. You are the master of all the devotees. You are the provider of the planetary systems, and therefore I am asking Your permission. You may accept me as fully surrendered unto You. I know very well that persons who are constantly engaged in chanting Your holy name attain release from all sinful reactions, and certainly persons who are fortunate enough to be personally touched by Your lotus feet are freed. Therefore I am sure that I am now relieved from the curse of the *brāhmaṇa* simply by being touched by Your lotus feet."

In this way, Vidyādhara got permission from Lord Kṛṣṇa to return to his home in the higher planetary system. After receiving this honor, he began to circumambulate the Lord. And after offering his respectful obeisances unto Him, he returned to his heavenly planet. Thus Nanda

Mahārāja also became relieved from the imminent danger of being devoured by the snake.

The cowherd men who had come to execute the ritualistic function of worshiping Lord Śiva and Ambikā finished their business and prepared to return to Vṛndāvana. While returning, they recalled the wonderful activities of Kṛṣṇa. By relating the incident of Vidyādhara's deliverance, they became more attached to Kṛṣṇa. They had come to worship Lord Śiva and Ambikā, but they became more and more attached to Kṛṣṇa. Similarly, the *gopīs* also worshiped goddess Kātyāyanī to become more and more attached to Kṛṣṇa. It is stated in the *Bhagavad-gītā* that persons who are attached to worshiping demigods like Lord Brahmā, Śiva, Indra and Candra, for some personal benefit, are less intelligent and have forgotten the real purpose of life. But the cowherd men, inhabitants of Vṛndāvana, were no ordinary men. Whatever they did, they did for Kṛṣṇa. If one worships demigods like Lord Śiva and Lord Brahmā to become more attached to Kṛṣṇa, that is approved. But if one goes to the demigods for some personal benefit, that is condemned.

After this incident, on a very pleasant night, both Kṛṣṇa and His elder brother Balarāma, who are inconceivably powerful, went into the forest of Vṛndāvana. They were accompanied by the damsels of Vrajabhūmi, and they began to enjoy each other's company. The young damsels of Vraja were very nicely dressed and anointed with pulp of sandalwood and decorated with flowers. The moon was shining in the sky, surrounded by glittering stars, and the breeze was blowing, bearing the aroma of *mallikā* flowers, and the bumblebees were mad after the aroma. Taking advantage of the pleasing atmosphere, both Kṛṣṇa and Balarāma began to sing very melodiously. The damsels became so absorbed in their rhythmical song that they almost forgot themselves; their hair loosened, their dresses slackened, and their garlands began to fall to the ground.

At that time, while they were so much absorbed, almost in madness, a demon associate of Kuvera (the treasurer of the heavenly planets) appeared on the scene. The demon's name was Śaṅkhāsura because on his head there was a valuable jewel resembling a conchshell. Just as the two sons of Kuvera were puffed up over their wealth and opulence and did not care for Nārada Muni's presence, this Śaṅkhāsura was also puffed up over material opulence. He thought that Kṛṣṇa and Balarāma were two ordinary cowherd boys enjoying the company of many beautiful girls. Generally, in the material world, a person with riches thinks that all beautiful women should be enjoyed by him. Śaṅkhāsura also thought that, since he belonged to the rich community of Kuvera, he, not Kṛṣṇa and Balarāma, should enjoy the company of so many beautiful girls. He therefore decided to take charge of them. He appeared before Kṛṣṇa and Balarāma and the damsels of Vraja and began to lead the girls away to the north. He commanded them as if he were their proprietor and husband, despite the presence of Kṛṣṇa and Balarāma. Being forcibly taken away by Śaṅkhāsura, the damsels of Vraja began to call the names of Kṛṣṇa and Balarāma for protection. The two brothers immediately began to follow them, taking up big logs in Their hands. "Don't be afraid, don't be afraid," They called to the *gopīs*. "We are coming at once to chastise this demon." Very quickly They reached Śaṅkhāsura. Thinking the brothers too powerful, Śaṅkhāsura left the company of the *gopīs* and ran for fear of his life. But Kṛṣṇa would not let him go. He entrusted the *gopīs* to the care of Balarāma and followed Śaṅkhāsura wherever he fled. Kṛṣṇa wanted to take the valuable jewel resembling a conchshell from the head of the demon. After following him a very short distance, Kṛṣṇa caught him, struck his head with His fist and killed him. He then took the valuable jewel and returned. In the presence of all the damsels of Vraja, He presented the valuable jewel to His elder brother Balarāma.

*Thus ends the Bhaktivedanta purport of the Thirty-third Chapter of* Kṛṣṇa, *"Vidyādhara Liberated and the Demon Śaṅkhāsura Killed."*

# 34 / The Gopīs' Feelings of Separation

The *gopīs* of Vṛndāvana were so attached to Kṛṣṇa that they were not satisfied simply with the *rāsa* dance at night. They wanted to associate with Him and enjoy His company during the daytime also. When Kṛṣṇa went to the forest with His cowherd boy friends and cows, the *gopīs* did not physically take part, but their hearts went with Him. And because their hearts went, they were able to enjoy His company through strong feelings of separation. To acquire this strong feeling of separation is the teaching of Lord Caitanya and His direct disciplic succession of Gosvāmīs. When we are not in physical contact with Kṛṣṇa, we can associate with Him like the *gopīs,* through feelings of separation. Kṛṣṇa's transcendental form, qualities, pastimes, and entourage are all identical with Him. There are nine different kinds of devotional service. Devotional service to Kṛṣṇa in feelings of separation elevates the devotee to the highest perfectional level, to the level of the *gopīs.*

It is stated in Śrīnivāsācārya's prayer to the six Gosvāmīs that they left the material opulences of government service and the princely status of life and went to Vṛndāvana, where they lived just like ordinary mendicants, begging from door to door. But they were so much enriched with the *gopīs'* feelings of separation that they enjoyed transcendental pleasure at every moment. Similarly, when Lord Caitanya was at Jagannātha Purī, He was in the role of Rādhārāṇī, feeling the separation of Kṛṣṇa. Those who are in the disciplic succession of the Mādhva-Gauḍīya-sampradāya should also feel the separation of Kṛṣṇa, worship His transcendental form, and discuss His transcendental teachings, His pastimes, His qualities, His entourage and His associations. The spiritual masters should enrich the devotees to the highest devotional perfection. Feeling constant separation while engaged in the service of the Lord is the perfection of Kṛṣṇa consciousness.

The *gopīs* used to discuss Kṛṣṇa amongst themselves, and their talks were as follows. "My dear friends," one *gopī* said, "do you know that when Kṛṣṇa lies on the ground He rests on His left elbow, and His head rests on His left hand. He moves His attractive eyebrows while playing His flute with His delicate fingers, and the sound He produces creates such a nice atmosphere that the denizens of the heavenly planets, who travel in space with their wives and beloved, stop their airplanes, for they are stunned by the vibration of the flute. The wives of the demigods who are seated in the planes then become very much ashamed of their singing and musical qualifications. Not only that, but they become afflicted with conjugal love, and their hair and tightened dresses immediately loosen."

Another *gopī* said, "My dear friends, Kṛṣṇa is so beautiful that the goddess of fortune always remains on His chest, and He is always adorned with a golden necklace. Beautiful Kṛṣṇa plays His flute in order to enliven the hearts of many devotees. He is the only friend of the suffering living entities. When He plays His flute, all the cows and other animals of Vṛndāvana, although engaged in eating, simply take a morsel of food in their mouths and stop chewing. Their ears raise up and they become stunned. They do not appear alive but like painted animals. Kṛṣṇa's flute playing is so attractive that even the animals become enchanted, and what to speak of ourselves."

Another *gopī* said, "My dear friends, not only living animals, but even inanimate objects like the rivers and lakes of Vṛndāvana also become stunned when Kṛṣṇa passes with peacock feathers on His head and His body smeared with the minerals of Vṛndāvana. With leaves and flowers decorating His body, He looks like some hero. When He plays on His flute and calls the cows with Balarāma, the River Yamunā stops flowing and waits for the air to carry dust from His lotus feet. The River Yamunā is unfortunate like us; it does not get Kṛṣṇa's mercy. The river simply remains stunned, stopping its waves just as we also stop crying out of frustration for Kṛṣṇa."

In the absence of Kṛṣṇa the *gopīs* were constantly shedding tears, but sometimes, when they expected that Kṛṣṇa was coming, they would stop crying. But when they saw that Kṛṣṇa was not coming, then again they would become frustrated and begin to cry. Kṛṣṇa is the original Personality of Godhead, the origin of all Viṣṇu forms, and the cowherd boys are all demigods. Lord Viṣṇu is always worshiped and surrounded by different demigods like Lord Śiva, Lord Brahmā, Indra, Candra, and others. When Kṛṣṇa traveled through the Vṛndāvana forest or walked on the Govardhana

Hill, He was accompanied by the cowherd boys. While walking, He played His flute, just to call His cows. Just by His association, the trees, plants and other vegetation in the forest immediately became Kṛṣṇa conscious. A Kṛṣṇa conscious person sacrifices everything for Kṛṣṇa. Although trees and plants are not very advanced in consciousness, by the association of Kṛṣṇa and His friends they also become Kṛṣṇa conscious. They then want to deliver everything—whatever they have—their fruits, flowers, and the honey incessantly falling from their branches.

When Kṛṣṇa walked on the bank of the Yamunā, He was seen nicely decorated with *tilaka* on His head. He was garlanded with different kinds of forest flowers, and His body was smeared by the pulp of sandalwood and *tulasī* leaves. The bumblebees became mad after the treasure and sweet nectar of the atmosphere. Being pleased by the humming sound of the bees, Kṛṣṇa would play His flute, and together the sounds became so sweet to hear that the aquatics, the cranes, swans and ducks and other birds were charmed. Instead of swimming or flying, they became stunned. They closed their eyes and entered a trance of meditation in worship of Kṛṣṇa.

One *gopī* said, "My dear friend, Kṛṣṇa and Balarāma are nicely dressed with earrings and pearl necklaces. They enjoy Themselves on the top of Govardhana Hill, and everything becomes absorbed in transcendental pleasure when Kṛṣṇa plays on His flute, charming the whole created manifestation. When He plays, the clouds stop their loud thundering, out of fear of Him. Rather than disturb the vibration of His flute, they respond with mild thunder and so congratulate Kṛṣṇa, their friend."

Kṛṣṇa is accepted as the friend of the cloud because both the cloud and Kṛṣṇa satisfy the people when they are disturbed. When the people are burning due to excessive heat, the cloud satisfies them with rain. Similarly, when people in materialistic life become disturbed by the blazing fire of material pangs, Kṛṣṇa gives them relief. The cloud and Kṛṣṇa, having the same bodily color also, are considered to be friends. Desiring to congratulate its superior friend, the cloud poured not water, but small flowers and covered the head of Kṛṣṇa to protect Him from the scorching sunshine.

One of the *gopīs* told mother Yaśodā, "My dear mother, your son is very expert among the cowherd boys. He knows all the different arts, how to tend the cows and how to play the flute. He composes His own songs, and to sing them He puts His flute to His mouth. When He plays, either in the morning or in the evening, all the demigods, like Lord Śiva, Brahmā, Indra and Candra, bow their heads and listen with great attention. Although they are very learned and expert, they cannot understand the musical arrangements of Kṛṣṇa's flute. They simply listen attentively and try to understand, but become bewildered and nothing more."

Another *gopī* said, "My dear friend, when Kṛṣṇa returns home with His cows, the footprint of the soles of His feet—with flag, thunderbolt, trident, and lotus flower—relieves the pain the earth feels when the cows traverse it. He walks in a stride which is so attractive, and He carries His flute. Just by looking at Him we become lusty to enjoy His company. At that time, our movements cease. We become just like trees and stand perfectly still. We even forget what we look like."

Kṛṣṇa had many thousands of cows, and they were divided into groups according to their colors. They were also differently named according to color. When He would return from the pasturing ground, He would find all the cows gathered. As Vaiṣṇavas count 108 beads, which represent the 108 individual *gopīs*, so Kṛṣṇa would also chant 108 different groups of cows.

"When Kṛṣṇa returns, He is garlanded with *tulasī* leaves," a *gopī* describes Him to a friend. "He puts His hand on the shoulder of a cowherd boy friend, and begins to blow His transcendental flute. The wives of the black deer become enchanted upon hearing the vibration of His flute, which resembles the vibration of the *vīṇā.* The deer come to Kṛṣṇa and become so charmed that they stand still, forgetting their homes and husbands. Like us, who are enchanted by the ocean of the transcendental qualities of Kṛṣṇa, the she-deer become enchanted by the vibration of His flute."

Another *gopī* told mother Yaśodā, "My dear mother, when your son returns home, He decorates Himself with the buds of the *kunda* flower, and just to enlighten and gladden His friends, He blows His flute. The breeze blowing from the south pleases the atmosphere because it is fragrant and very cool. Demigods like the Gandharvas and Siddhas take advantage of this atmosphere and offer prayers to Kṛṣṇa by sounding their bugles and drums. Kṛṣṇa is very kind to the inhabitants of Vrajabhūmi, Vṛndāvana, and when He returns with His cows and friends, He is remembered as the lifter of Govardhana Hill. Taking advantage of this opportunity, the most exalted demigods like Lord Brahmā and Lord Śiva come down to offer their evening prayers, and they accompany the cowherd boys in glorifying the qualities of Kṛṣṇa.

"Kṛṣṇa is compared with the moon, born in the ocean of the womb of Devakī. When He returns in the evening, it appears that He is fatigued, but He still tries to gladden the inhabitants of Vṛndāvana by His auspicious presence. When Kṛṣṇa returns, garlanded with flowers, His face looks beautiful. He walks into Vṛndāvana with a stride just like the elephant and slowly enters His home. Upon His return, the men, women, and cows of Vṛndāvana immediately forget the scorching heat of the day."

Such descriptions of Kṛṣṇa's transcendental pastimes and activities were remembered by the *gopīs* during His absence from Vṛndāvana. They give us some idea of Kṛṣṇa's attraction. Everyone and everything is attracted to Kṛṣṇa—that is the perfect description of Kṛṣṇa's attraction. The example of the *gopīs* is very instructive to persons who are trying to be absorbed in Kṛṣṇa consciousness. One can very easily associate with Kṛṣṇa simply by remembering His transcendental pastimes. Everyone has a tendency to love someone. That Kṛṣṇa should be the object of love is the central point of Kṛṣṇa consciousness. By constantly chanting the Hare Kṛṣṇa *mantra* and remembering the transcendental pastimes of Kṛṣṇa, one can be fully in Kṛṣṇa consciousness and thus make his life sublime and fruitful.

*Thus ends the Bhaktivedanta purport of the Thirty-fourth Chapter of* Kṛṣṇa, *"The Gopīs' Feelings of Separation."*

# Glossary

*Ācāryas*—spiritual masters who teach by their own personal behavior.

*Asura*—a demon or nondevotee.

*Ātmārāma*—a self-satisfied sage.

*Avatāra*—an incarnation of Godhead who descends from the spiritual world.

*Bhagavad-gītā*—the book which records the spiritual instructions given by Kṛṣṇa to His friend Arjuna on the Battlefield of Kurukṣetra.

*Bhakta*—devotee.

*Bhakti-yoga*—the *yoga* of devotional service to the Lord.

*Brahmā*—the first created living being in the universe.

*Brahmacārī*—a celibate student under the guidance of a spiritual master.

*Brahmajyoti*—the impersonal effulgence that emanates from the body of Kṛṣṇa.

*Brahman*—the impersonal feature of the Absolute Truth.

*Brāhmaṇas*—the spiritual order of society whose occupation is the cultivation of Vedic knowledge.

*Brahma-saṁhitā*—a scripture written by Lord Brahmā in which his authoritative prayers to the Lord are recorded.

*Caitanya Mahāprabhu*—the incarnation of Kṛṣṇa as His own devotee who comes in this age to teach the process of devotional service by chanting the holy name of God.

*Cāmara*—a yak-tail whisk.

*Deva*—a demigod or devotee.

*Ekādaśī*—a day of celebration which occurs twice a month and which is meant for increasing Kṛṣṇa consciousness.

*Gandharvas*—celestial denizens of the heavenly planets who sing very beautifully.

*Garuḍa*—the giant bird-carrier of Viṣṇu.

*Gopīs*—cowherd girls, specifically the transcendental girl friends of Lord Kṛṣṇa.

*Gṛhastha*—one who is in the householder order of spiritual life.

*Guru*—spiritual master.

*Jaya*—victory.

*Jñānī*—one who engages in mental speculation in pursuit of knowledge.

*Kadamba*—a tree which bears a round yellow flower and which is generally seen only in the Vṛndāvana area.

*Karma*—fruitive activities or their reactions.

*Karmī*—a fruitive worker.

*Kaumudī*—an especially fragrant flower found on the bank of the Yamunā River.

*Kaustubha*—a transcendental jewel worn around the neck of the Supreme Personality of Godhead.

*Kṛṣṇa-kathā*—narrations spoken by or about Kṛṣṇa.

*Kṣatriya*—the spiritual order of society whose occupation is governmental administration and military protection of the citizens.

*Kuṅkuma*—a sweetly flavored reddish powder which is thrown upon the bodies of worshipable persons.

*Līlā*—pastimes.

*Māgadhas*—professional singers present at sacrifices.

*Mahābhāgavata*—a highly advanced devotee.

*Mahāmantra*—the Hare Kṛṣṇa *mantra:* Hare Kṛṣṇa, Hare Kṛṣṇa, Kṛṣṇa Kṛṣṇa, Hare Hare/Hare Rāma, Hare Rāma, Rāma Rāma, Hare Hare.

*Mantra*—a transcendental sound vibration.

*Māyā (Mahāmāyā)*—the external energy of the Supreme Lord, which covers the conditioned soul and does not allow him to understand the Supreme Personality of Godhead.

*Māyāvāda*—the impersonalist or voidist philosophy.

*Māyāvādī*—one who adheres to the impersonalist or voidist philosophy and does not accept the eternal existence of the transcendental form of the Lord.

*Mukti*—liberation.

*Mukunda*—Lord Kṛṣṇa, who awards liberation and whose smiling face is like a *kunda* flower.

*Nirguṇa*—literally, without qualities (used to describe the Supreme Lord, who has no material qualities).

*Pāṇḍavas*—the five sons of King Pāṇḍu (Yudhiṣṭhīra, Arjuna, Bhīma, Nakula and Sahadeva).

*Paramahaṁsa*—(literally, the supreme swan) a devotee who can appreciate the spiritual essence of life, just as a swan extracts milk from water.

*Paramātmā*—the expansion of the Supreme Lord who lives in the hearts of all living entities.

*Pārijāta*—a type of flower found only on the heavenly planets.

*Prakṛta sahajiyā*—pseudo-devotees of Kṛṣṇa who fail to understand His absolute, transcendental position.

*Prāṇāyāma*—the yogic breathing exercises.

*Prasadam*—food first offered to the Supreme Lord and then distributed.

*Rasa*—a transcendental mellow relationship between the individual soul and the Supreme Lord.

*Rāsa-līlā*—Lord Kṛṣṇa's transcendental pastime of dancing with the *gopīs.*

*Samādhi*—trance, absorption in meditation upon the Supreme.

*Saṅkīrtana yajña*—the chanting of the holy names of God, which is the recommended sacrifice for this age.

*Sannyāsī*—one who is in the renounced order of spiritual life.

*Śāstras*—revealed scriptures.

*Sāyujya-mukti*—the liberation of merging into the existence of the Supreme Lord.

*Siddhi*—a mystic yogic perfection.

*Śiva*—the demigod in charge of annihilation and the mode of ignorance.

*Śrīmad-Bhāgavatam*—the authoritative Vedic scripture that deals exclusively with the pastimes of the Personality of Godhead and His devotees.

*Sudarśana*—the wheel which is the personal weapon of Viṣṇu or Kṛṣṇa.

*Śūdra*—the spiritual order of society who are not very intelligent and are unqualified for any work other than menial service.

*Śyāmasundara*—a name of Kṛṣṇa. *Śyāma* means blackish, and *sundara* means very beautiful.

*Tapasya*—austerity.

*Tilaka*—a clay mark that decorates the faces of Kṛṣṇa and His devotees.

*Tulasī*—a great devotee in the form of a plant who is very dear to Lord Kṛṣṇa.

*Vaiṣṇava*—a devotee of the Supreme Lord Viṣṇu or Kṛṣṇa.

*Vaiśya*—the agricultural community in Vedic culture, who protect cows and cultivate crops.

*Viṣṇu*—an all-pervasive, fully empowered expansion of Lord Kṛṣṇa, qualified by full truth, full knowledge and full bliss.

*Yajña*—sacrifice.

*Yoga*—the process of linking with the Supreme.

*Yogamāyā*—the principal internal (spiritual) potency of the Supreme Lord.

*Yogī*—one who practices *yoga.*

The vowels are pronounced almost as in Italian. The sound of the short *a* is like the *u* in b*u*t, the long *a* is like the *a* in f*a*r and held twice as long as the short *a*, and *e* is like the *a* in ev*a*de. Long *ī* is like the *i* in p*i*que. The vowel *ṛ* is pronounced like the *re* in the English word fib*re*. The *c* is pronounced as in the English word *ch*air, and the aspirated consonants (*ch, jh, dh,* etc.) are pronounced as in staun*ch-h*eart, he*dge-h*og, re*d-h*ot, etc. The two spirants *ś* and *ṣ* are pronounced like the English *sh*; *s* is pronounced as in *s*un.